THE COMPLETE KETO DIET COOKBOOK FOR BEGINNERS

By Samantha Capps

Contents

INTRODUCTION

I personally believe that cooking at home should be an important part of a healthy lifestyle. Although food is available everywhere, from fast-food restaurants to supermarkets, I've always enjoyed cooking and eating fresh, homemade foods. I think that nothing compares to a freshly cooked soup or a rich, old-fashioned cake from grandma's recipe book. Nothing compares to a hearty and delicious meal that is made with love! Nowadays, cooking is being observed like something that takes too much time. When did this all happen? Why did we stop cooking at home, reaching out for super-processed foods? Yes, it is easier to open a can or reheat food in the microwave than "slaving over a hot stove". In my opinion, that is such a shame. Home cooking is much healthier, much affordable and much tastier than processed foods, that's for sure. Moreover, family dinners bring people together around the table. We can talk and connect with each other, what's better way to spend your leisure time?

If you are considering a ketogenic diet, cooking at home is an absolute necessity! A few years ago, I decided to change my diet and find a nutrition plan that I can actually follow! I worked out, ate fat-free cheese and salads, and drink black coffee. However, I struggled to lose weight. So, I thought a ketogenic diet could be worth considering. I ate rich and delicious meals two or three times a day and consumed fat coffee every single day. I did not shy away from fat cheese and rich crustless pizza. Moreover, I indulged in snacks and desserts. Shortly after that, I dropped a dress size! I started losing pounds gradually and steadily. Once I achieved my goal weight, I made slight changes to my current eating habits. In fact, you don't need to make huge changes but there are some things you should keep in mind if you want to maintain your ideal weight. Just say goodbye to fast food and hello to barbecue, omelets, and fatty cheese! In fact, health and happiness are not just about ideal BMI. This is my ongoing lifestyle with new habits and a healthy mindset. At the end of the day, it's worth making an effort to look your best and feel your best.

After my personal experience with a ketogenic diet, I was motivated by a desire to help others and share my knowledge. Since I came up with unique combinations and inventive twists on traditional recipes, I decided to collect all of my favorite recipes. That's how this book was born! I hope this collection will become an integral part of your new lifestyle, helping you cook a wide range of keto foods, from simple salads to hearty casseroles and delectable desserts.

Basic Keto Diet Rules

A KETOGENIC DIET is a low-carbohydrate, moderate-protein, and high-fat nutrition plan. The fundamental goal of the keto diet is to force your body to stop burning glucose from the carbs. Once your body starts burning fat stores for energy and converts the fats to ketones, it gets into a state of ketosis. In fact, the ketosis is a natural process in which your body creates ketones and uses them for energy. Thus, you should consume minimal amounts of carbohydrates to lose weight without feeling hungry. In other words, you should limit carb intake to less than 20 grams of net carbs per day. Counting carbs is not the funniest thing in the world but you can use keto diet trackers and apps.

A keto diet plan is easy to follow as long as you stick to some general rules. The list of foods you are allowed to eat on a keto diet is rich, so I think it won't be difficult for you to start such a dietary regimen. You can't eat grains, rice, cereals, sugar, beans, root vegetables, and most of the fruits. Avoid trans fats and hydrogenated oil such as corn oil, cottonseed oil, vegetable shortening, and margarine. In addition, try to limit fried foods, packaged snacks, premade baked foods, and coffee creamers. When it comes to the packaged foods, always check the labels for hidden carbs. Remember, a well-organized keto pantry is half success! What foods are included in the ketogenic dietary regimen?

- **Above ground vegetables** – broccoli, celery, mushrooms, peppers, tomato, asparagus, onions, cauliflower, cabbage, bok choy, greens, arugula, and Brussels sprouts. These include canned and pickled vegetables (no sugar added);

- **Eggs;**

- **Dairy Products** –full-fat milk and cheese, heavy cream, full-fat yogurt, sour cream, and butter;

- **Meat** – pork, beef, veal, and poultry;

- **Fish and Seafood** – fresh and canned;

- **Nuts and seeds** – these include all types of nut and seed butters;

- **Oils & Fats** – olive, coconut, hemp, flaxseed, and avocado oil;

- **Fruit** – avocado and berries;

- **Sweeteners** –Stevia (zero carb), xylitol, erythritol, Splenda, Swerve, and monk fruit powder (zero carb);

- **Condiments and seasonings** – coconut aminos, mustard, vinegar, unsweetened cocoa powder, low-carb dressing, and herbs mix (no sugar added);

- **Vegetarian keto foods** – tofu, tempeh, coconut yogurt, unsweetened dairy-free milk, Shirataki noodles, and seaweed;

- **Beverages** – coffee, tea, keto smoothies, and sparkling water. **Alcoholic beverages** include rum, whiskey, vodka, brandy, and dry martini.

To sum up, this dietary regimen includes a good amount of high-quality protein, plenty of healthy fats, and low-carb foods.

Health Benefits of the Ketogenic Diet

Although there is no "one-size fits all" solution, there are some basic rules almost all experts agree on. We should start every day with a high-protein breakfast, avoid junk food and stay hydrated. Eating at home is the secret of healthy and skinny people! On the other hand, many studies have shown that processed food contributes to obesity problems, type 2 diabetes, cardiovascular disease, and so on. Researches have shown that families who cook at home are more likely to meet nutritional requirements.

There are a lot of sugar and trans fats in commercially prepared foods; plus, processed foods may contain some ingredients that cause allergies and sensitivities. When you prepare your food, you can take control of the ingredients you put in your body so try to cook homemade meals from scratch. Just simply forget poor quality restaurant foods! The ketogenic dietary regimen can revitalize your health and boost your immune system. Go organic whenever possible! Opt for natural and whole foods such as organic products, seasonal and fresh vegetables, wild-caught fish, and pasture-raised eggs.

When it comes to fats, consuming good fats is the key to success on a keto diet. The ketogenic diet promotes monounsaturated and polyunsaturated fats that can lower your risk for heart disease, reduce triglyceride levels, and lower blood pressure. Fatty fish such as mackerel, salmon, and sardines are excellent sources of omega-3 fatty acids. Opt for coconut oil, olive oil, nuts, seeds, and avocado that can increase good HDL (High-density lipoprotein). However, some healthcare professionals suggest that the keto diet can raise levels of bad LDL (Low density lipoprotein). In other words, the keto diet is not appropriate for people with high cholesterol since LDL can put people at risk of a heart attack.

The Ketogenic Diet for Weight Loss

The ketogenic diet is an effective way to lose weight in a short period of time. This is one of the best natural ways to lose weight and maintain a healthy and sustainable body weight. In addition to improving your eating habits and counting macros, being physically active on a regular basis can help you lose pounds fast and safely. On the ketogenic diet, you should do exercises that target fat cells. For example, practice cardio-vascular exercises on a daily basis or a minimum 150 minutes of moderate-intensity exercise per week. This can boost your metabolism and stimulate the leptin hormone that regulates your appetite. You should also perform weight resistance exercises because lifting weights burns off fat cells and strengthens your body.

If you are not losing weight on the ketogenic diet despite your best efforts, there are common mistakes that can sabotage your success.

Too many calories. One of the most common mistakes for those just starting the ketogenic diet is eating too much in general. Yes, you are right, you do not have to count your calories on a keto diet, but if you consume more calories than you burn, you will gain weight. For instance, the average adult needs about

2,000 calories a day. Here is the rule – excess calories will be stored as body fat! Besides being aware of calorie consumption, you should keep your cholesterol in check, too.

Too few calories. Yes, the most effective way to lose weight is to create a calorie deficit or eat fewer calories than you burn. However, an inadequate calorie intake or under-eating can slow down your metabolism and consequently keep you from losing weight. If your calorie intake dips too low, your body starts burning calories as slowly as possible to save its energy. It can also harm your health and cause anemia, hair loss, heart rhythm abnormalities, loss of menstrual periods, and psychological problems. To sum up, if you're not eating enough on a ketogenic diet, you can sabotage your weight-loss efforts.

Impatience. It takes time for your body to switch from running on carbs i.e. glucose to running on fat. When starting keto, your body has to burn any extra supplies of glucose before starting to use fat for fuel. This may slow the time it takes to enter ketosis, so be patient. In general, it takes 2 to 6 days but it depends on many factors. For example, people who typically eat high-carb foods may take longer to get into the state of ketosis (a week or longer).

Food allergies. If you're intolerant to milk, eggs, nuts, fish or crustacean shellfish, you can gain weight on a ketogenic diet. Food allergies and sensitivities can cause digestive problems and inflammation which can lead to an increase in body weight (an increase in fat deposits, excess water, and other issues). Another point to consider is the leptin resistance. If you are leptin resistant, you can struggle with weight loss on a keto diet. Stress, calorie restriction and overeating can trigger a leptin response.

Constant dehydration. Did you know that about 75 percent of Americans may be chronically dehydrated? Keeping the body hydrated contributes to many important functions of the body such as digestion, mood, and nutrient absorption. It helps the heart more easily pump blood and the muscles work properly. In fact, water is crucial to your overall health.

Once I achieve my healthy and sustainable weight, I could afford some extra carbs; however, I keep track of my calorie intake and practice cyclic ketogenic diet. It means that you should rotate low-carb days with moderate-carb and high-carb days. Further, I follow the most common ratio for macronutrients: about 60 percent of calories from fat, about 30 percent of calories from protein and 10 percent of calories from carbs.

My Favorite Keto Substitutes

With that being said, a healthy diet plan such as ketogenic no longer means dull and tasteless eating. Nor does it mean complicated to follow. Food technology and food science have resulted in the improvement of high-quality products so nearly every "regular and common" product, from bread to chocolate, has a keto substitute. However, you can make your homemade alternatives to rice and grain-based dishes. Here is a short list of my favorite keto substitutes, but I've got you covered with the best low carb swaps in these 600 recipes.

Pasta – In this collection, you will find the recipes for zoodles and veggie pasta. You can spiralize zucchini, cucumber or pumpkin and eat them with your favorite keto sauce, melted cheese or fried eggs. However, you can purchase keto pasta such as kelp noodles and shirataki noodles.

Baked goods, pizza, and bread – When I began my keto "lifestyle" I missed hamburgers and sandwiches with soft dinner roll or crusty, warm ciabatta. You can use low-carb cheese rolls, roasted eggplant rounds or grilled portobello mushrooms and fill them with your favorite fixings.

As for pizza and flatbread, you can use cauliflower, almond meal, coconut flour, ground psyllium husk powder, and ground nuts. I do not miss conventional bread anymore since it is usually low in micronutrients and high in carbs. Plus, refined wheat is definitely bad for your health. Some good alternatives include cloud bread (made of eggs and cream cheese) and nori sheets. Whether or not you have prior baking experience, this recipe collection is a very good place to start! You will find great keto baking ideas to convert your favorite recipes. As for tortilla, pancakes, and wraps, simply mix almond flour with milk, eggs, chia seeds, or flax meal. Other inventive ideas include kale, cabbage leaves, lettuce leaves, zucchini (sliced lengthwise) and so forth.

Snacks – We have so many options on the keto diet. You can make veggie chips using zucchini, Brussels sprouts, or kale. You can use pork rinds and cheese to make breadsticks. Cheese crisps are a real game changer! Here is my favorite – microwave pepperoni slices for about 1 minute and you are ready for a movie night. Such a brilliant idea!

Fried foods – When it comes to bread crumbs, I have several recommendations. You can use pork rinds, psyllium husk, and grated parmesan to make a good coating for fish, chicken tenders and fritters.

Other keto substitutes – Why settle for ordinary mashed potatoes when you can have mashed vegetables such as cauliflower, celery or broccoli? Cauli rice is a real game changer. This is a popular side dish on the ketogenic diet but you can also make casseroles, salads and Chinese foods. As for keto sushi, wrap sashimi and cauliflower rice in nori sheets. If you miss porridge, oatmeal and granola, you can make them with nuts, seeds, milk, and butter. Some other alternatives include flax crackers, fat bombs, and cheese taco shells.

3-Week Meal Plan

This is a sample menu for three weeks on a ketogenic diet plan.

DAY 1

Breakfast – Hard-Boiled Eggs with Avocado

Snack – Walnut and Chocolate Bites

Lunch – Home-Style Burgers; 1 handful of iceberg lettuce

Dinner – Cod Fillets with Sesame Sauce

DAY 2

Breakfast –1 slice of bacon; 1 hard-boiled egg; 1 shake with 1/2 cup of coconut milk and protein powder

Lunch – Oriental Spicy Turkey Soup; 1 serving of cauliflower rice

Dinner – Tuna and Ham Wraps; 1 medium tomato

Dessert – Chocolate Blechkuchen

DAY 3

Breakfast – Easy Greek Omelet

Lunch – Country-Style Pork Soup; Creamy Swiss Chard with Cheese

Snack – Pistachio Praline Truffles

Dinner – Ranch Tangy Wings; 1 keto dinner roll

DAY 4

Breakfast – Ham and Avocado Stuffed Eggs

Lunch – Beef Teriyaki Bowl; 1 serving of coleslaw

Dinner – Hearty Fisherman's Stew; Restaurant-Style Onions Rings

Dessert – Fudgy Mug Brownie

DAY 5

Breakfast – Breakfast Bacon and Kale Muffins

Snack – Herby Cheese Chips

Lunch – Filipino Pork Sinigang; 1 handful of mixed green salad with a few drizzles of a freshly squeezed lemon juice

Dinner – Favorite Monkfish Salad; 1 keto dinner roll

DAY 6

Breakfast – Breakfast Egg Cups

Lunch – Classic Fish Curry; 1 serving of cauliflower rice

Dinner – Herbed Chuck Roast

Dessert – Energy Chocolate Chip Candy

DAY 7

Breakfast – Favorite Breakfast Tabbouleh

Snack – Cheese and Prosciutto Fat Bombs

Lunch – Country-Style Beef Soup; 1 large tomato; 1 cup of fried mushrooms with 1 tablespoon of butter

Dinner – Italian Roasted Peppers with Cheese

DAY 8

Breakfast – Scrambled eggs; 1 tomato; 1/2 cup of Greek-style yogurt
Lunch – Old-Fashioned Pork Cutlets; 1 serving of cauliflower rice
Dinner – Chicken Mulligatawny
Dessert – Almond Butter Cookies

DAY 9

Breakfast – Cheesy Mexican Tortilla; 1/2 cup of unsweetened almond milk
Snack – Prawn Cocktail Skewers
Lunch – Paprika Pork Loin; 1 serving of cabbage salad
Dinner – Double Cheese Italian Chicken; 1 keto dinner roll

DAY 10

Breakfast – Deviled Eggs with Tuna
Snack – Beef-Stuffed Mini Peppers
Lunch – Hearty Fisherman's Stew; 1/2 chicken breast; 1 scallion; 1/2 tomato
Dinner – Famous New York Steak; a dollop of sour cream; 2 tablespoons tomato paste

DAY 11

Breakfast – 1 tablespoon of peanut butter; 1 slice of keto bread
Lunch – Easy Short Loin; 1 serving of cabbage salad
Dinner – Cod with Mustard Greens
Dessert – Blueberry Pot de Crème

DAY 12

Breakfast – Dukkah Frittata with Cheese
Snack – Cheesy Chicken Rolls
Lunch – Mustard Pork Roast; Cauliflower Tabbouleh Salad
Dinner – Sea Bass with Peppers; 1/2 cup of full-fat Greek yogurt

DAY 13

Breakfast – Keto Cauliflower Tots
Lunch – Italian Meatballs in Asiago Sauce; Braised Kale with Wine Sauce
Dinner – Peanut Butter Balls
Dessert – Favorite Keto Frisuelos

DAY 14

Breakfast – Breakfast Sausage and Cheese Bites
Lunch – Scotch Fillet with Marsala Wine; 1 handful of baby spinach with 1 teaspoon of mustard and 1 teaspoon of olive oil
Dinner – Easy Cheesy Broccoli Fritters
Dessert – Decadent Chocolate Soufflé

DAY 15

Breakfast – Frittata with Mediterranean Herbs; 1/2 cup of Greek-style yogurt
Snack – Ranch Blue Cheese Sauce
Lunch – Italian Meatloaf with Marinara Sauce; 1 serving of roasted keto veggies
Dinner – Garlicky Pork Roast; Roasted Asparagus Salad

DAY 16

Breakfast – Breakfast Keto Veggies; 1/2 cup of Greek-style yogurt
Lunch – Winter Pork Stew
Dinner – Turkey Crust Meatza
Dessert – Bavarian Vanilla Cream

DAY 17

Breakfast – Chia Smoothie Bowl
Snack – Deviled Eggs with Mustard Cream Cheese
Lunch – Easy Chicken Casserole; 1 fresh bell pepper
Dinner – Restaurant-Style Fish Masala; 1 cucumber

DAY 18

Breakfast – Cheesy Mini Frittatas with Sausage; 1/2 tomato
Snack – Saucy St. Louis-style Spareribs
Lunch – Authentic Japanese Katsudon; 1 serving of steamed broccoli
Dinner – Keto Mushroom Chili

DAY 19

Breakfast – Bombay Masala Frittata; 1 cucumber
Lunch – Traditional French Ragoût
Dinner – Easy Keto Quesadillas; Easy Insalata Caprese
Dessert – Pecan Pie Candy

DAY 20

Breakfast – Classic Italian Omelet; 1/2 medium tomato with 2-3 Kalamata olives
Lunch – Cabbage Stir-Fry; Easy Hungarian Meatballs; 1 dollop of sour cream
Snack – Cucumber and Pepper Bites
Dinner – Warm Shrimp and Vegetable Salad

DAY 21

Breakfast – Scrambled Eggs with Canadian Bacon; 1 serving of blue cheese
Lunch – Winter Turkey Soup; Easy Moroccan Tajine
Snack – Dijon Anchovies Fat Bombs
Dinner – Middle Eastern Shish Kebab

PORK

1. Harvest Pork Soup

(Ready in about 25 minutes | Servings 5)

Ingredients

5 cups vegetable broth
1/2 cup scallions, chopped
2 bell peppers, chopped

1 ½ pounds pork stew meat, cubed
1 celery stalk, chopped

Directions

Brush the bottom of a soup pot with nonstick cooking spray and heat up over medium-high flame.

Sear the meat for 5 minutes, stirring constantly. Add a splash of vegetable broth, scraping up any brown bits stuck to the bottom.

Add in the remaining ingredients; bring to a boil.

Reduce the heat to a simmer and cover; let it simmer until everything is thoroughly warmed for 15 to 16 minutes.

Spoon into serving bowls and serve immediately. Bon appétit!

Per serving: 303 Calories; 18.3g Fat; 3.5g Carbs; 29.1g Protein; 0.6g Fiber

2. Spanish-Style Pork Cutlets

(Ready in about 15 minutes | Servings 2)

Ingredients

2 pork cutlets
2 garlic cloves, minced
1 Spanish onion, chopped

1 Spanish pepper, deveined and sliced
1/2 teaspoon hot sauce

Directions

Spritz a saucepan with nonstick cooking spray and preheat it over medium-high heat.

Sear the pork cutlets for about 4 minutes or until golden-brown on both sides.

Reduce the heat to medium and add the garlic, Spanish onion, pepper, and hot sauce; continue cooking until the vegetables have softened, for a further 3 minutes.

Season with salt and black pepper and serve warm. Enjoy!

Per serving: 403 Calories; 24.1g Fat; 3.4g Carbs; 40.1g Protein; 0.7g Fiber

3. Spanish Pork Stew (Olla Podrida)

(Ready in about 45 minutes | Servings 4)

Ingredients

1 ½ pounds pork ribs
2 Spanish peppers, chopped
1 yellow onion, chopped

8 ounces button mushrooms, sliced
1 cup tomato puree

Directions

Heat 1 tablespoon of the olive oil in a stockpot over moderate flame. Sear the pork ribs for 4 to 5 minutes per side or until they achieve the reddish-brown exterior; reserve.

Heat another tablespoon of the olive oil and sauté Spanish peppers and onion until tender and aromatic for 4 to 6 minutes.

Pour in a splash of wine to scrape up the browned bits that stick to the bottom of the pot if desired.

Add the mushrooms and tomato puree to the pot. When your mixture reaches boiling, reduce the temperature to a simmer.

Add the reserved pork ribs back to the stockpot. Continue to cook for 30 to 35 minutes longer or until cooked through. Enjoy!

Per serving: 395 Calories; 10.3g Fat; 5g Carbs; 44.3g Protein; 4.8g Fiber

4. Pork with Tangy Herb Butter

(Ready in about 20 minutes | Servings 6)

Ingredients

6 pork medallions
2/3 cup butter, at room temperature

1/2 teaspoon dried thyme, crushed
2 cloves garlic, smashed
1 tablespoon lemon juice

Directions

Heat 1 tablespoon of olive oil until sizzling. Brown the pork medallions for 4 to 5 minutes per side.

Season the pork medallions with salt and black pepper to taste.

Mix the butter with thyme, garlic, and lemon juice. Serve warm pork with well-chilled butter. Bon appétit!

Per serving: 451 Calories; 31.7g Fat; 0.8g Carbs; 39.5g Protein; 0.2g Fiber

5. Pork Steak with Cabbage and Bacon

(Ready in about 20 minutes | Servings 5)

Ingredients

5 ounces bacon, diced
1 onion, sliced
1 pound pork steak, cut into strips

4 cloves garlic, sliced
4 cups green cabbage, shredded

Directions

Sear the bacon in a large sauté pan that is preheated over high heat; sear until crisp or about 5 minutes.

Now, stir in the onion and pork strips allow it to cook for 3 to 4 minutes or until the meat is no longer pink.

Add in garlic and continue to sauté for 2 minutes more or until fragrant. Afterwards, stir in the cabbage, cover, and continue to cook for a further 5 minutes.

Season with coarse sea salt and black pepper. Bon appétit!

Per serving: 384 Calories; 25g Fat; 6.4g Carbs; 24.7g Protein; 1.6g Fiber

6. Spicy Bolognese with Peppers

(Ready in about 55 minutes | Servings 6)

Ingredients

1 pound ground pork
1 bell pepper, chopped
1 habanero pepper, chopped
1/2 cup scallions, finely chopped
2 vine-ripe tomatoes, pureed

Directions

Brush your saucepan with nonstick cooking oil; heat the oil over a medium-high heat.

Then, sear the ground pork until no longer pink or about 5 minutes; crumble with a fork or wide spatula to ensure even cooking.

Add in the peppers and scallions and continue to cook until they are just tender. Add in pureed tomatoes and 1 cup of chicken stock.

Reduce the temperature to medium-low. Allow it simmer for 35 to 40 minutes, stirring periodically to ensure even cooking. Bon appétit!

Per serving: 225 Calories; 16.1g Fat; 3.8g Carbs; 13.5g Protein; 0.9g Fiber

7. Authentic Japanese Katsudon

(Ready in about 1 hour 35 minutes | Servings 7)

Ingredients

2 pounds pork ribs
2 bell peppers, chopped
1 brown onion, roughly chopped
2 cloves garlic, minced
4 cups dashi

Directions

Heat 2 tablespoons of sesame oil until sizzling. Once hot, brown the pork ribs until they achieve the reddish-brown exterior approximately 7 minutes per side; set aside, keeping warm.

Then, cook the peppers, onions, and garlic until tender or 3 to 4 minutes.

Add the pork ribs back the pot. Season with the salt and black pepper. Pour in dashi. When your mixture reaches boiling, reduce the temperature to a simmer.

Cook for 65 minutes longer or until the meat is fall-apart and fork-tender.

Stir in the mirin if desired, cover, and let it sit for 5 minutes. Ladle into individual bowls. Enjoy!

Per serving: 232 Calories; 11.3g Fat; 3.5g Carbs; 27.8g Protein; 0.9g Fiber

8. Old-Fashioned Pork Cutlets

(Ready in about 25 minutes | Servings 2)

Ingredients

1 tablespoon lard, softened at room temperature
2 pork cutlets, 2-inch-thick
1/3 cup dry red wine
2 garlic cloves, sliced
1 teaspoon juniper berries

Directions

Melt the lard in a pan over a moderate heat. Once hot, sear the pork cutlets until just browned about 7 minutes; reserve.

Pour in a splash of wine to deglaze the pan. Add in the garlic and juniper berries; continue to sauté until aromatic or for 30 seconds

Add the pork cutlets back to the pan.

Let it simmer over medium-low heat until the sauce has thickened and reduced. Bon appétit!

Per serving: 369 Calories; 20.6g Fat; 1.1g Carbs; 40.1g Protein; 0.1g Fiber

9. Traditional French Ragoût

(Ready in about 40 minutes | Servings 2)

Ingredients

3/4 pound pork butt, cut into bite-sized cubes
1/2 cup leeks, chopped
1 red bell pepper, deveined and chopped
2 cloves garlic, pressed
2 vine-ripe tomatoes, pureed

Directions

Brush the sides and bottom of a stockpot with 1 tablespoon of melted lard. Heat the lard over medium-high heat.

Once hot, sear the pork cubes, stirring occasionally, for 5 minutes.

Then, stir in the leeks, pepper, and garlic, and continue cooking until they have softened, an additional 5 minutes.

Season with the salt and ground black pepper; add in mustard seeds and celery seeds, if desired.

Add pureed tomatoes and turn the heat to simmer. Simmer the pork ragout for 25 to 30 minutes l or until through.ly cooked. Serve warm and enjoy!

Per serving: 389 Calories; 24.3g Fat; 5.4g Carbs; 33.1g Protein; 1.3g Fiber

10. Country-Style Pork Soup

(Ready in about 25 minutes | Servings 2)

Ingredients

1/2 cup scallions, chopped
1 bell pepper, deveined and chopped
1/2 pound ground pork (84% lean)
2 cups beef bone broth
2 cups mustard greens, torn into pieces

Directions

Heat 1 tablespoon of olive oil in a heavy-bottomed pot over a moderate heat. Once hot, sweat the scallions and peppers until just tender, 2 to 3 minutes.

Fold in the ground pork and cook for 4 to 6 minutes longer or until browned; crumble with a fork.

Pour in the beef bone broth and bring to a rapid boil. Then, cover, and reduce the temperature to simmer. Let it simmer for 10 to 11 minutes.

Lastly, stir in the mustard greens; remove from heat. Let it sit, covered, until mustard greens are wilted. Bon appétit!

Per serving: 344 Calories; 25.2g Fat; 6.3g Carbs; 23.1g Protein; 2.9g Fiber

11. Grandma's Pork Medallions

(Ready in about 20 minutes | Servings 2)

Ingredients

1 ounce bacon, diced
2 pork medallions
1/2 cup chicken bone broth
1/3 pound red cabbage, shredded
2 garlic cloves, sliced

Directions

Preheat a Dutch pot over moderate flame. Sear the bacon for about 3 minutes and reserve, leaving the pan drippings.

Cook the pork medallions in the pan drippings until they are nicely browned all over. Add in a splash of chicken bone broth to scrape up the browned bits that stick to the bottom of Dutch pot.

Fold in red cabbage and garlic, and turn the heat to medium-low. Continue to cook for 10 to 12 minutes, stirring occasionally.

Salt to taste and adjust the seasonings. Divide between individual bowls and top with the reserved bacon. Serve warm.

Per serving: 528 Calories; 31.8g Fat; 6.3g Carbs; 51.2g Protein; 2.6g Fiber

12. Italian Ground Pork Soup

(Ready in about 30 minutes | Servings 5)

Ingredients

1 pound ground pork
1 celery stalk, chopped
1 fresh Italian pepper, deveined and chopped
2 shallots, chopped
5 cups beef bone broth

Directions

Preheat a soup pot over a medium-high heat; brush the sides and bottom with nonstick cooking oil.

Once hot, brown the ground pork for about 5 minutes, stirring and crumbling with a fork; set aside.

In the pan drippings, sauté the celery, Italian pepper, and shallot until they have just softened. Add in the reserved ground pork.

Pour in the beef bone broth and bring to a boil. Immediately turn the heat to simmer, and continue to cook for 20 to 25 minutes longer.

Season with salt and black pepper and garnish with fresh cilantro just before serving. Bon appétit!

Per serving: 292 Calories; 20.6g Fat; 1.6g Carbs; 23.6g Protein; 0.3g Fiber

13. Paprika Pork Loin

(Ready in about 25 minutes | Servings 4)

Ingredients

1 pound pork loin shoulder, cut into bite-sized cubes
1/4 cup red wine
4 cloves garlic, minced
1/2 teaspoon paprika
1 tablespoon hot sauce

Directions

Heat the 1 tablespoon of olive oil in a pan over a medium heat. Then, sear the pork approximately 5 minutes, stirring frequently; reserve.

Pour in a splash of wine and stir with a wooden spoon to deglaze the pan. Then, sauté the garlic until aromatic.

Stir in the paprika and hot sauce along with the reserved pork. Partially cover and cook over medium-low heat approximately 12 minutes until the sauce has reduced by half. Bon appétit!

Per serving: 302 Calories; 18g Fat; 2.6g Carbs; 30.4g Protein; 0.4g Fiber

14. Herbed Pork Meatloaf

(Ready in about 1 hour 10 minutes | Servings 6)

Ingredients

1 ½ pounds ground pork
1/2 cup scallions, chopped
1/4 cup flax seed meal
2 eggs, beaten
3 ounces herbed tomato sauce

Directions

Preheat an oven to 365 degrees F. Then, brush the sides and bottom of a baking pan with nonstick cooking spray.

Mix the ground pork, scallions, flax seed meal, and eggs in a bowl; mix until everything is well incorporated.

Spoon the meatloaf mixture into the greased pan and bake for 30 minutes Spread the herbed tomato sauce on top of the meatloaf.

Bake for a further 25 to 28 minutes. Bon appétit!

Per serving: 344 Calories; 23.1g Fat; 2.8g Carbs; 30g Protein; 1g Fiber

15. Mexican Chili Con Carne

(Ready in about 50 minutes | Servings 4)

Ingredients

2 ounces bacon, diced
1 pound ground pork
1 red onion, chopped
2 ripe tomatoes, crushed
1 teaspoon chipotle powder

Directions

Preheat Dutch oven over a medium-high flame. Fry the bacon until crisp and set aside.

Now, sauté the onion and ground pork in the pan drippings for about 5 minutes.

Stir in the ground cumin and garlic and continue to sauté for 30 seconds more or until aromatic.

Then, add in tomatoes and chipotle powder. Pour in 1/2 cup of chicken broth, partially cover and cook for 40 minutes more or until cooked through.

You can add some extra broth or water during the cooking, as needed. Enjoy!

Per serving: 389 Calories; 29.9g Fat; 5.3g Carbs; 22.2g Protein; 1.6g Fiber

16. Spicy Pork Meatballs

(Ready in about 25 minutes | Servings 2)

Ingredients

1/2 pound ground pork
1/2 cup scallions, chopped
2 ounces bacon rinds

1 garlic clove, minced
1 teaspoon taco seasoning
blend

Directions

Mix all ingredients until everything is well incorporated. Shape the meat mixture into golf-ball-sized balls.

In a lightly greased nonstick skillet, sear the meatballs over medium-high heat until golden brown on all sides.

Bon appétit!

Per serving: 557 Calories; 50.1g Fat; 2.3g Carbs; 0.5g Protein; 0.9g Fiber

17. Decadent Saucy Filet Mignon

(Ready in about 15 minutes | Servings 6)

Ingredients

2 teaspoons lard, at room temperature
Flaky salt and ground black pepper, to season

2 pounds pork filet mignon, cut into bite-sized chunks
1 cup double cream
1 tablespoon Dijon mustard

Directions

In a frying pan, melt the lard over medium-high heat; now, sear the filet mignon until it achieves the reddish-brown exterior. Add the salt and pepper to taste.

Add in the cream and mustard and immediately reduce the heat to simmer.

Next, let it simmer, partially covered, for a further 5 to 7 minutes or until the sauce has reduced by half. Enjoy!

Per serving: 301 Calories; 16.6g Fat; 2.3g Carbs; 34.2g Protein; 0.2g Fiber

18. Mustard Pork Roast

(Ready in about 1 hour 15 minutes | Servings 5)

Ingredients

1 ½ tablespoons olive oil
2 pounds pork loin roast, trimmed
1 tablespoon pork rub seasoning blend

1 tablespoon stone-ground mustard
1 tablespoon fresh lemon juice

Directions

Massage the pork with the olive oil on all sides.

Then, spread the pork rub seasoning blend, mustard, and lemon juice all over the roast.

Grill the pork over indirect heat for about 55 minutes or so or until cooked through. Bon appétit!

Per serving: 386 Calories; 20.1g Fat; 0.1g Carbs; 48g Protein; 0.1g Fiber

19. Cheesy and Spicy Pork Patties

(Ready in about 20 minutes | Servings 6)

Ingredients

1 ½ cups Romano cheese, grated
2 pounds ground pork
2 garlic cloves, finely minced

1/2 cup onion, finely minced
1 serrano pepper, deseeded and minced

Directions

Thoroughly combine all of the ingredients; season with salt and pepper to taste; add in mustard seeds and thyme if desired.

Shape the mixture into six patties using your hands.

Cook on the preheated grill for about 15 minutes turning once or twice. Bon appétit!

Per serving: 515 Calories; 35.4g Fat; 2.6g Carbs; 44.3g Protein; 0.2g Fiber

20. Filipino Pork Sinigang

(Ready in about 45 minutes | Servings 4)

Ingredients

1 pound pork ribs, boneless and cut into small pieces
2 garlic cloves, minced

1 shallot, chopped
1 cup fresh tomatoes, pureed
3 cups chicken stock

Directions

Preheat a lightly buttered stock pot over moderate heat.

Now, sear the pork ribs for about 5 minutes per side. Stir in the garlic and shallot and let it cook for a further 4 minutes.

Pour in tomato sauce and chicken stock. Bring to a boil and reduce the heat to simmer.

Let it simmer, covered, for 28 to 32 minutes. Serve with 1 cup of cauliflower "rice" if desired.

Per serving: 203 Calories; 8.4g Fat; 3.7g Carbs; 27.1g Protein; 1.1g Fiber

21. Old-Fashioned Pork Stew

(Ready in about 1 hour | Servings 5)

Ingredients

2 pounds pork stew meat
2 garlic cloves, minced
1 yellow onion, chopped

1 cup tomatoes, pureed
4 cups chicken bone broth

Directions

Sear the pork meat in a lightly greased soup pot over medium-high flame for about 5 minutes; reserve.

Then, sweat the garlic and onion in the pan drippings until they have softened.

Pour in a splash of dry sherry to scrape up the browned bits that stick to the bottom of the pot.

Add the pureed tomatoes and chicken bone broth to the pot; bring to a rapid boil and immediately reduce to simmer.

Continue to cook, partially covered, for 10 minutes longer. Season with salt and freshly ground black pepper.

Return the reserved pork to the pot, and continue to cook for a further 30 to 40 minutes. Garnish with fresh cilantro just before serving and enjoy!

Per serving: 332 Calories; 14.7g Fat; 3.9g Carbs; 41g Protein; 0.8g Fiber

22. Garlicky Pork Roast

(Ready in about 1 hour + marinating time | Servings 2)

Ingredients

1 pound pork shoulder
1 teaspoon Mediterranean herb blend
4 tablespoons red wine
1 shallot, peeled and chopped
1/2 head garlic, peeled and separated into cloves

Directions

Place the pork shoulder, Mediterranean herbs, and red wine in a ceramic dish; add in 2 tablespoons of lemon juice and mustard seeds if desired.

Now, let it sit in the refrigerator at least 3 hours.

Transfer the pork shoulder to a greased baking pan; reserve the marinade. Scatter the shallot and garlic around the pork shoulder

Season with salt and black pepper and roast in the preheated oven at 395 degrees F for 12 to 16 minutes. Baste the pork with the reserved marinade.

Turn the temperature to 320 degrees F and continue to roast for a further 40 minutes. Bon appétit!

Per serving: 497 Calories; 35.3g Fat; 2.5g Carbs; 40.2g Protein; 0.6g Fiber

23. Traditional Hungarian Paprikash

(Ready in about 55 minutes | Servings 4)

Ingredients

1 pound pork stew meat, cut into bite-sized chunks
1 red onion, chopped
2 bell peppers, deseeded and chopped
1 teaspoon Hungarian spice blend
4 cups chicken bone broth

Directions

Preheat a stockpot over a medium-high heat. Brown the meat for 4 to 5 minutes, stirring occasionaly.

Season with the Hungarian spice blend and reserve the meat. Now, sauté the onion and bell peppers until they have softened.

Return the reserved meat to the stockpot.

Pour in the broth and bring to a boil. Turn the heat to simmer and continue to cook, partially covered, for 45 to 48 minutes. Enjoy!

Per serving: 270 Calories; 15.5g Fat; 5.6g Carbs; 25.5g Protein; 0.8g Fiber

24. Easy Hungarian Meatballs

(Ready in about 20 minutes | Servings 5)

Ingredients

1 onion, chopped
2 garlic cloves, minced
1 pound ground pork
1/2 pound ground beef
1 teaspoon Hungarian spice blend

Directions

Start by reheating your oven to 390 degrees F.

Mix all ingredients until everything is well combined. Then, roll the meatballs with oiled hands.

Arrange the meatballs on a parchment-lined baking sheet. Bake approximately 13 minutes or until they are browned an all sides.

Bon appétit!

Per serving: 377 Calories; 23.9g Fat; 2.4g Carbs; 35.7g Protein; 0.4g Fiber

25. Zucchini Noodles Bolognese

(Ready in about 30 minutes | Servings 3)

Ingredients

2 zucchinis, spiralized
3 teaspoons olive oil
3/4 pound ground pork
2 medium-sized tomatoes, pureed
2 cloves garlic, pressed

Directions

Warm the olive oil in a pan over moderate heat. Once hot, brown the ground pork for 4 minutes, stirring and crumbling periodically.

Add in the garlic and continue to sauté for 30 seconds or so. Add in the pureed tomatoes.

When your mixture reaches boiling, reduce the temperature to a simmer. Now, continue to simmer an additional 18 to 20 minutes.

Afterwards, fold in the zucchini noodles; let them cook for a further 2 minutes. Bon appétit!

Per serving: 357 Calories; 28.7g Fat; 4g Carbs; 20.2g Protein; 1.1g Fiber

26. Mediterranean Pork Roast

(Ready in about 20 minutes | Servings 6)

Ingredients

2 pounds pork roast, sliced
1/2 cup vegetable broth
2 scallions, chopped
2 Italian peppers, chopped
2 teaspoons Italian seasoning mix

Directions

Preheat a lightly greased pan over moderate flame and sear the pork for about 4 minutes on each side; reserve.

Add in vegetable broth to deglaze the pan.

Now, stir in the Italian peppers and scallions; continue to sauté for 3 to 4 minutes more, until they have softened.

Sprinkle with Italian seasoning mix; add the reserved pork and some extra broth or water if needed.

Continue to cook, covered, for 8 to 12 minutes more or until everything is thoroughly cooked. Bon appétit!

Per serving: 255 Calories; 10.9g Fat; 3.4g Carbs; 24.4g Protein; 0.6g Fiber

27. Pork Loin Roast with Aromatic Sauce

(Ready in about 50 minutes | Servings 7)

Ingredients

3 pounds pork loin
1/2 cup cooking wine
2 bell peppers, sliced

2 cups herbed tomato sauce, sugar-free
2 cloves garlic

Directions

Begin by preheating your oven to 350 degrees F. Then, brush a baking pan with a nonstick spray.

Lower the pork loin into the prepared baking pan. Add in cooking wine and roast for 25 minutes.

Stir in peppers, herbed tomato sauce and garlic; bake for a further 20 minutes until the pork reaches the temperature of 145 degrees F.

Let the pork rest for 10 minutes before cutting and serving. Enjoy!

Per serving: 350 Calories; 17.1g Fat; 5.6g Carbs; 44g Protein; 3.4g Fiber

28. Char Seiw Pork Meatballs

(Ready in about 20 minutes | Servings 4)

Ingredients

1 pound ground pork
1 shallot, chopped
1 teaspoon sriracha sauce

2 garlic cloves, minced
1 teaspoon five-spice powder

Directions

Thoroughly combine all ingredients until well mixed. Shape the mixture into meatballs with am ice cream scoop.

Heat 1 tablespoon of sesame oil in a large pan or wok over medium heat. Once hot, sear the meatballs until all sides are browned, about 6 minutes; work in batches.

Serve on a nice serving platter and enjoy!

Per serving: 366 Calories; 30.9g Fat; 1.6g Carbs; 19.4g Protein; 0.3g Fiber

29. Pork Fajita Wraps

(Ready in about 15 minutes | Servings 6)

Ingredients

1 ½ pounds ground pork
2 bell peppers, chopped
2 cloves garlic, finely chopped

1/2 cup yellow onions, chopped
18 endive spears, rinsed

Directions

Heat 2 tablespoons of olive oil in a wok over moderate heat.

Brow the ground pork for 3 to 4 minutes, crumbling with a spatula.

Add in the peppers, garlic, and onions. Continue to saute an additional 5 minutes, stirring frequently.

Divide the meat mixture between endive spears and serve.

Per serving: 432 Calories; 30.1g Fat; 6g Carbs; 33.2g Protein; 3.2g Fiber

30. Turkish Lahana Sarmasi

(Ready in about 1 hour 30 minutes | Servings 8)

Ingredients

16 cabbage leaves
1 medium-sized leek, chopped
1 ½ pounds ground pork

1 tablespoon Turkish spice mix
2 cups chicken bone broth

Directions

Cook the cabbage leaves in the salted boiling water until they are just tender; rinse them and set aside.

Then, cook the leek and ground meat about 4 minutes or until the leeks are tender and the meat has browned.

Add in Turkish spice mix. Divide the meat mixture between cabbage leaves and roll them up.

Pour the broth over the cabbage rolls and add the bay leaf if desired; cover with a piece of foil and let it simmer, covered, for 1 hour 15 minutes. Enjoy!

Per serving: 278 Calories; 21.7g Fat; 5.1g Carbs; 15.8g Protein; 1.3g Fiber

31. Pork and Scallion Omelet

(Ready in about 20 minutes | Servings 5)

Ingredients

2 tablespoons butter, melted
1 pound ground pork
5 eggs

2 tablespoons full-fat milk
4 scallions, sliced

Directions

Melt the butter in an oven-proof skillet over moderate heat. Sear the ground pork until for 4 to 5 minutes.

Stir in the scallions and continue to sauté for 2 to 3 minutes more.

Then, whisk the eggs and milk until frothy; pour the egg/milk mixture into the skillet. Let it cook for 3 minutes.

Turn the omelet over and let it cook for 3 to 4 minutes more. Afterwards, broil your omelet for 3 to 4 minutes until eggs are set and puffy.

Serve warm and enjoy!

Per serving: 354 Calories; 28.1g Fat; 2.5g Carbs; 21.5g Protein; 0.5g Fiber

32. Beer-Braised Pork

(Ready in about 1 hour 35 minutes | Servings 6)

Ingredients

2 pounds Boston butt, cut into cubes
1 tablespoon olive oil
1 teaspoon mustard powder
1 cup beer
Sea salt and freshly ground black pepper, to taste

Directions

Heat the olive oil in a cast-iron skillet until sizzling. Once hot, sear the Boston butt for 6 minutes or until no longer pink in the center.

Season the pork with mustard powder, salt, and black pepper. Slowly pour in the beer.

When mixture reach boiling, reduce the heat to simmer; allow it to simmer for 80 minutes or until cooked through.

Preheat your oven to broil. Now, broil the pork about 5 minutes. Let it rest for 10 minutes before slicing and serving.

Per serving: 238 Calories; 10.9g Fat; 1.5g Carbs; 28.5g Protein; 0.1g Fiber

33. Southern Pork with Cabbage

(Ready in about 25 minutes | Servings 2)

Ingredients

1 tablespoon lard, room temperature
1/2 pound pork tenderloin
1/3 cup vegetable broth
1 tablespoon pork chop seasoning
4 ounces cabbage, sliced into strips

Directions

Melt the lard medium-high heat.

Season the pork tenderloin with pork chop seasoning. Now, brown the pork for about 12 minutes or cooked through; reserve.

Then, bring vegetable broth and cabbage to a boil. Immediately reduce the temperature and let it simmer for about 10 minutes until the cabbage is crisp-tender.

Taste and adjust seasonings. Serve with the reserved pork. Bon appétit!

Per serving: 254 Calories; 10.8g Fat; 5.7g Carbs; 31.8g Protein; 1.6g Fiber

34. Classic Pork Cutlets

(Ready in about 15 minutes | Servings 4)

Ingredients

2 tablespoons olive oil
4 pork cutlets
1/2 teaspoon paprika
Sea salt and ground black pepper, to taste
1/4 cup cream of onion soup

Directions

Heat the olive oil in a pan over medium-high heat. Then, sear the pork cutlets for about 5 minutes, turning periodically.

Stir in the cream of onion soup, salt, black pepper, and paprika. Continue to cook for 3 to 4 minutes more.

Garnish with freshly snipped chives if desired. Bon appétit!

Per serving: 395 Calories; 24.4g Fat; 0.8g Carbs; 40.3g Protein; 0.1g Fiber

35. Pork, Bacon and Shallot Omelet

(Ready in about 15 minutes | Servings 5)

Ingredients

6 eggs, whisked
2 ounces bacon, diced
1 pound ground pork
1 teaspoon ginger-garlic paste
1 shallot, chopped

Directions

Fry the bacon in the preheated skillet until it is crisp and releases easily from the bottom of your skillet.

Fold in the ground pork, ginger-garlic paste, and shallot; continue to cook for 5 minutes longer or until cooked through.

Pour the whisked eggs over the meat mixture; continue to cook, partially covered, for 4 to 5 minutes per side until the eggs are set. Bon appétit!

Per serving: 393 Calories; 28g Fat; 0.8g Carbs; 31.4g Protein; 0.1g Fiber

36. Cheesy Pulled Pork

(Ready in about 20 minutes | Servings 2)

Ingredients

1 teaspoon lard, melted at room temperature
3/4 pork Boston butt, sliced
2 garlic cloves, pressed
2 bell peppers, deveined and sliced
4 tablespoons cream cheese

Directions

Melt the lard in a saucepan over medium-high flame. Sear the pork for about 10 minutes, turning it over to ensure even cooking.

Turn the heat to medium-low; continue to cook another 4 to 5 minutes. Shred the pork with two forks.

Add the garlic and bell peppers to the pan; continue to cook an additional 3 minutes or until cooked through.

Serve with cream cheese. Enjoy!

Per serving: 370 Calories; 21.9g Fat; 5.1g Carbs; 34.9g Protein; 1g Fiber

37. Tender Pork in Peppery Sauce

(Ready in about 15 minutes | Servings 2)

Ingredients

2 pork loin steaks
2 bell peppers, deseeded and chopped
1 shallot, chopped
1 teaspoon Italian seasoning mix
1/4 cup Greek-style yogurt

Directions

Melt 1 teaspoon of lard in a nonstick skillet over medium-high heat. Sear the pork loin until for about 5 to 7 minutes or until browned; reserve.

Pour in 1/2 cup of the beef bone broth (or wine) to deglaze the pan. Add bell peppers and shallot and continue to cook for 3 to 4 minutes or until they have softened.

Season with Italian seasoning mix.

Turn the heat to medium-low and fold in Greek yogurt; let it simmer for 2 or 3 minutes until thoroughly cooked. Enjoy!

Per serving: 447 Calories; 19.2g Fat; 6g Carbs; 62.2g Protein; 1.3g Fiber

38. Chinese-Style Pork Ribs

(Ready in about 2 hours 10 minutes | Servings 5)

Ingredients

2 pounds St. Louis-style pork ribs
1 teaspoon Chinese five-spice
1 tablespoon coconut aminos soy sauce
1 cup tomato sauce, no sugar added
2 tablespoons Swerve sweetener

Directions

Season the pork ribs with Chinese five-spice and place them on a baking pan. Brush with 4 tablespoons of sesame oil and wrap in a piece of foil.

Bake in the preheated oven at 365 degrees F for 80 minutes (the pork must reach an internal temperature of 145 degrees F).

Then, whisk the coconut aminos, tomato sauce, and Swerve sweetener; brush the mixture over the pork ribs.

Turn the temperature to 410 degrees F. Continue to bake an additional 25 minutes. Bon appétit!

Per serving: 370 Calories; 21.2g Fat; 4.3g Carbs; 38.8g Protein; 1.1g Fiber

39. Pork Stuffed Tomatoes

(Ready in about 50 minutes | Servings 4)

Ingredients

4 ounces pork sausage, sliced
1 onion, chopped
1 garlic clove, minced
4 tomatoes
6 ounces Colby cheese, shredded

Directions

Brown the pork sausage over medium-high heat for 5 to 6 minutes, breaking the meat apart with a spatula.

Add in the onion and garlic and continue to sauté cook for 3 to 4 minutes more. Season with salt and black pepper to taste.

Now, slice a thin piece off the top of each tomato using a sharp kitchen knife. Scoop out the pulp and divide the filling between tomatoes.

Arrange the stuffed tomatoes in a foil-lined baking pan. Bake in the preheated oven at 350 degrees F for about 35 to 40 minutes.

Top with Colby cheese and continue to bake an additional 5 minutes. Bon appétit!

Per serving: 300 Calories; 21.9g Fat; 9g Carbs; 14.3g Protein; 2g Fiber

40. Favorite Pork Shoulder with Broccoli

(Ready in about 50 minutes | Servings 6)

Ingredients

2 pounds pork shoulder, cut into slices
2 cups broccoli florets
2 bell peppers, deseeded and quartered
4 cloves garlic, halved
1 yellow onion, quartered

Directions

Heat 2 tablespoons of olive oil in a saucepan over medium-high flame. Now, brown the pork for 5 minutes.

Add vegetables and turn the heat to medium-low; Add in 1/2 cup of water or chicken broth. Season with the salt and pepper to taste. Add red pepper flaked if desired.

Let it cook, partially covered, for 35 to 40 minutes (the pork must reach an internal temperature of 145 degrees F).

Serve the pork shoulder with the cooking juices and enjoy!

Per serving: 476 Calories; 31.4g Fat; 4.5g Carbs; 40.5g Protein; 0.9g Fiber

41. Puerto Rican Sancocho

(Ready in about 40 minutes | Servings 6)

Ingredients

1/2 pound Chorizo sausage, sliced
1 ½ pounds pork stew meat, cut into bite-sized pieces
1/2 cup shallots, chopped
1 chipotle pepper, deseeded and minced
2 ripe tomatoes, crushed

Directions

Melt 1 tablespoon of lard in a stockpot over medium-high flame. Then, brown Chorizo sausage and pork for 5 to 7 minutes; reserve.

Then, stir in the shallots and chipotle pepper; continue to sauté for 3 to 4 minutes or until tender and aromatic.

Season with salt and black pepper to taste. Add in tomatoes along with the reserved pork and Chorizo sausage.

Cover with 4 cups of water and reduce the heat to simmer. Partially cover and continue to simmer for 30 to 35 minutes.

Serve with pimento olives if desired.

Per serving: 305 Calories; 17.7g Fat; 2.8g Carbs; 31.4g Protein; 0.8g Fiber

42. Paprika Pork with Romano Cheese

(Ready in about 15 minutes | Servings 6)

Ingredients

2 tablespoons sesame oil
6 pork cutlets
1 cup Romano cheese, preferably freshly grated
2 eggs, whisked
1 tablespoon paprika

Directions

Season the pork with salt and black pepper to taste.

Dip each pork cutlet into the eggs, then roll in the cheese mixture, pressing to coat well. Season with paprika.

Warm the sesame oil in a saucepan over a medium-high heat.

Cook for 4 to 5 minutes on each side. Serve immediately.

Per serving: 454 Calories; 21.5g Fat; 1.1g Carbs; 60.7g Protein; 0.4g Fiber

43. Mediterranean Ground Pork Salad

(Ready in about 15 minutes | Servings 5)

Ingredients

1 ½ pounds ground pork
2 scallions, sliced
2 bell peppers, deveined and sliced
1 cucumber, sliced
1 tablespoon Mediterranean herb mix

Directions

Heat 1 tablespoon of the olive oil in a cast-iron skillet over moderate flame. Then, brown the ground pork for 5 to 6 minutes or until no longer pink; transfer the browned pork to a salad bowl.

Add in the scallions, peppers, and cucumber. Season with Mediterranean herb mix. Toss your salad with about 2 tablespoons of olive oil and balsamic vinegar to taste.

Serve immediately.

Per serving: 455 Calories; 38.2g Fat; 2.7g Carbs; 23.7g Protein; 0.7g Fiber

44. Tuscan Meatballs with cheese

(Ready in about 45 minutes | Servings 4)

Ingredients

1 pound lean ground pork
1/2 cup Romano cheese, grated
1 egg
1 Italian pepper, chopped
1 tablespoon Italian seasoning blend

Directions

Thoroughly combine all ingredients until everything is well incorporated. Roll the mixture into 16 balls.

Melt 1 tablespoon of lard in a nonstick skillet over medium-high heat.

Cook the meatballs until well browned on all sides or 9 to 14 minutes; work in batches. Bon appétit!

Per serving: 263 Calories; 13.8g Fat; 4.7g Carbs; 30g Protein; 0.5g Fiber

45. Pork Carnitas with Herbs

(Ready in about 3 hours | Servings 4)

Ingredients

1 cup tomato sauce
3 tablespoons apple cider vinegar
1 tablespoon Taco seasoning blend
1/2 teaspoon chipotle powder
1 ½ pounds Boston butt

Directions

Start by preheating your oven to 310 degrees F.

Place tomato sauce, apple cider vinegar, seasonings and Boston butt in a lightly greased baking dish.

Bake for about 2 hours 40 minutes, turning occasionally to ensure even cooking.

Then, shred the pork and serve with cooking juices. Enjoy!

Per serving: 338 Calories; 21.2g Fat; 4.4g Carbs; 30.8g Protein; 1.2g Fiber

46. Easy Roasted Pork Shoulder

(Ready in about 4 hours + marinating time | Servings 4)

Ingredients

2 pounds pork shoulder
2 tablespoons coconut aminos
1/2 cup red wine
1 tablespoon Dijon mustard
1 tablespoon Mediterranean spice mix

Directions

Place the ingredients a ceramic dish. Allow it to marinate in your refrigerator for at least 2 hours.

Put the rack into a roasting pan. Lower the marinated pork onto the rack. Roast in the preheated oven at 410 degrees F for 30 minutes.

Turn the heat to 340 degrees F. Continue to roast an additional 3 hours, basting with the marinade. Bon appétit!

Per serving: 609 Calories; 40.1g Fat; 0.6g Carbs; 57g Protein; 0.1g Fiber

47. Thai Pork Chop Salad

(Ready in about 20 minutes + marinating time | Servings 6)

Ingredients

2 pounds pork rib chops
1 cup pork marinade
6 cups lettuce, torn into small pieces
1 bell pepper, deseeded and sliced
1/2 cup sour cream, for garnish

Directions

Place the marinade and pork in a ceramic dish. Let it marinate in your refrigerator for at least 2 hours.

Heat 1 tablespoon of olive oil in an oven-proof skillet over a moderate flame. Sear the pork rib chops for about 10 minutes, flipping them over to ensure even cooking.

Season with salt and black pepper. Transfer the skillet to the preheated oven and roast the pork for 15 minutes or until thoroughly cooked.

Transfer pork chops to a cutting board.

Shred the pork chops and transfer to a salad bowl. Add the lettuce, bell pepper, and sour cream. Toss to combine and serve well-chilled.

Enjoy!

Per serving: 296 Calories; 14.2g Fat; 6g Carbs; 35.3g Protein; 1.4g Fiber

48. Buttery Pork Chops with Mushrooms

(Ready in about 20 minutes | Servings 2)

Ingredients

1/3 pound pork loin chops
1/2 stick butter, room temperature
1/2 cup Swiss cheese, shredded
1/2 cup white onion, chopped
4 ounces button mushrooms, sliced

Directions

Warm 1/4 of the butter stick in a saucepan over moderate heat. Now, sauté the onions and mushrooms until the onions are caramelized and the mushrooms are aromatic, about 5 to 6 minutes. Set aside.

Warm the remaining 1/4 of the butter stick. Once hot, cook the pork for about 10 to 12 minutes. \

Add the onion mixture back to the skillet. Afterwards, top pork chops with Swiss cheese, cover and let it sit in the residual heat until cheese has melted. Enjoy!

Per serving: 494 Calories; 39.8g Fat; 5.3g Carbs; 28.6g Protein; 2g Fiber

49. Asian Pork Bowl

(Ready in about 20 minutes | Servings 6)

Ingredients

6 eggs

2 pounds ground pork

1 teaspoon ginger-garlic paste

1 red onion, chopped

1/2 Chinese cabbage, shredded

Directions

Heat 2 tablespoons of the sesame oil in a skillet over medium-high flame. Once hot, fry the eggs for about 5 minutes; set aside.

In the same skillet, heat another 2 tablespoons of sesame oil. Now, cook the ground pork, breaking the meat apart with a fork.

Add in the ginger-garlic paste, onion, and Chinese cabbage; continue to cook for a further 6 to 7 minutes or until the vegetables are tender.

Remove from heat and add 4 tablespoon of rice wine if desired. Stir to combine and top with fried eggs.

Serve garnished with 1/2 cup of roasted peanuts if desired.

Per serving: 538 Calories; 41.9g Fat; 4.9g Carbs; 34.1g Protein; 1.6g Fiber

50. Indian Spicy Pork

(Ready in about 15 minutes | Servings 4)

Ingredients

1 pound pork shoulder, sliced

2 dried Kashmiri red chillies, roasted

1/2 cup ground pork rinds

1/2 cup parmesan cheese, grated

2 eggs

Directions

Season the pork shoulder with salt and ground black pepper to taste.

Then, mix Kashmiri red chillies, pork rinds and parmesan cheese. In another shallow bowl, whisk the eggs.

Now, dip the pork into the egg; then, dredge the pork in the pork rind mixture, pressing to coat well.

Melt 2 tablespoons of tallow in a nonstick skillet over medium-high flame. Cook the pork slices for about 7 minutes, flipping them over to ensure even cooking. Bon appétit!

Per serving: 478 Calories; 34.7g Fat; 2.2g Carbs; 36.4g Protein; 0.1g Fiber

51. Authentic Mexican Pork

(Ready in about 45 minutes | Servings 4)

Ingredients

2 pounds pork butt, cut into 2-inch cubes

1/2 cup dry red wine

1/2 cup tomato sauce

1 tablespoons Taco seasoning mix

4 tablespoons scallions, chopped

Directions

Preheat a lightly greased Dutch oven with nonstick cooking spray over medium-high heat; now, sear the pork until no longer pink.

Now, add the remaining ingredients to the stockpot. Add 1/2 cup of chicken broth and stir to combine well.

Wrap in a piece of foil and bake at 360 degrees F for 30 to 35 minutes.

Afterwards, place the pork under the preheated broil for 8 minutes, until the top is slightly crisp. Enjoy!

Per serving: 477 Calories; 16.2g Fat; 5.7g Carbs; 67.7g Protein; 2.2g Fiber

52. Winter Pork Stew

(Ready in about 40 minutes | Servings 4)

Ingredients

1/4 cup leeks, chopped

1 bell pepper, seeded and chopped

1 pound pork stew meat, cubed

2 garlic cloves, minced

1/4 cup of creme fraiche

Directions

Melt 2 tablespoons of lard in a heavy-bottomed pot over medium heat. Then, cook the leeks, garlic, and peppers for 4 to 5 minutes.

Add the pork to the pot and cook an additional 5 minutes, stirring periodically.

Pour in 2 cups of water or vegetable broth. Continue to cook over low-medium heat for 25 to 30 minutes.

Stir in creme fraiche, cover with the lid, and let it sit in the residual heat. Serve warm.

Per serving: 351 Calories; 22.7g Fat; 2.7g Carbs; 32.3g Protein; 2g Fiber

53. Pork Belly with Peppers

(Ready in about 20 minutes | Servings 4)

Ingredients

1 pound skinless pork belly, poke holes with fork

2 bell peppers, seeded and sliced

2 cloves garlic, pressed

1/2 cup shallots, sliced

1 teaspoon dried Mediterranean herb mix

Directions

Rub Mediterranean herb mix all over the pork belly; sprinkle with the salt and black pepper to taste.

Lower the pork into a foil-lined baking dish. Top the pork with garlic, shallots, and peppers.

Roast in the preheated oven at 380 degrees F for 15 to 20 minutes. Serve warm.

Per serving: 607 Calories; 60g Fat; 4.4g Carbs; 11.4g Protein; 1.5g Fiber

54. Classic Italian Meatloaf

(Ready in about 1 hour | Servings 5)

Ingredients

1 1/3 pound ground pork
1/2 cup yellow onions, chopped
1 egg

1 cup parmesan cheese, preferably freshly grated
1 tablespoon Italian seasoning mix

Directions

Mix all ingredients until everything is well incorporated. Scrape the mixture into a lightly greased baking pan.

Bake in the preheated oven at 360 degrees F for 50 to 55 minutes. Serve warm.

Per serving: 426 Calories; 28.1g Fat; 5.2g Carbs; 34.6g Protein; 0.9g Fiber

55. Pork with Dijon Sauce

(Ready in about 20 minutes | Servings 4)

Ingredients

1 pound pork fillets
2 scallions, chopped
2 cloves garlic, minced

1/2 cup dry white wine
2 tablespoons whole-grain Dijon mustard

Directions

Melt 2 tablespoon of butter in a nonstick skillet over a moderate flame. Now, sear the pork for 3 to 4 minutes per side; reserve.

Next, sauté the scallions and garlic in the pan drippings for 1 to 2 minutes. Pour in white wine to scrape up the browned bits that stick to the bottom of the skillet.

Add in Dijon mustard along with the reserved pork; partially cover and cook for a further 12 minutes or until the sauce has reduced by half.

Serve the pork fillets garnished with the sauce. Bon appétit!

Per serving: 343 Calories; 17.5g Fat; 5.4g Carbs; 40g Protein; 1g Fiber

56. Greek Hoirino me Selino

(Ready in about 20 minutes | Servings 6)

Ingredients

1 ½ pounds pork shoulder, and cut into small chunks
1 cup tomato puree
1/2 cup shallots, chopped

5 cups chicken stock
1 tablespoon Greek seasoning mix

Directions

Heat 1 tablespoon of olive oil in a soup pot over medium-high heat. Once hot, brown the pork for 4 to 5 minutes.

Stir in the shallots and continue to sauté for 4 minutes more or until it has softened.

Stir in Greek seasoning mix, chicken stock, and tomato puree. When the mixture reaches boiling, immediately reduce the heat to simmer.

Cover and continue to simmer for 10 to 15 minutes or until everything is thoroughly cooked.

Serve with a dollop of Greek yogurt, if desired.

Per serving: 214 Calories; 11.5g Fat; 2.6g Carbs; 24.7g Protein; 0.7g Fiber

57. Pork in Sherry Sauce

(Ready in about 20 minutes | Servings 4)

Ingredients

1 pound pork cutlets
2 tablespoons sherry
1/4 cup sour cream

1/4 cup beef bone broth
1 teaspoon mustard

Directions

Season the pork cutlets with salt and black pepper to taste.

Melt 1 tablespoon of lard in a saucepan over medium-high flame; once hot, cook pork cutlets for 3 to 4 minutes per each side. Set aside, keeping them warm.

Deglaze the saucepan with sherry. Stir in the cream, beef broth, and mustard. Partially cover and let it simmer until the sauce has thickened and reduced slightly, approximately 10 minutes.

Stir in the reserved pork and let it simmer for 5 minutes more. Serve warm.

Per serving: 288 Calories; 17.3g Fat; 1.1g Carbs; 29.9g Protein; 0.9g Fiber

58. Cheeseburger and Mushroom Bowl

(Ready in about 20 minutes | Servings 4)

Ingredients

2 slices Canadian bacon, chopped
1/2 cup shallots, sliced
1 pound ground pork

6 ounces Cremini mushrooms, sliced
1/2 cup cream cheese

Directions

Preheat a frying pan over medium heat. Then, fry the bacon for 3 to 4 minutes, crumbling with a fork; reserve.

Sauté the shallots in the bacon fat for about 3 minutes. Stir in the ground pork and continue to cook for 4 to 5 minutes more, stirring frequently.

Season the pork with salt and black pepper. Add in mushrooms along with 1/2 cup of water or broth. Cook, covered, for 10 minutes longer over medium-low heat.

Remove from heat and fold in cream cheese; stir to combine well, top with the reserved bacon and serve!

Per serving: 463 Calories; 60g Fat; 4.7g Carbs; 36.2g Protein; 1g Fiber

59. Classic Mexican Tacos

(Ready in about 20 minutes | Servings 4)

Ingredients

1 tablespoon lard
8 ounces mixed ground meat
(pork and turkey)
4 tablespoons sour cream

12 lettuce leaves
4 tablespoons roasted tomatillo
salsa

Directions

Place the ground meat in a bowl and season with the salt and black pepper to taste.

In a saucepan, warm the lard over medium-high heat. Now, cook the ground meat for 5 to 6 minutes, stirring continuously and crumbling with a spatula.

Fold in the roasted tomatillo salsa and stir again. Remove from heat.

Afterwards, divide the meat mixture between lettuce leaves. Top with sour cream and serve.

Per serving: 330 Calories; 26.3g Fat; 4.9g Carbs; 17.9g Protein; 1.1g Fiber

60. French Pork Daube

(Ready in about 50 minutes | Servings 4)

Ingredients

1 pound pork belly, cut into
bite-sized chunks
1/2 pound ripe tomatoes,
pureed

2 scallions, chopped
1 teaspoon garlic, minced
1 tablespoon Herbes de
Provence

Directions

Heat up a soup pot over medium-high heat. Now, sear the pork for about 5 minutes, stirring frequently to ensure even cooking.

Add in pureed tomatoes, scallions, garlic, and Herbes de Provence. Pour in 2 cups of water or broth and bring to a rapid boil.

Then, immediately reduce the heat to medium-low. Continue to simmer for 35 to 40 minutes or until everything is cooked through.

Divide among soup bowls and garnish with 8 niçoise olives if desired. Enjoy!

Per serving: 615 Calories; 61g Fat; 2.7g Carbs; 12.9g Protein; 0.8g Fiber

61. Rich Ground Pork Casserole

(Ready in about 40 minutes | Servings 6)

Ingredients

2 pounds ground pork
1 bell pepper, deseeded and
chopped
1 leek, chopped

2 eggs, beaten
1 1/2 cups cream cheese, at
room temperature

Directions

In a nonstick skillet, warm 1 tablespoon of butter over moderate flame. Then, brown the ground pork until no longer pink or about 4 minutes.

Stir in the peppers and leek and continue to sauté for 6 to 7 minutes, stirring frequently.

Pour in 1/2 cup of water or chicken bone broth; continue to cook for 6 to 7 minutes. Scrape the mixture into a greased casserole dish.

Then, whisk the eggs and cream cheese until well combined. Pour the egg mixture into the prepared casserole dish.

Bake in the preheated oven at 340 degrees F for about 9 minutes until bubbly and golden brown on the top. Let it sit for 10 minutes before slicing and serving.

Per serving: 620 Calories; 50g Fat; 5.7g Carbs; 33.9g Protein; 0.7g Fiber

62. Pork and Mushroom Skillet

(Ready in about 20 minutes | Servings 3)

Ingredients

1 onion, sliced
2 cups button mushrooms,
sliced
3 pork medallions

1 tomato, sliced
1 bell pepper, deveined and
sliced

Directions

In a cast-iron skillet, heat 2 tablespoon of olive oil over medium-high heat. Once hot, sweat the onions until they are just tender and translucent.

Stir in the mushrooms and continue to cook for 2 minutes more or until they are tender and aromatic.

Add in the pork medallions tomato, and bell pepper; season with the salt and pepper and let it cook for about 13 minutes.

Garnish with fresh parsley if desired. Bon appétit!

Per serving: 364 Calories; 17.3g Fat; 4.6g Carbs; 45g Protein; 0.9g Fiber

POULTRY

63. Oriental Spicy Turkey Soup

(Ready in about 20 minutes | Servings 5)

Ingredients

1 Bird's eye chili, deseeded and chopped

2 Oriental sweets peppers, deseeded and chopped

2 green onions, chopped

1 teaspoon five-spice powder

1 pound turkey thighs, deboned and cut into halves

Directions

Heat 2 tablespoons of olive oil in a soup pot over medium-high flame. Then, sauté the peppers and onions until just tender and aromatic or about 3 minutes.

Add in turkey thighs and five-spice powder; pour in 5 cups of water or vegetable broth.

Reduce the heat to medium-low, cover, and let it simmer cook for 15 minutes more. Serve warm and enjoy!

Per serving: 180 Calories; 7.5g Fat; 6.7g Carbs; 21.4g Protein; 1.2g Fiber

64. Old-Fashioned Stuffed Chicken

(Ready in about 30 minutes | Servings 2)

Ingredients

2 chicken fillets, skinless and boneless

1 teaspoon Herbes de Provence

2 (1-ounce) slices bacon

2 (1-ounce) slices cheddar cheese

1 tomato, sliced

Directions

Rub the chicken fillets with Herbes de Provence.

Then, fry the bacon slices for a few minutes or until just tender; chop with a knife.

Place the fried bacon and cheddar cheese on chicken fillets and roll them up; secure with a kitchen twine.

Arrange the stuffed chicken in a parchment-lined baking pan. Add the tomatoes around the chicken rolls.

Roast in the preheated oven at 380 degrees F for 30 minutes, turning them over once or twice. Bon appétit!

Per serving: 401 Calories; 23.9g Fat; 3.7g Total Carbs; 41.2g Protein; 1.2g Fiber

65. Home-Style Chicken Kebab

(Ready in about 20 minutes + marinating time | Servings 2)

Ingredients

2 Roma tomatoes, chopped

1 pound chicken thighs, boneless, skinless and halved

2 tablespoons olive oil

1/2 cup Greek-style yogurt

1 ½ ounces Swiss cheese, sliced

Directions

Place the chicken thighs, yogurt, tomatoes, and olive oil in a glass storage container. You can add in mustard seeds, cinnamon, and sumac, if desired.

Cover tightly and allow it to marinate in the refrigerator for 3 to 4 hours.

Thread the chicken thighs onto skewers, creating a thick log shape. Grill the kebabs over medium-high heat for 3 or 4 minutes on each side.

Use an instant-read thermometer to check the doneness of meat; it should read about 165 degrees F.

Top with the cheese; continue to cook for 4 minutes or until cheesy is melted. Enjoy!

Per serving: 498 Calories; 23.2g Fat; 6.2g Carbs; 61g Protein; 1.7g Fiber

66. Traditional Hungarian Gulyás

(Ready in about 1 hour 10 minutes | Servings 2)

Ingredients

1/2 cup celery ribs, chopped

1 ripe tomato, pureed

1 tablespoon spice mix for goulash

2 (1-ounce) slices bacon, chopped

1/2 pound duck legs, skinless and boneless

Directions

Heat a heavy-bottomed pot over medium-high flame; then, fry the bacon for about 3 minutes. Stir in the duck legs and continue to cook until they are nicely browned on all sides.

Shred the meat and discard the bones. Set aside.

In the pan drippings, sauté the celery for about 3 minutes, stirring with a wide spatula. Add in pureed tomatoes and spice mix for goulash; add in the reserved bacon and meat.

Pour 2 cups of water or chicken broth into the pot.

Turn the heat to medium-low, cover, and continue to simmer for 50 minutes more or until everything is cooked thorough. Serve warm and enjoy!

Per serving: 363 Calories; 22.3g Fat; 5.1g Carbs; 33.2g Protein; 1.4g Fiber

67. Winter Turkey Soup

(Ready in about 1 hour 15 minutes | Servings 2)

Ingredients

1/2 pound turkey thighs
1 cup cauliflower, broken into small florets

1 large-sized leek, chopped
1 teaspoon Turkish spice mix
1 whole egg

Directions

Place the turkey thighs in a heavy-bottomed pot over medium-high heat; add in 2 ½ cups of water bring the mixture to a boil.

Then, reduce the heat to medium-low and continue to cook for about 35 minutes; shred the meat with two forks, discarding the skin and bones.

Stir in the cauliflower, leeks, and spices. Continue to cook an additional 30 minutes.

Afterwards, fold in the egg and whisk until it is well mixed into the soup. Enjoy!

Per serving: 216 Calories; 8.1g Fat; 6.8g Carbs; 25.2g Protein; 2.1g Fiber

68. Greek Chicken Stifado

(Ready in about 35 minutes | Servings 2)

Ingredients

2 ounces bacon, diced
1 teaspoon poultry seasoning mix
2 vine-ripe tomatoes, pureed

3/4 pound whole chicken, boneless and chopped
1/2 medium-sized leek, chopped

Directions

Cook the bacon in the preheated skillet over medium-high heat. Fold in the chicken and continue cook for 5 minutes more until it is no longer pink; set aside.

In the same skillet, sauté the leek until it has softened or about 4 minutes. Stir in the poultry seasoning mix and 2 cups of water or chicken broth.

Now, reduce the heat to medium-low and continue to simmer for 15 to 20 minutes.

Add in tomatoes along with the reserved meat. Continue to cook for a further 13 minutes or until cooked through. Bon appétit!

Per serving: 352 Calories; 14.3g Fat; 5.9g Carbs; 44.2g Protein; 2.4g Fiber

69. Easy Chicken Casserole

(Ready in about 30 minutes | Servings 2)

Ingredients

2 ripe tomatoes, chopped
3/4 pound chicken breast fillets, chopped into bite-sized chunks

1/2 cup heavy whipping cream
2 garlic cloves, sliced
1/2 teaspoon Korean spice mix

Directions

Preheat your oven to 380 degrees F

Spritz a casserole dish with nonstick spray. Add the chicken, garlic, Korean spice mix to the casserole dish.

Top with tomatoes and heavy whipping cream

Bake in for 22 to 27 minutes or until the sauce is piping hot and thickened. Bon appétit!

Per serving: 410 Calories; 20.7g Fat; 6.2g Carbs; 50g Protein; 1.5g Fiber

70. Tangy Chicken with Scallions

(Ready in about 40 minutes | Servings 4)

Ingredients

3 tablespoons butter, melted
1 pound chicken drumettes
2 tablespoons white wine

1 garlic clove, sliced
1 tablespoon fresh scallions, chopped

Directions

Arrange the chicken drumettes on a foil-lined baking pan. Brush with melted butter.

Add in the garlic and wine. Season with salt and black pepper to taste. Bake in the preheated oven at 400 degrees F for about 30 minutes or until an internal temperature reaches about 165 degrees F.

Serve garnished with scallions and enjoy!

Per serving: 209 Calories; 12.2g Fat; 0.4g Carbs; 23.2g Protein; ; 1.9g Fiber

71. Double Cheese Italian Chicken

(Ready in about 20 minutes | Servings 2)

Ingredients

2 chicken drumsticks
2 cups baby spinach
1 teaspoon Italian spice mix

1/2 cup cream cheese
1 cup Asiago cheese, grated

Directions

In a saucepan, heat 1 tablespoon of oil over medium-high heat. Sear the chicken drumsticks for 7 to 8 minutes or until nicely browned on all sides; reserve.

Pour in 1/2 cup of chicken bone broth; add in spinach and continue to cook for 5 minutes more until spinach has wilted.

Add in Italian spice mix, cream cheese, Asiago cheese, and reserved chicken drumsticks; partially cover and continue to cook for 5 more minutes. Serve warm.

Per serving: 589 Calories; 46g Fat; 5.8g Carbs; 37.5g Protein; 2g Fiber

72. Chicken and Green Cabbage Soup

(Ready in about 55 minutes | Servings 6)

Ingredients

2 tablespoons butter
1 (3-pound) whole chicken
1/2 onion, chopped

2 celery stalks, chopped
2 cups green cabbage, sliced into strips

Directions

Cook the chicken with 6 cups of water over moderate heat for 13 to 17 minutes. Turn the heat to medium-low and cook for 10 to 15 minutes longer; reserve.

Next, chop the meat into small chunks and discard the bones.

Warm the butter in a heavy-bottomed pot over moderate flame. Cook the celery and onion until they have softened.

Season with salt and pepper; add the reserved chicken and broth to the pot; let it simmer for 10 to 13 minutes.

Afterwards, fold in the cabbage and continue to simmer, partially covered, for a further 15 minutes. Bon appétit!

Per serving: 265 Calories; 23.8g Fat; 4.3g Carbs; 9.3g Protein; 1g Fiber

73. Middle Eastern Shish Kebab

(Ready in about 20 minutes + marinating time | Servings 5)

Ingredients

2 pounds chicken tenders, cut into bite-sized cubes
1/2 cup ajran

1 tablespoon mustard
1/2 cup tomato sauce
Turkish spice mix

Directions

Place chicken tenders with the remaining ingredients in a ceramic dish. Cover and let it marinate for 4 hours in your refrigerator.

Thread chicken tenders onto skewers and place on the preheated grill them until golden brown on all sides approximately 15 minutes.

Serve immediately and enjoy!

Per serving: 274 Calories; 10.7g Fat; 3.3g Carbs; 39.3g Protein; 0.8g Fiber

74. Capocollo and Garlic Chicken

(Ready in about 40 minutes | Servings 5)

Ingredients

2 pounds chicken drumsticks, skinless and boneless, butterflied
10 thin slices of capocollo

1 garlic clove, peeled and halved
Coarse sea salt and ground black pepper, to taste
1/2 teaspoon smoked paprika

Directions

Rub garlic halves over the surface of chicken drumsticks. Season with paprika, salt, and black pepper.

Place a slice of capocollo on each chicken drumsticks and roll them up; secure with a kitchen twine.

Bake in the preheated oven at 410 degrees F for 30 to 35 minutes until your chicken begin to brown. Bon appétit!

Per serving: 485 Calories; 33.8g Fat; 3.6g Carbs; 39.2g Protein; 1g Fiber

75. Chicken Thigh Salad

(Ready in about 20 minutes + chilling time | Servings 2)

Ingredients

2 chicken thighs, skinless
1 tablespoon red wine vinegar
1/4 cup mayonnaise

2 spring onion stalks, chopped
1/2 head Romaine lettuce, torn into pieces

Directions

In the preheated skillet cook the chicken thighs until crunchy on the outside. Discard the bones and transfer the meat to a salad bowl.

Add Dijon mustard, if desired.

Stir in the other ingredients. Serve chilled and enjoy!

Per serving: 456 Calories; 29g Fat; 6.7g Carbs; 40.1g Protein; 3.7g Fiber

76. Cheesy Mexican-Style Chicken

(Ready in about 25 minutes | Servings 6)

Ingredients

1 ½ pounds chicken breasts, cut into bite-sized cubes
2 ripe tomatoes, pureed
4 ounces sour cream

6 ounces Cotija cheese, crumbled
1 Mexican chili pepper, finely chopped

Directions

Preheat your oven to 390 degrees F.

In a saucepan, heat 2 tablespoons of olive oil over a medium-high heat. Cook the chicken breasts for about 10 minutes, stirring frequently to ensure even cooking.

Then, add in Mexican chili pepper and cook until it has softened.

Add in the pureed tomatoes and continue to cook, partially covered, for 4 to 5 minutes. Season with Mexican spice mix. Transfer the mixture to a lightly greased baking dish.

Top with the sour cream and Cotija cheese. Bake in the preheated oven for about 15 minutes or until hot and bubbly. Enjoy!

Per serving: 354 Calories; 23.2g Fat; 6g Carbs; 29.3g Protein; 0.6g Fiber

77. Asian Saucy Chicken

(Ready in about 25 minutes | Servings 4)

Ingredients

1 tablespoon sesame oil
4 chicken legs
1/4 cup Shaoxing wine

2 tablespoons brown erythritol
1/4 cup spicy tomato sauce

Directions

Heat the sesame oil in a wok over medium-high heat. Fry the chicken until golden in color; reserve.

Add Shaoxing wine to deglaze the pan.

Add in erythritol and spicy tomato sauce, and bring the mixture to a boil. Then, immediately reduce the heat to medium-low.

Let it simmer for about 10 minutes until the sauce coats the back of a spoon. Add the chicken back to the wok.

Continue to cook until the chicken is sticky and golden or about 4 minutes. Enjoy!

Per serving: 367 Calories; 14.7g Fat; 3.5g Carbs; 51.2g Protein; 1.1g Fiber

78. Duck Stew Olla Tapada

(Ready in about 30 minutes | Servings 3)

Ingredients

1 red bell pepper, deveined and chopped
1 pound duck breasts, boneless, skinless, and chopped into small chunks

1/2 cup chayote, peeled and cubed
1 shallot, chopped
1 teaspoon Mexican spice mix

Directions

In a clay pot, heat 2 teaspoons of canola oil over a medium-high flame. Sauté the peppers and shallot until softened about 4 minutes.

Add in the remaining ingredients; pour in 1 ½ cups of water or chicken bone broth. Once your mixture starts boiling, reduce the heat to medium-low.

Let it simmer, partially covered, for 18 to 22 minutes, until cooked through. Enjoy!

Per serving: 228 Calories; 9.5g Fat; 3.3g Carbs; 30.6g Protein; 1g Fiber

79. Cheesy Ranch Chicken

(Ready in about 20 minutes | Servings 4)

Ingredients

2 chicken breasts
1/2 tablespoon ranch seasoning mix
4 slices bacon, chopped

1/2 cup Monterey-Jack cheese, grated
4 ounces Ricotta cheese, room temperature

Directions

Preheat your oven to 360 degrees F.

Rub the chicken with ranch seasoning mix.

Heat a saucepan over medium-high flame. Now, sear the chicken for about 8 minutes. Lower the chicken into a lightly greased casserole dish.

Top with cheese and bacon and bake in the preheated oven for about 10 minutes until hot and bubbly. Serve with freshly snipped scallions, if desired.

Per serving: 295 Calories; 19.5g Fat; 2.9g Carbs; 25.5g Protein; 0.4g Fiber

80. Turkey Crust Meatza

(Ready in about 35 minutes | Servings 4)

Ingredients

1/2 pound ground turkey
2 slices Canadian bacon
1 tomato, chopped

1 tablespoon pizza spice mix
1 cup Mozzarella cheese, grated

Directions

Mix the ground turkey and cheese; season with salt and black pepper and mix until everything is well combined.

Press the mixture into a foil-lined baking pan. Bake in the preheated oven at 380 degrees F for 25 minutes.

Top the crust with Canadian bacon, tomato, and pizza spice mix. Continue to bake for a further 8 minutes.

Let it rest a couple of minutes before slicing and serving. Bon appétit!

Per serving: 360 Calories; 22.7g Fat; 5.9g Carbs; 32.6g Protein; 0.7g Fiber

81. Simple Turkey Goulash

(Ready in about 45 minutes | Servings 6)

Ingredients

2 tablespoons olive oil
1 large-sized leek, chopped
2 cloves garlic, minced

2 pounds turkey thighs, skinless, boneless and chopped
2 celery stalks, chopped

Directions

In a clay pot, heat 2 olive oil over a medium-high flame. Then, cook the leeks until tender and translucent.

Then, continue to sauté the garlic for 30 seconds to 1 minute.

Stir in the turkey, celery, and 4 cups of water. Once your mixture starts boiling, let it simmer, partially covered, for about 40 minutes.

Bon appétit!

Per serving: 220 Calories; 7.4g Fat; 2.7g Carbs; 35.5g Protein; 1g Fiber

82. Fajita with Zucchini

(Ready in about 20 minutes | Servings 4)

Ingredients

1 red onion, sliced
1 teaspoon Fajita seasoning mix

1 pound turkey cutlets
1 zucchini, spiralized
1 chili pepper, chopped

Directions

In a nonstick skillet, heat 1 tablespoon of the olive oil over a medium-high flame. Cook the turkey cutlets for 6 to 7 minutes on each side. Slice the meat into strips and reserve.

Heat another tablespoon of olive oil and sauté the onion and chili pepper until they are just tender. Sprinkle with Fajita seasoning mix.

Add in the zucchini and the reserved turkey; let it cook for 4 minutes more or until everything is cooked through. Serve with 1/2 cup of salsa, if desired. Enjoy!

Per serving: 212 Calories; 9.2g Fat; 5.6g Carbs; 26g Protein; 1.2g Fiber

83. Easiest Turkey Meatballs Ever

(Ready in about 1 hour 20 minutes | Servings 4)

Ingredients

1 egg, whisked
4 spring onions, finely chopped
1/2 cup parmesan cheese, grated

1 tablespoon Italian spice mix
1 pound ground turkey

Directions

Thoroughly combine all ingredients. Roll the turkey mixture into balls and place them in your refrigerator for 1 hour.

In a cast-iron skillet, heat 2 tablespoons of olive oil over medium-high heat. Sear the meatballs for 12 minutes or until nicely browned on all sides.

Bon appétit!

Per serving: 366 Calories; 27.7g Fat; 3g Carbs; 25.9g Protein; 0.5g Fiber

84. Greek-Style Chicken Drumettes

(Ready in about 30 minutes | Servings 2)

Ingredients

1 tablespoon olive oil
6 Kalamata olives, pitted and sliced
1 pound chicken drumettes

6 ounces tomato sauce
1 teaspoon Greek seasoning blend

Directions

Rub the chicken drumettes with Greek seasoning blend.

In a nonstick skillet, heat the olive oil over medium-high flame. Sear the chicken for about 10 minutes until nicely brown.

Add in the olives and tomato sauce. Stir and continue to cook, partially covered, for about 18 minutes until everything is thoroughly heated. Bon appétit!

Per serving: 341 Calories; 14.3g Fat; 3.6g Carbs; 47g Protein; 1.1g Fiber

85. Chicken Tawook Salad

(Ready in about 20 minutes | Servings 2)

Ingredients

2 chicken breasts
4 tablespoons apple cider vinegar
1 cup grape tomatoes, halved

1 Lebanese cucumber, thinly sliced
2 tablespoons extra-virgin olive oil

Directions

Preheat a grill to medium-high and oil a grill grate. Grill the chicken for about 13 minutes, turing them over a few times.

Slice the chicken into the bite-sized chunks and transfer them to a serving bowl. Add in the vinegar, tomatoes, cucumber, and olive oil. Toss to combine well.

Serve at room temperature or well-chilled. Bon appétit!

Per serving: 403 Calories; 18g Fat; 5.3g Carbs; 51.6g Protein; 1.6g Fiber

86. Greek Chicken with Peppers

(Ready in about 20 minutes | Servings 2)

Ingredients

2 chicken drumsticks, boneless and skinless
2 bell peppers, deveined and halved

1 small chili pepper, finely chopped
2 tablespoons Greek aioli
6 Kalamata olives, pitted

Directions

Rub the chicken with 1 tablespoon of extra-virgin olive oil. Season with salt and black pepper to taste.

Grill the chicken drumsticks for 8 to 9 minutes; add the bell peppers and grill them for a further 6 minutes.

Place the meat and peppers in a serving bowl; add in chili pepper and Greek aioli. Top with Kalamata olives and serve.

Per serving: 403 Calories; 31.4g Fat; 5g Carbs; 24.5g Protein; 1.1g Fiber

87. Colorful Chicken Chowder

(Ready in about 50 minutes | Servings 6)

Ingredients

1 tablespoon olive oil
6 chicken wings
1 cup mixed frozen vegetables (celery, onions, and pepper)

1 tablespoon poultry seasoning mix
1 whole egg

Directions

Heat the olive oil in a heavy-bottomed pot over medium-high heat. Then, brown the chicken for 10 minutes or until no longer pink; set them aside.

Then, cook the vegetables in the pan drippings until they are crisp-tender.

Season with poultry seasoning mix and turn the heat to medium-low; continue to simmer for a further 40 minutes or until everything is thoroughly cooked.

Chop the chicken and discard the fat and bones.

Whisk the egg into the cooking liquid. Add the reserved chicken back to the pot. Taste and adjust the seasonings. Enjoy!

Per serving: 283 Calories; 18.9g Fat; 2.6g Carbs; 25.4g Protein; 0.5g Fiber

88. Chicken Frittata with Asiago Cheese and Herbs

(Ready in about 30 minutes | Servings 4)

Ingredients

1 pound chicken breasts, cut into small strips
4 slices of bacon
1 cup Asiago cheese, shredded
6 eggs
1/2 cup yogurt

Directions

Preheat an oven-proof skillet. Then, fry the bacon until crisp and reserve. Then, in the pan drippings, cook the chicken for about 8 minutes or until no longer pink.

Add the reserved bacon back to the skillet.

In a mixing dish, thoroughly combine the eggs and yogurt; season with Italian spice mix.

Pour the egg mixture over the chicken and bacon. Top with cheese and bake in the preheated oven at 380 degrees F for 22 minutes until hot and bubbly.

Let it rest a couple of minutes before slicing and serving. Bon appétit!

Per serving: 484 Calories; 31.8g Fat; 5.8g Carbs; 41.9g Protein; 0.7g Fiber

89. Stuffed Chicken with Sauerkraut and Cheese

(Ready in about 35 minutes | Servings 5)

Ingredients

5 chicken cutlets
1 cup Romano cheese, shredded
2 garlic cloves, minced
5 Italian peppers, deveined and chopped
5 tablespoons sauerkraut, for serving

Directions

Spritz a baking pan with 1 tablespoon of the olive oil. Brush the chicken with another tablespoon of olive oil.

Season the chicken with Italian spice mix. You can spread Dijon mustard on one side of each chicken cutlet, if desired.

Divide the garlic, peppers and Romano cheese between chicken cutlets; roll them up.

Bake at 360 degrees F for 25 to 33 minutes until nicely brown on all sides. Serve with the sauerkraut and serve. Bon appétit!

Per serving: 376 Calories; 16.7g Fat; 5.8g Carbs; 47g Protein; 1g Fiber

90. Cream of Chicken Soup

(Ready in about 40 minutes | Servings 5)

Ingredients

1/2 cup Italian peppers, deseeded and chopped
1/2 cup green cabbage, shredded
5 chicken thighs
1/2 cup celery, chopped
7 ounces full-fat cream cheese

Directions

Add Italian peppers, cabbage, chicken thighs, and celery to a large clay pot.

Pour in 5 cups of water or chicken broth.

Partially cover and let it simmer over medium-high heat approximately 30 minutes. Transfer the chicken to a cutting board,

Shred the chicken and return it to the pot. Add in full-fat cream cheese and stir until everything is well incorporated.

Ladle into serving bowls and enjoy!

Per serving: 514 Calories; 38g Fat; 5.4g Carbs; 35.3g Protein; 0.5g Fiber

91. Lemony and Garlicky Chicken Wings

(Ready in about 25 minutes + marinating time | Servings 4)

Ingredients

8 chicken wings
2 garlic cloves, minced
1/4 cup leeks, chopped
2 tablespoons lemon juice
1 teaspoon Mediterranean spice mix

Directions

Place all ingredients in a ceramic dish. Cover and let it sit in your refrigerator for 2 hours.

Brush the chicken wings with melted ghee. Grill the chicken wings for 15 to 20 minutes, turning them occasionally to ensure even cooking. Enjoy!

Per serving: 131 Calories; 7.8g Fat; 1.8g Carbs; 13.4g Protein; 0.3g Fiber

92. Creamiest Chicken Salad Ever

(Ready in about 1 hour 20 minutes | Servings 3)

Ingredients

1 chicken breast, skinless
1/4 mayonnaise
1/4 cup sour cream
2 tablespoons Cottage cheese, room temperature
1/2 avocado, peeled and cubed

Directions

Cook the chicken in a pot of salted water. Remove from the heat and let the chicken sit, covered, in the hot water for 10 to 15 minutes.

Slice the chicken into bite-sized strips. Toss with the remaining ingredients.

Place in the refrigerator for at least one hour. Serve well chilled. Enjoy!

Per serving: 400 Calories; 35.1g Fat; 5.6g Carbs; 16.1g Protein; 1g Fiber

93. Thai Turkey Curry

(Ready in about 1 hour | Servings 4)

Ingredients

1 pound turkey wings, boneless and chopped
2 cloves garlic, finely chopped
1 Thai red chili pepper, minced
1 cup unsweetened coconut milk, preferably homemade
1 cup turkey consommé

Directions

In a saucepan, warm 2 teaspoons of sesame oil. Once hot, brown turkey about 8 minutes or until it is golden brown.

Add in the garlic and Thai chili pepper and continue to cook for a minute or so.

Add coconut milk and consommé. Season with salt and black pepper to taste. Continue to cook for 40 to 45 minutes over medium heat. Serve warm and enjoy!

Per serving: 295 Calories; 19.5g Fat; 2.9g Carbs; 25.5g Protein; 1g Fiber

94. Baked Teriyaki Turkey

(Ready in about 15 minutes | Servings 2)

Ingredients

3/4 pound lean ground turkey
1 brown onion, chopped
1 red bell pepper, deveined and chopped
1 serrano pepper, deveined and chopped
1/4 cup keto teriyaki sauce

Directions

Cook the ground turkey in the preheated pan over medium-high heat; cook for about 5 minutes until no longer pink.

Now, sauté the onion and peppers for 3 minutes more. Add in teriyaki sauce and bring the mixture to a boil.

Immediately remove from the heat; add in the cooked ground turkey and sautéed mixture.

Serve warm and enjoy!

Per serving: 410 Calories; 27.1g Fat; 6.6g Carbs; 36.5g Protein; 1g Fiber

95. Ranch Turkey with Greek Sauce

(Ready in about 20 minutes | Servings 4)

Ingredients

2 eggs
1 tablespoon Ranch seasoning blend
1/2 cup almond meal
1 pound turkey tenders, 1/2-inch thick
1/2 cup Greek keto sauce

Directions

In a shallow bowl, whisk the eggs with Ranch seasoning blend.

In another shallow bowl, place the almond meal. Dip the turkey tenders into the Ranch egg mixture.

Then, press them into the almond meal; press to coat well.

Heat 2 tablespoons of olive oil in a pan over medium-high heat. Brown turkey tenders for 3 to 4 minutes on each side.

Serve the turkey tenders with Greek keto sauce. Enjoy!

Per serving: 396 Calories; 27.5g Fat; 3.9g Carbs; 33.1g Protein; 1.9g Fiber

96. Mediterranean Herbed Chicken

(Ready in about 20 minutes | Servings 5)

Ingredients

2 tablespoons butter, softened at room temperature
5 chicken legs, skinless
2 scallions, chopped
1 tablespoon Mediterranean spice mix
1 cup vegetable broth

Directions

In a saucepan, melt 1 tablespoon of butter over a medium-high flame. Now, brown the chicken legs for about 10 minutes, turning them periodically.

Add in the remaining tablespoon of butter, scallions, Mediterranean spice mix, and broth. When your mixture reaches boiling, reduce the temperature to a simmer.

Continue to simmer for 10 to 11 minutes until cooked through. Taste and adjust the seasoning. Bon appétit!

Per serving: 370 Calories; 16g Fat; 0.9g Carbs; 51g Protein; 0.2g Fiber

97. Saucy Chicken with Marsala Wine

(Ready in about 20 minutes | Servings 2)

Ingredients

2 chicken fillets
1/4 cup marsala wine
1 cup broccoli florets
1/4 tomato paste
1/2 cup double cream

Directions

Heat 1 tablespoon of olive oil in a sauté pan over medium-high heat. Once hot, sear the chicken for 10 minutes, flipping them over once or twice.

Add marsala wine and deglaze the pot. Add in the broccoli and tomato paste. Reduce the heat to simmer.

Continue to simmer for a further 5 to 7 minutes. Lastly, stir in the double cream. Season with paprika, salt, and black pepper to taste.

Bon appétit!

Per serving: 347 Calories; 20.4g Fat; 4.7g Carbs; 35.3g Protein; 1.4g Fiber

98. Chicken Mulligatawny

(Ready in about 35 minutes | Servings 4)

Ingredients

2 tablespoons ghee
1 pound chicken thighs, boneless and skinless
1 tablespoon Indian spice mix
1 celery stalk, chopped
1 cup milk

Directions

Melt the butter in a soup pot over medium-high flame. Brown the chicken thighs until nicely browned on all sides about 6 minutes.

Add in Indian spice mix and celery; stir to combine and reduce the heat to simmer; continue to simmer for 30 minutes more.

Pour in the milk and stir to combine well. Bon appétit!

Per serving: 343 Calories; 26.7g Fat; 3.8g Carbs; 20.9g Protein; 0.2g Fiber

99. Naga Chicken Salad Ole

(Ready in about 20 minutes + chilling time | Servings 6)

Ingredients

1/2 cup dry white wine
1 ½ pounds chicken breasts
1 Spanish naga chili pepper, chopped

1/4 cup mayonnaise
2 cups arugula

Directions

Place the chicken breasts and wine in a deep saucepan. Then, cover the chicken with water, and bring to a boil.

When your mixture reaches boiling, reduce the temperature to a simmer.

Let it simmer, partially covered, for about 13 minutes or until cooked through.

Shred the chicken, discarding the bones and poaching liquid. Place in a salad bowl and add naga chili pepper, arugula, and mayonnaise to the bowl.

Add Spanish peppers, if desired and stir to combine well.

Serve well-chilled and enjoy!

Per serving: 278 Calories; 16.1g Fat; 4.9g Carbs; 27.2g Protein; 0.9g Fiber

100. Oven-Roasted Chimichurri Chicken

(Ready in about 40 minutes + marinating time | Servings 5)

Ingredients

1 ½ pounds chicken tenders
1/2 cup fresh parsley, chopped
2 garlic cloves, minced

1/4 cup olive oil
4 tablespoons white wine vinegar

Directions

Blend the parsley, olive oil, vinegar, and garlic in your food processor until the smooth and uniform sauce forms. Pierce the chicken with a small knife.

Add chicken and 1/2 of the chimichurri sauce to a glass dosh and let them marinate for 2 hours in your refrigerator.

Spritz a baking pan with nonstick cooking spray. Place the chicken in the baking pan. Season with salt and black pepper.

Bake in the preheated oven at 360 degrees F for 35 minutes or until an internal temperature reaches about 165 degrees F.

Serve with the reserved chimichurri sauce. Bon appétit!

Per serving: 305 Calories; 14.7g Fat; 0.8g Carbs; 27.9g Protein; 0.2g Fiber

101. Classic Garlicky Chicken Drumettes

(Ready in about 40 minutes + marinating time | Servings 5)

Ingredients

1/4 cup coconut aminos
1 tablespoon olive oil
1 tablespoon apple cider vinegar

2 cloves garlic, minced
5 chicken drumettes

Directions

Thoroughly combine, coconut aminos, olive oil, apple cider vinegar, and garlic in a glass dish. Allow it to marinate for 2 hours in your refrigerator

Place the chicken in a foil-lined baking dish. Season with salt and black pepper to taste.

Bake in the preheated oven at 410 degrees F for 35 minutes, basting the chicken with the reserved marinade. Bon appétit!

Per serving: 266 Calories; 19.3g Fat; 0.8g Carbs; 20.3g Protein; 0.2g Fiber

102. Turkey Chili with Monterey Jack Cheese

(Ready in about 40 minutes | Servings 5)

Ingredients

1 ½ pounds ground turkey
1 onion, diced
1 cup spicy tomato sauce

5 ounces Monterey Jack cheese, shredded
2 medium Italian peppers, deveined and sliced

Directions

Preheat a Dutch oven over medium-high heat. Cook the ground turkey and onion for 5 to 6 minutes until no longer pink.

Add in a splash of red wine to scrape up the browned bits that stick to the bottom of the pan. Stir in Italian peppers and tomato sauce.

When your mixture starts to boil, turn the heat to simmer. Continue to simmer, partially covered, for 30 to 35 minutes.

Top with Monterey Jack cheese and place under preheated broil for 5 minutes until hot and bubbly. Enjoy!

Per serving: 390 Calories; 25.3g Fat; 4.8g Carbs; 33.7g Protein; 1.3g Fiber

103. Swiss Turkey and Pepper Timbale

(Ready in about 30 minutes | Servings 5)

Ingredients

1 yellow onion, thinly sliced
1 cup bell peppers, sliced
1 ½ pounds turkey breast

1 cup double cream
1/2 cup Swiss cheese, shredded

Directions

In a saucepan, heat 2 teaspoons of the olive oil over medium-high heat. Sauté the onion and peppers until they have softened and reserve.

In the same saucepan, heat 1 teaspoon of olive oil; now, sear the turkey breasts until nicely browned on all sides.

Place the peppers and onions on the bottom of a lightly greased baking pan. Add the turkey breast on top.

Mix double cream with 1 cup of chicken bone broth and spoon the mixture over the turkey breasts.

Bake in the preheated oven at 360 degrees F for about 18 minutes.

Top with the Swiss cheese and continue to bake for a further 6 minutes or until bubbly and golden brown on top. Bon appétit!

Per serving: 464 Calories; 28.5g Fat; 4.5g Carbs; 45.4g Protein; 0.3g Fiber

104. Chicken and Vegetable Souvlaki

(Ready in about 20 minutes | Servings 6)

Ingredients

2 tablespoons olive oil
1 tablespoon stone-ground mustard
1 ½ pounds chicken, skinless, boneless and cubed
2 red onions, cut into wedges
3 bell pepper, cut into 1-inch pieces

Directions

In a mixing bowl, combine the olive oil, mustard and chicken cubes. Drizzle with 4 tablespoons of dry sherry.

Alternate skewering the chicken and vegetables and season them with salt and black pepper.

Cook your souvlaki on the preheated grill, flipping a few times to ensure even cooking. Serve warm.

Per serving: 200 Calories; 8.1g Fat; 7g Carbs; 24.3g Protein; 1.3g Fiber

105. Hungarian Chicken Paprikash

(Ready in about 35 minutes | Servings 5)

Ingredients

2 pounds chicken drumsticks
1 cup marinara sauce, sugar-free
1 Hungarian wax pepper, chopped
1 bell pepper, deseeded and chopped
1/2 cup leeks, sliced

Directions

Heat 2 tablespoons of olive oil in a heavy-bottomed pot over medium-high flame. Then, brown the chicken drumsticks until no longer pink or about 8 minutes; shred the meat and discard the bones.

Then, cook the peppers and leeks in the pan drippings until they have softened or 4 to 5 minutes.

Add in the marinara sauce along with 4 cups of water or vegetable broth; season with salt and black pepper, if desired.

Fold in the reserved chicken and bring to a boil; turn the heat to simmer, let it simmer for 20 minutes more or until heated through. Enjoy!

Per serving: 358 Calories; 22.2g Fat; 4.4g Carbs; 33.3g Protein; 0.7g Fiber

106. Sri Lankan Curry

(Ready in about 30 minutes | Servings 5)

Ingredients

2 tablespoons coconut oil
1 ½ pounds chicken tenders, cut into chunks
1/2 cup coconut milk
1/2 cup chicken broth
1 tablespoon curry powder

Directions

Melt the coconut oil in a saucepan or wok over medium-high heat. Then, cook the chicken tenders for 6 to 7 minutes, stirring periodically to ensure even cooking.

Now, add in coconut milk, chicken broth and curry powder, bringing to a boil.

Turn the heat to medium-low and allow it to simmer for a further 20 minutes. Garnish with fresh cilantro just before serving, if desired. Enjoy!

Per serving: 370 Calories; 16g Fat; 0.9g Carbs; 51g Protein; 0.2g Fiber

107. Traditional Japanese Ramen

(Ready in about 35 minutes | Servings 6)

Ingredients

1 tablespoon peanut oil
1 pound chicken thigs
4 ounces enokitake or enoki mushrooms
4 garlic cloves, chopped
2 tablespoons sake

Directions

Warm the peanut oil in a large soup pot over medium-high flame. Then, sear the chicken thighs for about 8 minutes, turning them over once or twice.

Add in 6 cups of dashi, enokitake, and garlic. When the soup reaches boiling, turn the heat to a simmer. Then, let it simmer for another 30 minutes.

Shred the chicken and return it to the pot. Pour in the sake and stir to combine well.

Taste, adjust the seasonings and serve warm.

Per serving: 199 Calories; 13.7g Fat; 2.4g Carbs; 14.7g Protein; 0.6g Fiber

108. Summer Turkey Drumstick

(Ready in about 20 minutes + marinating time | Servings 2)

Ingredients

1 turkey drumstick, skinless and boneless
1 tablespoon whiskey
1/4 cup chicken marinade, no sugar added
1 brown onion, peeled and chopped
1 teaspoon Mediterranean spice mix

Directions

Place the turkey, marinade, and whiskey in a ceramic dish; add in 1 tablespoon of stone ground mustard, if desired.

Cover and refrigerate for 2 hours.

Then, preheat your grill to the hottest setting.

Grill the turkey for 12 to 15 minutes per side. Season with Mediterranean spice and serve with brown onion. Bon appétit!

Per serving: 388 Calories; 19.5g Fat; 6g Carbs; 42g Protein; 1.4g Fiber

109. Greek-Style Roasted Chicken with Herbs

(Ready in about 25 minutes | Servings 5)

Ingredients

1 ½ pounds chicken drumettes
2 tablespoons olive oil
2 cloves garlic, minced

1 red onion, cut into wedges
1 tablespoon Mediterranean spice mix

Directions

Preheat your oven to 410 degrees F. Brush the sides and bottom a baking dish with 1 tablespoon of olive oil.

In a nonstick skillet, heat the remaining tablespoon of olive oil over medium heat. Sear the chicken drumettes for 10 to 12 minutes, turning them over periodically to ensure even cooking.

Place the chicken in a baking dish. Add in the garlic, spices, and red onion.

Roast in the preheated oven for about 15 minutes or until nicely browned on top. Serve and enjoy!

Per serving: 218 Calories; 9.1g Fat; 4.2g Carbs; 28.6g Protein; 0.7g Fiber

110. Garlicky Roasted Chicken Drumsticks

(Ready in about 50 minutes | Servings 6)

Ingredients

4 cloves garlic, minced
Sea salt and ground black pepper, to taste

1 tablespoon fresh thyme leaves
1 stick unsalted butter, softened
2 pounds chicken drumsticks

Directions

Start by preheating your oven to 395 degrees F.

Mix the garlic, salt, black pepper, thyme, and butter. Rub the mixture all over the chicken drumsticks.

Place the chicken drumsticks on a foil-lined baking dish. Bake in the preheated oven for 35 to 40 minutes.

Afterwards, place under the preheated broiler for 3 minutes to get nice, crisp skin. Bon appétit!

Per serving: 343 Calories; 24.2g Fat; 1.6g Carbs; 28.2g Protein; 0.2g Fiber

111. Chicken Breasts in Creamy Mushroom Sauce

(Ready in about 15 minutes | Servings 4)

Ingredients

2 chicken breast, skinless and boneless, cut into bite-sized pieces
2 garlic cloves, pressed

1 tablespoon olive oil
1 yellow onion, chopped
1/2 cup cream of mushroom soup

Directions

Heat the olive oil in a nonstick skillet over medium-high flame. Once hot, cook the onion for about 4 minutes or until caramelized and softened.

Then, cook the garlic for 30 seconds more.

Sear the chicken breast approximately 5 minutes, stirring continuously to ensure even cooking. Pour in the cream of mushroom soup.

Turn the heat to a simmer and continue to cook until the sauce has reduced and thickened about 8 minutes. Serve warm chicken topped with the sauce. Enjoy!

Per serving: 335 Calories; 20.8g Fat; 4.3g Carbs; 30.9g Protein; 0.6g Fiber

112. Easy Cocktail Party Meatballs

(Ready in about 25 minutes | Servings 4)

Ingredients

1 tablespoon Italian seasoning blend
1 egg, beaten

2 cloves garlic, minced
1/2 cup leeks, minced
1 pound ground turkey

Directions

Thoroughly combine all ingredients in a bowl.

Shape the mixture into small balls and transfer them to a foil-lined baking pan. Brush the meatballs with olive oil.

Bake in the preheated oven at 390 degrees F for about 20 minutes. Serve with toothpicks or cocktail sticks.

Per serving: 216 Calories; 11.2g Fat; 3.6g Carbs; 24.3g Protein; 0.5g Fiber

113. Chinese Duck with Onion

(Ready in about 25 minutes | Servings 4)

Ingredients

1 tablespoon sesame oil
1 ½ pounds duck breast
1 white onion, chopped

3 teaspoons soy sauce
1/4 cup rice wine

Directions

Preheat your oven to 395 degrees F.

Using a sharp knife, score the duck breast skin in a tight crosshatch pattern.

Heat the sesame oil in a wok over medium-high heat. Now, sauté the onion until softened and aromatic.

Add the duck breast to the wok and cook for about 15 minutes or until nicely brown on the top.

Pour in rice wine to scrape up the browned bits that stick to the bottom of the wok. Transfer duck breasts to a lightly greased baking pan; add the soy sauce to the baking pan.

Roast in the preheated oven for 10 minutes and serve warm. Enjoy!

Per serving: 263 Calories; 11.3g Fat; 3.7g Carbs; 34.4g Protein; 0.5g Fiber

114. Chicken Drumstick Soup

(Ready in about 30 minutes | Servings 2)

Ingredients

1 stalk celery, chopped
1/2 white onion, chopped
1 teaspoon poultry seasoning mix
1 tablespoon fresh cilantro, chopped
2 chicken drumsticks, skinless and boneless

Directions

Place the chicken in a medium-sized soup pot. Add enough water to cover the chicken by about two inches.

Now, add in celery, onion, and poultry seasoning mix. Bring to a boil; then, immediately reduce the heat to a simmer and continue cooking for about 40 minutes.

Serve with fresh cilantro. Enjoy!

Per serving: 166 Calories; 4.9g Fat; 3.3g Carbs; 25.6g Protein; 0.7g Fiber

115. Oven-Roasted Buffalo Chicken

(Ready in about 1 hour | Servings 6)

Ingredients

1/2 cup melted butter
2 tablespoons white vinegar
1/2 cup hot sauce
1/4 teaspoon granulated garlic
2 pounds chicken drumettes

Directions

Preheat your oven to 330 degrees F. Lightly oil the sides and bottom of a baking pan. Place the chicken drumettes in the baking pan.

Whisk the melted butter, white vinegar, hot sauce, and garlic. Add in the salt and black pepper to taste and whisk until everything is well combined.

Pour the sauce over the chicken drumettes and bake for 50 to 55 minutes, flipping them once or twice to ensure even cooking. Bon appétit!

Per serving: 288 Calories; 20.6g Fat; 1.4g Carbs; 23.5g Protein; 0.4g Fiber

116. Chicken Drumsticks with Tomato

(Ready in about 1 hour 15 minutes | Servings 5)

Ingredients

2 pounds chicken drumsticks, boneless, skinless
2 garlic cloves, minced
1/2 cup tomato paste
1/2 cup chicken broth
2 fresh scallions, chopped

Directions

Spritz a baking pan with 1 tablespoon of olive oil.

Place the chicken drumsticks in the prepared baking pan. Drizzle 1 tablespoon of olive oil over chicken drumsticks.

Add the garlic, tomato paste, and chicken broth to the pan.

Bake in the preheated oven at 340 degrees F for about 65 minutes or until nicely brown and crisp on the top. Garnish with fresh scallions and enjoy!

Per serving: 352 Calories; 22.1g Fat; 2.5g Carbs; 33.3g Protein; 0.5g Fiber

117. Creamed Chicken Salad

(Ready in about 20 minutes + chilling time | Servings 4)

Ingredients

2 chicken breasts, skinless and boneless
1 teaspoon Dijon mustard
2 teaspoons freshly squeezed lemon juice
1 cup mayonnaise, preferably homemade
4 scallions, trimmed and thinly sliced

Directions

Place the chicken in a stockpot; cover with water by 1 inch and bring to a boil.

Then, continue to simmer for 13 to 16 minutes (a meat thermometer should read 165 degrees F).

When cool enough to handle, cut the chicken into strips and place them in a serving bowl. Toss the chicken with the remaining ingredients.

Serve with fresh coriander if desired. Bon appétit!

Per serving: 536 Calories; 49g Fat; 3.1g Carbs; 19g Protein; 0.5g Fiber

118. Rustic Italian Stuffed Turkey

(Ready in about 1 hour | Servings 6)

Ingredients

1 ½ pounds turkey breasts
6 ounces Asiago cheese, sliced
2 tablespoons extra-virgin olive oil
1 tablespoon Italian seasoning mix
2 bell peppers, thinly sliced

Directions

Start by preheating your oven to 370 degrees F. Brush the inside of a baking dish with 1 tablespoon of olive oil.

Sprinkle the turkey breast with the Italian seasoning mix; season with salt and black pepper to taste.

Create slits in turkey breasts to make a pocket; stuff them with Asiago cheese and bell peppers. You can add minced garlic if desired.

Drizzle the turkey breasts with the remaining tablespoon of olive oil.

Bake for 55 minutes or until thoroughly cooked. Let it stand for 10 minutes before slicing and serving.

Garnish with Italian parsley if desired and serve.

Per serving: 347 Calories; 22.2g Fat; 3g Carbs; 32g Protein; 0.5g Fiber

119. Chicken with Tomato and Romano Cheese

(Ready in about 15 minutes | Servings 3)

Ingredients

1/2 pound chicken fillets
1 egg, whisked
3 ounces Romano cheese, grated
2 ounces pork rinds, crushed
1 large-sized Roma tomato, pureed

Directions

In a shallow dish, place the whisked egg.

In the second shallow dish, mix Romano cheese and crushed pork rinds; season with salt, black pepper, cayenne pepper, and dried parsley.

Dip the chicken fillets into the egg mixture; then, roll the chicken over the breading mixture until well coated.

In a frying pan, heat 2 tablespoons of olive oil over medium-high heat. Once hot, fry the chicken fillets for about 3 minutes per side.

Place the chicken in a lightly greased baking pan. Spread pureed tomato over the top. Bake for a further 3 minutes. Bon appétit!

Per serving: 359 Calories; 23.6g Fat; 5.8g Carbs; 30.4g Protein; 1.1g Fiber

120. Indian Chicken Masala

(Ready in about 30 minutes | Servings 5)

Ingredients

1 ½ pounds chicken breasts, cut into bite-sized pieces
1 teaspoon garam masala
10 ounces tomato puree
1/2 cup heavy cream
1 onion, chopped

Directions

Spritz a saucepan with a nonstick cooking spray and preheat over medium-high heat. Now, sear the chicken breasts until nicely browned on both sides.

Remove the chicken to the sides of the saucepan and sauté the onions for about 3 minutes or until translucent and tender.

Stir in the garam masala and tomato puree. Cook for 9 to 10 minutes until the sauce is reduced by two-thirds.

Add in the heavy cream and stir for about 12 minutes or until thoroughly heated. Bon appétit!

Per serving: 294 Calories; 17.2g Fat; 4.6g Carbs; 29.3g Protein; 1.1g Fiber

121. Authentic Italian Puttanesca

(Ready in about 25 minutes | Servings 5)

Ingredients

1 ½ pounds chicken wings, boneless
2 cups marinara sauce, no sugar added
1 bell pepper, chopped
1 red onion, chopped
1/4 cup parmesan cheese, preferably freshly grated

Directions

In a saucepan, heat 2 tablespoons of olive oil over a moderate flame. Once hot, sauté the peppers and onions until tender and translucent.

Stir in the chicken and marinara sauce; you can add garlic and capers, if desired; continue to simmer for 18 to 22 minutes.

Serve garnished with parmesan cheese. Bon appétit!

Per serving: 265 Calories; 11.4g Fat; 6.5g Carbs; 32.5g Protein; 1.4g Fiber

122. Chicken with Wine-Mushroom Sauce

(Ready in about 50 minutes | Servings 4)

Ingredients

1 ½ pounds whole chicken, skinless and boneless
1 medium-sized leek, chopped
2 cups button mushrooms, sliced
1/4 cup dry red wine
1 cup marinara sauce, no sugar added

Directions

In a frying pan, heat 1 tablespoon of olive oil over medium-high heat. Sear the chicken until golden brown or about 9 minutes; reserve.

Then, cook the leek and mushrooms until they tender and aromatic or about 5 minutes. Pour in red wine to deglaze the pan.

Return the chicken to the frying pan. Season with salt and black pepper. Add in marinara sauce and stir to combine well.

Reduce the temperature to medium-low and let it cook for 25 to 30 minutes or until cooked through. Serve and enjoy!

Per serving: 426 Calories; 29.2g Fat; 5.7g Carbs; 33.3g Protein; 1.1g Fiber

123. Gourmet Italian Turkey Fillets

(Ready in about 20 minutes | Servings 5)

Ingredients

2 eggs
1 cup sour cream
1 teaspoon Italian seasoning blend

1/2 cup grated parmesan cheese
2 pounds turkey fillets

Directions

Beat the eggs until frothy and light. Add in the sour cream and continue whisking until pale and well mixed.

In another bowl, mix the Italian seasoning blend and parmesan cheese; mix to combine well.

Dip the turkey fillets into the egg mixture; then, coat them with the parmesan mixture.

Fry turkey fillets in the greased sauté pan until golden brown and cooked through. Bon appétit!

Per serving: 335 Calories; 12.8g Fat; 5.3g Carbs; 47.7g Protein; 0.1g Fiber

124. Mediterranean Chicken with Thyme and Olives

(Ready in about 1 hour 15 minutes | Servings 5)

Ingredients

2 pounds whole chicken
1 teaspoon lemon zest, slivered
1 cup oil-cured black olives, pitted

4 cloves garlic
1 bunch fresh thyme, leaves picked

Directions

Begin by preheating your oven to 360 degrees F. Then, spritz the sides and bottom of a baking dish with nonstick cooking oil.

Sprinkle the chicken with paprika, lemon zest, salt, and black pepper. Bake for 60 minutes.

Scatter black olives, garlic, and thyme around the chicken and bake an additional 10 to 13 minutes; a meat thermometer should read 180 degrees F. Bon appétit!

Per serving: 235 Calories; 7.5g Fat; 2.7g Carbs; 37.3g Protein; 1g Fiber

125. Duck with Zucchini and Marinara Sauce

(Ready in about 30 minutes | Servings 4)

Ingredients

1 ½ pounds duck breasts, chopped into small chunks
1/2 cup leeks, sliced
1 medium zucchini, sliced

1 bell pepper, sliced
1 cup marinara sauce, no sugar added

Directions

Melt 2 tablespoons of butter in a sauté pan over a moderate flame. Brown the duck breasts for about 7 minutes, stirring frequently.

Add in the leeks, zucchini, and pepper; continue to sauté for a further 3 to 4 minutes or until fragrant and tender.

Add in marinara sauce. Reduce the heat to a simmer and continue to cook for a further 11 minutes.

Serve warm.

Per serving: 274 Calories; 13.3g Fat; 3g Carbs; 34.3g Protein; 0.6g Fiber

BEEF

126. Home-Style Burgers

(Ready in about 20 minutes | Servings 6)

Ingredients

2 ounces bacon, chopped
1 shallot, chopped
4 tablespoons almond meal
1 ½ pounds ground chuck
2 garlic cloves, minced

Directions

Mix all ingredients in a bowl until well combined. Season with salt and black pepper and form the mixture into 6 patties.

Preheat a grill pan that is previously greased with a nonstick cooking spray. Cook your burgers over a medium-high heat for about 5 minutes per side.

Serve on keto buns and enjoy!

Per serving: 325 Calories; 21.5g Fat; 1.3g Carbs; 29.9g Protein; 0.4g Fiber

127. Beef Teriyaki Bowl

(Ready in about 15 minutes | Servings 6)

Ingredients

1 ½ pounds bottom round steak, cut into bite-sized pieces
1 onion, sliced
1 zucchini, sliced
1 package (0.07-ounce) stevia
2 tablespoons rice vinegar

Directions

In a wok, heat 1 tablespoons of the sesame oil over medium-high flame. Sear the beef for about 7 minutes until no longer pink; reserve.

Heat 1/2 tablespoon of sesame oil and cook the onion and zucchini for 4 to 5 minutes or until tender.

Mix stevia and rice vinegar to make the sauce; add in 2 tablespoons of coconut aminos, if desired.

Add the sauce to the wok along with the reserved beef. Cook for 3 to 4 minutes more or until warmed thorough. Serve and enjoy!

Per serving: 207 Calories; 11g Fat; 1.1g Carbs; 24.2g Protein; 0.1g Fiber

128. Country-Style Beef Soup

(Ready in about 45 minutes | Servings 4)

Ingredients

3/4 pound chuck, cut into bite-sized cubes
1/2 tablespoon lard, at room temperature
4 cups beef bone broth
1 celery rib, chopped
1/2 cup scallions, chopped

Directions

Melt the lard in a soup pot over a medium-high heat. Now, sear the beef for 5 to 6 minutes, stirring periodically to ensure even cooking; reserve.

After that, sauté the celery and scallions in the pan drippings for about 3 minutes or until they've softened. Deglaze the pan with the beef broth.

Return the reserved beef to the soup pot, bringing to a rolling boil. Reduce the heat to medium-low and let it cook approximately 30 minutes.

Divide between individual bowls. Bon appétit!

Per serving: 181 Calories; 8.6g Fat; 2.1g Carbs; 23.2g Protein; 0.5g Fiber

129. Steak and Pepper Salad

(Ready in about 15 minutes | Servings 5)

Ingredients

1 ½ pounds beef sirloin steaks, sliced into bite-sized strips
2 bell peppers, sliced
2 tablespoons soy sauce
1 ½ tablespoons fresh lemon juice
2 tomatoes, sliced

Directions

Brush the sides and bottom of your wok with a nonstick cooking spray.

Then, stir fry the beef for 6 to 7 minutes, shaking the wok. Add in peppers and continue to cook an additional 2 minutes or until the peppers are crisp-tender.

Place the cooked beef and pepper in a serving bowl.

Toss with the soy sauce, lemon juice, and tomatoes. Serve at and enjoy!

Per serving: 276 Calories; 15.3g Fat; 4.4g Carbs; 29g Protein; 1.1g Fiber

130. Classic Family Cheeseburgers

(Ready in about 15 minutes | Servings 3)

Ingredients

1 pound ground beef
3 slices Colby cheese
1 tablespoon olive oil
1 white onion, sliced
1 teaspoon burger seasoning mix

Directions

With oiled hands, mix the ground beef with the burger seasoning mix; season with salt and black pepper to taste.

Roll the mixture into 3 equal patties.

Heat the olive oil in a grill pan over medium-high heat. Then, grill your burgers for 5 to 6 minutes, flipping them over with a a wide spatula.

Top with cheese and cook for 5 minutes more or until cheese has melted. Serve with onions and enjoy!

Per serving: 533 Calories; 35.1g Fat; 4.8g Carbs; 46g Protein; 0.8g Fiber

131. Roast Beef a la Cacerola

(Ready in about 40 minutes | Servings 5)

Ingredients

5 ounces Chorizo sausage, chopped
2 eggs, whisked
2 pounds ground chuck

8 ounces Manchego cheese, grated
2 vine-ripe tomatoes, pureed

Directions

Melt 2 tablespoon of butter in a fruing pan over a medium-high heat. Brown Chorizo sausage and ground chuck for about 5 minutes until no longer pink.

Sprinkle with steak seasoning blend; add in tomatoes and stir to combine.

Continue to cook for 7 to 8 minutes over medium-low heat. Transfer the mixture into a buttered baking dish.

Top with Manchego cheese and bake for about 17 to 20 minutes or until hot and bubbly on the top. Enjoy!

Per serving: 585 Calories; 40.1g Fat; 6.2g Carbs; 48g Protein; 1.1g Fiber

132. Asian-Style Beef Brisket

(Ready in about 15 minutes | Servings 3)

Ingredients

3/4 pound beef brisket, cut into small pieces
2 cups button mushrooms, sliced

3 scallions, sliced
1 celery, cut into matchsticks
1 teaspoon Five-spice powder

Directions

Heat 1 tablespoon of peanut oil in a medium-sized sauce pan over a medium-high heat. Next, cook the beef brisket for 5 to 6 minutes, shaking the pan frequently.

Add a splash of Shaoxing wine (about 4 tablespoons) and deglaze the pan.

Stir in the mushrooms, scallions, and celery and continue to cook for 3 to 5 minutes more until they have softened.

Season with Five-spice powder. Enjoy!

Per serving: 277 Calories; 21.5g Fat; 2.7g Carbs; 17.4g Protein; 0.8g Fiber

133. Rustic Thai Beef Curry

(Ready in about 35 minutes | Servings 6)

Ingredients

1 ½ pounds ground chuck
1 tablespoon Thai curry powder

1 medium broccoli head, chopped into florets
1 ½ cups tomato sauce
1 shallot, chopped

Directions

In a saucepan, melt 2 teaspoons of tallow (or coconut oil) until sizzling. Once hot, cook the ground meat until no longer pink, breaking it with a fork or wide spatula.

Stir in the remaining ingredients. Reduce the heat to simmer; let it simmer over medium-low heat for 20 to 25 minutes or until warmed through.

Garnish with a small handful of Thai basil. Enjoy!

Per serving: 216 Calories; 10.6g Fat; 5.2g Carbs; 24.8g Protein; 2.5g Fiber

134. Classic Corned Beef Brisket

(Ready in about 3 hours 15 minutes | Servings 8)

Ingredients

2 stalks celery, sliced
3 pounds corned beef brisket
2 tablespoons olive oil

1/2 cup beef bone broth
1 cup ale beer

Directions

Add the, celery and beef brisket to a resealable bag; add in Montreal streak seasoning and shake to coat well. Place the seasoned beef in a foil-lined baking pan.

Add in the olive oil, beef bone broth, and beer.

Meanwhile, preheat your oven to 360 degrees F. Wrap in foil and bake in the preheated oven for 50 minutes.

Reduce the temperature of your oven and bake an additional 2 hours at 310 degrees F. Your brisket is cooked when it reaches an internal temperature of 190 degrees F.

Tate and adjust the seasonings. Then, place the brisket under the preheated broil for about 8 minutes.

Let it stand for 10 minutes before slicing across the grain. Serve with the cooking juices and enjoy!

Per serving: 435 Calories; 33.8g Fat; 4g Carbs; 27.3g Protein; 2g Fiber

135. Hearty Beef and Vegetable Stew

(Ready in about 45 minutes | Servings 2)

Ingredients

1 ounce bacon, diced
1 cup herb pasta sauce, no sugar added

3/4 pound well-marbled beef chuck, boneless and cut into 1-1/2-inch pieces
1 parsnip, chopped
2 bell pepper, chopped

Directions

In a Dutch oven, cook the bacon over medium-high heat; reserve.

In the bacon grease, brown the beef pieces for about 4 minutes or until nicely browned; reserve.

Then, sauté the parsnip and peppers for 4 minutes more until they have softened. Season with salt and black pepper to taste. Add in herb pasta sauce along with reserved beef.

When your mixture reaches boiling, reduce the heat to simmer. Let it simmer for about 30 minutes or until everything is thoroughly cooked.

Serve garnished with the reserved bacon. Bon appétit!

Per serving: 372 Calories; 16.8g Fat; 5.4g Carbs; 41g Protein; 4g Fiber

136. Easy Beef Ragù

(Ready in about 25 minutes | Servings 6)

Ingredients

1 ½ pounds ground beef
2 cups beef bone broth
1 celery rib, chopped

1 bell pepper, deseeded and chopped
2 cups tomato sauce with garlic, no sugar added

Directions

Cook ground beef in a lightly greased pot for 5 to 6 minutes until no longer pink; reserve.

In the pan drippings, cook the celery and the peppers until they are tender.

Stir in the tomato sauce and beef bone broth; season with Italian herb mix and bring to a boil.

Reduce heat to medium-low and add the reserved beef to the pot. Then, continue to cook until the sauce has reduced by half. Bon appétit!

Per serving: 349 Calories; 21.8g Fat; 4.9g Carbs; 34g Protein; 2.4g Fiber

137. Beef with Harvest Vegetables

(Ready in about 20 minutes | Servings 5)

Ingredients

2 tablespoons olive oil
1 ½ pounds chuck, cut into bite-sized cubes

2 bell peppers, deveined and sliced
2 cups cauliflower florets
1 red onion, sliced

Directions

In a saucepan, heat the olive oil over medium-high flame. Sear the beef for 4 to 5 minutes until no longer pink; set aside.

Then, cook the peppers, cauliflower, and onion in the pan drippings until tender, adding about 1/4 cup of water if needed.

Bring to a boil and immediately reduce the heat to medium-low. Now, let it simmer for 10 minutes or until the cooking liquid has evaporated. Bon appétit!

Per serving: 261 Calories; 14.3g Fat; 4g Carbs; 30.1g Protein; 1.2g Fiber

138. One-Skillet Ground Beef

(Ready in about 20 minutes | Servings 7)

Ingredients

2 ounces bacon, diced
1/2 cup Spanish onion, chopped

2 pounds ground beef
2 zucchinis, sliced
2 cups tomato sauce with garlic

Directions

In a cast-iron skillet, fry the bacon for 3 to 4 minutes until the fat is released; reserve.

In the bacon grease, cook the ground beef for 4 to 5 minutes. Then, stir in the zucchinis and Spanish onion; continue to sauté for 4 to 5 minutes more or until they have softened.

Stir in the sauce puree and season with salt and pepper.

When the mixture reaches boiling, reduce the heat to simmer. Continue to cook, partially covered, for 7 to 8 minutes longer.

Garnish with Kalamata olives, if desired. Enjoy!

Per serving: 338 Calories; 17.8g Fat; 7.6g Carbs; 36.2g Protein; 1.5g Fiber

139. Herbed Chuck Roast

(Ready in about 3 hours 10 minutes | Servings 5)

Ingredients

2 ½ pounds chuck roast
1 ½ tablespoons lard, room temperature

1/2 cup celery, chopped
1/2 cup leeks, sliced
2 vine-ripe tomatoes, pureed

Directions

Start by preheating your oven to 340 degrees F.

In a heavy-bottomed pot, melt the lard over medium-high heat. Now, sauté the celery and leek for 4 to 5 minutes.

Transfer the mixture to a lightly greased casserole dish.

Add in the tomatoes and chuck roast. Sprinkle everything with Italian herb mix. Roast in the preheated oven for 3 hours.

Slice the beef against the grain and serve warm. Bon appétit!

Per serving: 359 Calories; 16.4g Fat; 5.1g Carbs; 47.5g Protein; 1.2g Fiber

140. The Best Porterhouse Steak Ever

(Ready in about 20 minutes + marinating time | Servings 6)

Ingredients

4 tablespoons olive oil
2 pounds porterhouse steak, cut into 6 thin slices

1/2 cup steak marinade
4 tablespoons rice vinegar
2 cloves garlic, pressed

Directions

Place the porterhouse steak, marinade, rice vinegar, garlic, and 2 tablespoons of olive oil in a large ceramic dish; let it marinate in your refrigerator for 5 hours or overnight.

Then, brush the porterhouse steak and rack with the remaining 2 tablespoon of olive oil; grill the porterhouse steak over medium heat for about 15 minutes, basting with the reserved marinade.

Your meat thermometer should read 145 degrees F.

Season with salt and pepper. Enjoy!

Per serving: 299 Calories; 17.7g Fat; 1.1g Carbs; 31.5g Protein; 0.1g Fiber

141. Kid-Friendly Sloppy Joes

(Ready in about 45 minutes | Servings 8)

Ingredients

2 pounds ground beef
1 teaspoon garlic, minced
1 shallot, chopped
1 Italian pepper, chopped
1 cup marinara sauce

Directions

Heat 2 tablespoons of olive oil in a nonstick skillet over a moderate heat. Now, cook the ground beef for 5 to 6 minutes, crumbling with a fork or wooden spatula.

Add in the shallot and continue to sauté for 3 to 4 minutes or until tender.

Stir in marinara sauce, Italian pepper, and garlic; bring to a rolling boil. Reduce the heat to medium-low and partially cover.

Now, continue to simmer for 30 minutes longer. Serve on keto buns and enjoy!

Per serving: 248 Calories; 16g Fat; 2.6g Carbs; 22.7g Protein; 0.8g Fiber

142. Authentic Tex-Mex Chili

(Ready in about 35 minutes | Servings 6)

Ingredients

1 medium-sized leek, chopped
1 celery rib, sliced
1 bell pepper, sliced
2 pounds ground chuck
2 tomatoes, pureed

Directions

Melt 2 teaspoon of tallow in a heavy-bottomed pot over moderate heat. Sauté the leek, celery, and bell pepper for about 5 minutes until they have softened.

Add in ground chuck and tomatoes; pour in 2 cups of chicken broth. Season with the salt and black pepper to taste. Bring to a boil.

Turn the heat to simmer; continue to cook for 30 to 35 minutes more or until cooked through. Enjoy!

Per serving: 270 Calories; 13.6g Fat; 5g Carbs; 33g Protein; 0.9g Fiber

143. Old-Fashioned Hamburger Soup

(Ready in about 1 hour | Servings 7)

Ingredients

2 ½ pounds ground chuck
1 stalk celery, chopped
1 yellow onion, chopped
2 ripe tomatoes, pureed
3 bouillon cubes

Directions

In a large pot, heat 2 tablespoons of sesame oil over medium-high heat. Brown the ground chuck for about 5 minutes, stirring and breaking apart with a fork.

Add in the celery and onion and continue to sauté for 4 to 5 minutes more. Stir in the tomatoes and bouillon cubes. Pour in 7 cups of water and stir to combine well.

Turn the heat to a simmer and continue to cook, partially covered, for about 45 minutes, stirring periodically.

Divide between individual bowls and serve warm.

Per serving: 301 Calories; 17.7g Fat; 3.3g Carbs; 32.5g Protein; 0.8g Fiber

144. Stuffed Mushrooms with Beef and Cheese

(Ready in about 25 minutes | Servings 5)

Ingredients

20 button mushrooms, stems removed
6 ounces ground beef
1 garlic clove, minced
1/3 cup goat cheese, crumbled
2 tablespoons shallot, minced

Direction

Start by preheating your oven to 365 degrees F.

Thoroughly combine ground beef, cheese, shallot, and garlic in a mixing bowl. Season with salt and black pepper.

Divide the filling between mushrooms.

Bake in the preheated oven for about 20 minutes and serve at room temperature. Enjoy!

Per serving: 148 Calories; 8.4g Fat; 4.8g Carbs; 14.1g Protein; 1.1g Fiber

145. Pot Roast with Mashed Vegetables

(Ready in about 1 hour 25 minutes | Servings 5)

Ingredients

2 tablespoons butter
1 tablespoon steak seasoning mix
2 pounds beef chuck roast
1/2 pound parsnips, chopped
1/3 pound cauliflower florets

Directions

Start by preheating your oven to 365 degrees F.

Rub the chuck roast with steak seasoning mix on all sides. Place the chuck roast on a parchment-lined baking pan.

Bake in the preheated oven for 50 minutes. Let it rest for 10 minutes before slicing.

In the meantime, boil the cauliflower and parsnip in a saucepan around 30 minutes.

Discard the water and drain well. Fold in the butter and puree to your desired consistency. Serve mashed vegetables with the roast beef and enjoy!

Per serving: 324 Calories; 15.1g Fat; 6.5g Carbs; 38.4g Protein; 2.8g Fiber

146. Easy Szechuan Beef

(Ready in about 20 minutes | Servings 4)

Ingredients

1 shallot, sliced
2 tablespoons sesame oil
1 teaspoon ginger-garlic paste
3 teaspoons tamari sauce
1 ½ pounds shoulder top blade, cut into strips

Directions

In a wok, warm the sesame oil over medium-high flame. Cook the beef for about 5 minutes, shaking your wok continuously.

Now, stir in the ginger garlic paste and shallot; continue cooking for 3 to 4 minutes more or until they have softened. Season with salt and Szechuan pepper to taste.

Add in the tamari sauce along with the reserved beef; continue to cook for 5 to 6 minutes longer. Devour!

Per serving: 302 Calories; 16.6g Fat; 3.7g Carbs; 35.2g Protein; 0.7g Fiber

147. The Best Chilean Cazuela

(Ready in about 1 hour 20 minutes | Servings 6)

Ingredients

1 ½ pounds beef brisket, cut into cubes
1 red onion, chopped
2 celery stalks, chopped
2 fresh Italian peppers, chopped
2 cups marinara sauce

Directions

Heat 2 tablespoons of olive oil in a soup pot over medium-high heat. Sear the beef for about 6 minutes, stirring periodically to ensure even cooking.

Add in the onion, celery, and Italian peppers; continue to cook for 3 to 4 minutes, stirring frequently.

Stir in marinara sauce and reduce the heat to medium-low. Continue to simmer, partially covered, for about 1 hour 10 minutes.

Serve warm and enjoy!

Per serving: 286 Calories; 21.4g Fat; 5g Carbs; 17.5g Protein; 1.1g Fiber

148. Chinese Beef Stir Fry

(Ready in about 15 minutes | Servings 3)

Ingredients

1/2 pound ground chuck
1 teaspoon tamari soy sauce
1 garlic clove, minced
1 shallot, minced
4 ounces brown mushrooms, sliced

Directions

Heat sesame oil in a wok over a moderate heat. Brown the ground chuck for about 5 minutes, crumbling with a spatula. Reserve.

Then, cook the mushrooms, garlic and shallot for a further 4 minutes or until they have softened. Add in tamari soy sauce along with reserved beef.

Reduce the heat to a simmer and continue to cook for about 3 minutes, stirring continuously. Serve immediately.

Per serving: 179 Calories; 10.4g Fat; 5.8g Carbs; 16.5g Protein; 1g Fiber

149. Easy Beef Stroganoff

(Ready in about 1 hour | Servings 4)

Ingredients

1 pound beef stew meat, cut across grain into strips
1 cup tomato sauce with garlic and onion
2 celery stalks, chopped
4 ounces fresh mushrooms, sliced
1/2 cup sour cream

Directions

Melt 2 tablespoons of lard in a heavy-bottomed pot over moderate heat. Brown the meat on all sides for 5 to 6 minutes.

Then, cook the celery until just tender. Add in the mushrooms and cook for 3 minutes more or until tender and aromatic.

Add in tomato sauce with garlic and onion and reduce the heat to simmer. Continue to cook for 50 to 55 minutes.

Remove from the heat and serve with sour cream. Bon appétit!

Per serving: 303 Calories; 17.2g Fat; 5.6g Carbs32.4g Protein; 0.9g Fiber

150. Beef Teriyaki with Chinese Cabbage

(Ready in about 15 minutes | Servings 2)

Ingredients

3/4 pound flank steak, thinly sliced
1 yellow onion, thinly sliced
1/2 cup keto teriyaki sauce
1 teaspoon sesame oil
1/2 cup Chinese cabbage, shredded

Directions

Heat the sesame oil in a wok over medium-high heat; sear the steak and onion for 5 to 6 minutes.

Add in Chinese cabbage and continue to cook for a further 3 minutes.

Add in keto teriyaki sauce. Let it simmer for about 5 minutes or until the sauce has reduced and thickened.

Stir to coat and serve immediately. Devour!

Per serving: 304 Calories; 13.7g Fat; 5.2g Carbs; 37.2g Protein; 0.8g Fiber

151. Dad's Beef Goulash

(Ready in about 3 hours 10 minutes | Servings 6)

Ingredients

2 pounds flank steak, cut against the grain into 6 pieces
1 onion, chopped
1 cup marinara sauce
1 celery stalk, chopped
2 bell peppers, chopped

Directions

In a soup pot, melt 1 tablespoon of lard over medium-high flame. Then, sear the beef approximately 10 minutes, stirring frequently to ensure even cooking; set aside.

In the pan drippings, sauté the celery, bell peppers, and onions for about 3 minutes or until they have softened.

Add in marinara sauce along with reserved beef; stir to coat well.

Bake in the preheated oven at 310 degrees F for 2 hours 45 minutes or until the beef is fork-tender. Bon appétit!

Per serving: 254 Calories; 9.8g Fat; 6.3g Carbs; 33.4g Protein; 1.2g Fiber

152. Party Cheeseburger Dip

(Ready in about 30 minutes | Servings 10)

Ingredients

1 shallot, chopped
1 pound ground beef
1 cup tomato sauce with onions and garlic
8 ounces mascarpone cheese
8 ounces Colby cheese, shredded

Directions

Heat 1 tablespoon of olive oil in a frying pan over a moderate flame.

Once hot, cook the shallot and ground beef for 5 minutes until the shallot is tender and translucent and beef is nicely browned.

Spoon the mixture into a lightly greased casserole dish. Add in tomato sauce along with salt and black pepper.

Bake in the preheated oven at 330 degrees F for about 15 minutes.

Top with mascarpone and Colby cheese and bake an additional 6 minutes until hot and bubbly on top.

Serve at room temperature and enjoy!

Per serving: 264 Calories; 17g Fat; 4.9g Carbs; 21.3g Protein; 0.4g Fiber

153. Beef Stuffed Peppers

(Ready in about 45 minutes | Servings 2)

Ingredients

1/2 pound ground beef

2 bell peppers, deveined and halved

2 tomatoes, pureed

1 garlic clove, minced

Sea salt and ground black pepper, to taste

Directions

Brown the ground beef in a preheated saucepan for about 5 minutes, breaking apart with a spatula.

Then, sauté the minced garlic for a minute or so. Sprinkle with salt and ground black pepper.

Spoon the filling into the peppers. Place the peppers in a lightly greased backing dish. Pour in the pureed tomatoes and 1/4 cup of water.

Bake in the preheated oven at 365 degrees F approximately 35 to 40 minutes. Bon appétit!

Per serving: 260 Calories; 14.6g Fat; 6.4g Carbs; 24.2g Protein; 2.2g Fiber

154. Classic Pot-Au-Feu

(Ready in about 25 minutes | Servings 5)

Ingredients

1 ½ pounds skirt steak, slice into strips

2 tablespoons olive oil

1 cup beef bone broth

2 garlic cloves, pressed

1 large-sized leek, chopped

Directions

Heat the olive oil in a heavy-bottomed pot over medium-high flame. Now, brown the skirt steak for about 6 minutes; reserve.

Add the garlic and leeks to the pot; continue to cook in the pan drippings for 3 to 4 minutes. Pour in the beef bone broth, bringing to a boil.

Add the reserved beef back to the pot; turn the temperature to medium-low. Continue to simmer for about 13 minutes until the cooking liquid has thickened and reduced.

Ladle into serving bowls and enjoy!

Per serving: 368 Calories; 22.3g Fat; 3.1g Carbs; 36.8g Protein; 0.3g Fiber

155. Provençal Beef Cassoulet

(Ready in about 1 hour 20 minutes | Servings 5)

Ingredients

1 ½ pounds shoulder steak, cut into cubes

1 cup red Burgundy wine

1 tablespoon Herbs de Provence

1 celery stalk, chopped

1 onion, chopped

Directions

Spritz a soup pot with nonstick cooking oil. Then, cook the steak for about 10 minutes over a medium-high heat.

Add a splash of wine to deglaze the pot.

Stir in celery, onion, and Herbs de Provence along with 3 cups of water; stir to combine. Turn the heat to simmer.

Let it simmer for 1 hour 10 minutes. Enjoy!

Per serving: 217 Calories; 5.5g Fat; 3.9g Carbs; 30g Protein; 0.4g Fiber

156. Traditional Beef Gulyás

(Ready in about 1 hour 10 minutes | Servings 6)

Ingredients

1 ½ pounds beef shoulder, cut into bite-sized pieces

2 tablespoons olive oil

2 ripe tomatoes, pureed

2 cloves garlic, minced

1/2 cup leeks, chopped

Directions

In a stock pot, heat 1 tablespoon of the olive oil over medium-high flame. Cook beef shoulder for 10 minutes, stirring continuously; reserve.

Add a splash of broth to deglaze the pan. Heat the remaining tablespoon of olive oil; sauté the leeks until softened or about 5 minutes.

Add in garlic and continue to cook for a minute or so. Season with salt and black pepper to taste. Add in pureed tomatoes.

Turn the heat to simmer and add the reserved beef to the pot; let it simmer for 50 to 55 minutes or until thoroughly cooked. Serve and enjoy!

Per serving: 195 Calories; 9.5g Fat; 3.3g Carbs; 25.2g Protein; 0.9g Fiber

157. Sticky and Saucy Back Ribs

(Ready in about 30 minutes + marinating time | Servings 4)

Ingredients

2 pounds back ribs

1/2 cup beef bone broth

1 tablespoon monk fruit powder

2 tablespoons coconut aminos

2 tablespoons dry red wine

Directions

Thoroughly combine all of the above ingredients; allow it to marinate in the refrigerator for 3 hours.

Brush back ribs with 2 tablespoons of olive oil.

Then, cook the ribs on the preheated grill over moderate heat for 5 to 6 minutes on each side, basting them with the reserved marinade. Enjoy!

Per serving: 570 Calories; 42.4g Fat; 2.1g Carbs; 45g Protein; 0.3g Fiber

158. Beef Salad Bowl

(Ready in about 20 minutes | Servings 5)

Ingredients

2 pounds beef strips
1/2 pound cabbage, shredded
1 celery stalk, sliced
4 scallions, chopped
1 cup ale

Directions

Heat 1 tablespoon of olive oil in a large pot over medium-high flame. Now, sear the beef until nicely browned on all sides.

Stir in the ale and celery and reduce the temperature to medium-low. Now, let it simmer for 10 minutes, stirring periodically.

Transfer the mixture to a salad bowl; toss with the scallions and cabbage. Drizzle with 1 tablespoon of lime juice and olive oil; toss to combine.

Bon appétit!

Per serving: 321 Calories; 11.8g Fat; 5.8g Carbs; 43.6g Protein; 1.9g Fiber

159. American Roast Beef

(Ready in about 2 hours 10 minutes | Servings 6)

Ingredients

2 pounds boneless chuck roast, trimmed
8 garlic cloves, halved
1 ½ cups beef bone broth
1/2 cup low-carb marinara sauce
1 tablespoon steak rub

Directions

Strat by preheating your oven to 365 degrees F.

Place the beef in a lightly oiled roasting pan. Now, scatter the garlic cloves around the chuck roast.

Mix the remaining ingredients and pour the mixture over the chuck roast. Wrap in a piece of aluminum foil.

Roast in the preheated oven approximately 2 hours. A meat thermometer should read 140 degrees F for rare meat or 160 degrees F for medium.

Let it rest for 10 minutes before slicing and serving. Devour!

Per serving: 265 Calories; 13.9g Fat; 3.2g Carbs; 31.8g Protein; 0.5g Fiber

160. Mexican Taco Bake

(Ready in about 55 minutes | Servings 2)

Ingredients

1/2 pound blade steak, sliced into strips
1 ½ cups medium salsa
1/2 tablespoon Taco seasoning mix
3/4 cup Manchego cheese, shredded
1 cup cauliflower florets

Directions

Heat 1 tablespoon of canola oil in a medium pot over moderate flame. Sear blade steak for about 7 minutes, stirring occasionally.

Fold in cauliflower and continue to sauté for 5 minutes longer or until it is crisp-tender.

Add in Taco seasoning mix and salsa. Turn the temperature to simmer; partially cover and let it simmer for 30 to 35 minutes.

Place the mixture into a baking dish; top with the Manchego and bake for 12 minutes or until the edges are bubbling. Enjoy!

Per serving: 452 Calories; 32.1g Fat; 7.1g Carbs; 39.2g Protein; 2.1g Fiber

161. Classic Sunday Roast

(Ready in about 55 minutes + marinating time | Servings 5)

Ingredients

2 pounds bottom round roast
1 tablespoon pot roast seasoning mix
4 tablespoons olive oil
1 tablespoon prepared horseradish, strained
1/2 cup beef stock

Directions

Cut slits in the bottom round roast using a small knife.

In a mixing bowl, combine pot roast seasoning. olive oil, and horseradish.; add the salt and black pepper to taste.

Let the roast sit in your refrigerator overnight. Place the roast in a baking pan; pour in the beef stock.

Roast the beef in the preheated oven at 425 degrees F for 30 minutes. Now, lower the temperature to 370 degrees F and roast for a further 11 to 16 minutes. Bon appétit!

Per serving: 405 Calories; 20.6g Fat; 0.7g Carbs; 51.1g Protein; 0.1g Fiber

162. Cheesy Zucchini Lasagna

(Ready in about 45 minutes | Servings 7)

Ingredients

1 large-sized zucchini, sliced
2 ½ pounds ground chuck
7 eggs, whisked
1 shallot, chopped
1 ½ cups Asiago cheese, shredded

Directions

Heat 2 tablespoons of olive oil in a sauce pan over medium-high flame; then, sear the ground chuck for about 5 minutes.

Then, stir in the shallot and continue to cook for 3 to 4 minutes more or until it has softened. Sprinkle with 1 tablespoon of the steak seasoning blend.

Spread 1/3 of the beef mixture on the bottom of a lightly greased baking dish. Top with the layer of zucchini slices. Repeat until you run out of the filling and zucchini.

Spoon the eggs over the top. Top with the cheese and cover with a piece of foil. Bake in the preheated oven at 365 degrees F for 18 to 20 minutes.

Remove the aluminum foil and bake for a further 13 minutes until it is golden around edges. Bon appétit!

Per serving: 467 Calories; 31.8g Fat; 3.3g Carbs; 42g Protein; 0.4g Fiber

163. Scotch Fillet with Marsala Wine

(Ready in about 15 minutes + marinating time | Servings 4)

Ingredients

2 tablespoons butter, unsalted and softened
4 Scotch fillet steaks, about 1-inch thick
1/2 cup Marsala wine
1/4 cup Spanish olives, pitted and halved
2 Spanish peppers, sliced

Directions

Pat the fillet dry with kitchen towels and place in a glass dish. Add in Marsala wine; season with salt and black pepper. Let it sit in your refrigerator for 4 hours.

Melt the butter in a saucepan over medium-high heat.

Next, cook fillet steaks the for 4 minutes per side; add in Spanish peppers and cook for a further 3 minutes, adding the marinade and stirring periodically.

Serve with Spanish olives. Enjoy!

Per serving: 426 Calories; 21.8g Fat; 5.6g Carbs; 49g Protein; 1.4g Fiber

164. Mediterranean Roast Beef

(Ready in about 2 hours 35 minutes | Servings 8)

Ingredients

2 ½ pounds beef chuck roast, cut into bite-sized pieces
1 cup condensed cream of mushroom soup
1 Italian pepper, deseeded and sliced
1 celery stalk, sliced
1/2 cup leeks, sliced

Directions

Begin by preheating an oven to 330 degrees F.

Heat 1 tablespoon of olive oil in a saucepan. Brown beef chuck roast over medium-high flame. Place the beef chuck roast in a large roasting pan.

Scatter the leeks, pepper and celery around the beef.

Add in the cream of mushroom soup along with 1 cup of water. Sprinkle with salt and black pepper.

Bake approximately 2 hours 20 minutes or until the meat is fall-apart. Bon appétit!

Per serving: 353 Calories; 18.2g Fat; 3.7g Carbs; 43g Protein; 0.5g Fiber

165. Old-Fashioned Steak

(Ready in about 8 hours 15 minutes | Servings 6)

Ingredients

2 tablespoons peanut oil
2 pounds bone-in rib eye steaks (1 1/2-inch thick)
2 cloves garlic, pressed
1/2 cup rice wine
1 cup cream of mushroom soup

Directions

In your slow cooker, heat the oil in until sizzling; now, sear the steaks for about 3 minutes per side.

Stir in the garlic, rice wine, and cream of mushroom soup. Set the cooker on Low, cover, and cook for 7 to 8 hours.

Preheat your broiler for 5 minutes and position the oven rack.

Broil the meat for 8 to 9 minutes. Check doneness using an instant-read thermometer and enjoy!

Per serving: 448 Calories; 36.1g Fat; 1.6g Carbs; 28.2g Protein; 0.1g Fiber

166. Meatballs with French Sauce

(Ready in about 45 minutes | Servings 6)

Ingredients

4 ounces bacon, diced
2 pounds ground beef
1/2 cup Parmigiano-Reggiano cheese, grated
1/2 cup tomato puree
1/2 cup French onion soup

Directions

Mix the bacon, ground beef, and Parmigiano-Reggiano cheese until well combined.

Cook your meatballs in a lightly greased grill pan over medium-high heat for about 6 minutes.

Then, in a mixing bowl, whisk tomato puree and French onion soup. Pour the sauce over the meatballs.

Reduce the heat to medium-low and let it simmer, partially covered, for 30 to 33 minutes or until cooked through. Bon appétit!

Per serving: 434 Calories; 25.2g Fat; 5.2g Carbs; 44.4g Protein; 1g Fiber

167. American-Style BBQ Ribs

(Ready in about 1 hour 45 minutes | Servings 2)

Ingredients

1/2 pound beef ribs
1 teaspoon American-style mustard
1 leek, sliced
1/4 teaspoon stevia powder
3/4 cup vegetable broth

Directions

In a grill pan, heat 1 tablespoon of olive oil over medium-high flame. Cook the ribs for about 4 minutes per side; stir in the leek and continue to sauté for 3 to 4 minutes.

Add a splash of wine to scrape up the browned bits that stick to the bottom of the pot, if desired. Then, add in broth and stir to combine well.

Reduce the temperature to medium-low, partially cover, and let it simmer for 35 to 40 minutes longer. Season with the salt and black pepper to taste.

Place the ribs along with the cooking liquid in a foil-lined baking dish.

Add in stevia and American-style mustard. Bake in the preheated oven at 310 degrees F for 50 to 55 minutes, flipping them occasionally.

Garnish with fresh chives if desired. Bon appétit!

Per serving: 481 Calories; 41g Fat; 5.9g Carbs; 19.9g Protein; 1.3g Fiber

168. Mini Spinach Meatloaves

(Ready in about 35 minutes | Servings 2)

Ingredients

1 bunch spinach, chopped
1/2 pound lean ground beef
2 tablespoons tomato paste
1/4 cup almond meal
1 egg, beaten

Directions

Thoroughly combine the ingredients until everything is well incorporated.

Divide the meat mixture into lightly greased muffin cups. Bake in the preheated oven at 365 degrees F for 25 minutes.

Bon appétit!

Per serving: 439 Calories; 18.4g Fat; 8.4g Carbs; 40.1g Protein; 5g Fiber

169. Buttery Steak with Broccoli

(Ready in about 15 minutes + marinating time | Servings 3)

Ingredients

2 tablespoons butter, room temperature
1/2 pound broccoli, cut into florets
1/2 cup steak marinade
1/2 pound skirt steak, sliced into pieces
1/2 cup scallions, chopped

Directions

Place the steak marinade and beef in a ceramic bowl; let it marinate in your refrigerator for 3 hours.

In a frying pan, melt 1 tablespoon of butter over medium-high heat. Then, sauté the broccoli for 2 to 3 minutes or until it is crisp-tender; reserve.

Heat the remaining tablespoon of butter in the pan. Now, sauté the scallions until tender for 2 to 3 minutes; reserve.

Brown skirt steak, adding a small amount of the reserved marinade.

Stir in the reserved vegetables and continue to cook until everything is thoroughly warmed. Bon appétit!

Per serving: 331 Calories; 24.7g Fat; 4.5g Carbs; 24.1g Protein; 2.8g Fiber

170. French-Style Beef with Onion Gravy

(Ready in about 1 hour 25 minutes | Servings 8)

Ingredients

3 tablespoons peanut oil
1/2 cup of red wine
4 garlic cloves, halved
4 pounds beef sirloin
1 onion, sliced

Directions

Rub the garlic halves all over the beef; season with the salt and black pepper. Add in 2 tablespoons of peanut oil and let it to marinate in your refrigerator for 3 hours.

Then, heat the remaining tablespoon of peanut oil in a sauce pan over medium-high heat. Now, sear the meat until nicely browned all sides.

Place the beef sirloin in a lightly greased baking pan; pour in 1 cup of water or vegetable broth. Bake in the preheated oven at 365 degrees F for about 55 minutes.

In the meantime, heat a sauce pan over a low heat and sweat the onion for 15 minutes until caramelized.

Now, whisk in red wine and let it simmer until the sauce has reduced by half. Spoon the sauce over the beef and enjoy!

Per serving: 532 Calories; 34.6g Fat; 3.2g Carbs; 45.8g Protein; 0.8g Fiber

171. Chunky Beef and Cheese Casserole

(Ready in about 30 minutes | Servings 6)

Ingredients

1 yellow onion, chopped
1 ½ pounds ground chuck
2 cups double cream
1 ¼ cups Monterey Jack cheese, shredded
1 cup marinara sauce

Directions

In a saucepan, melt 1 teaspoon of butter over medium-high flame. Cook the onion and beef until the onion is tender and translucent and the beef is no longer pink.

Add in marinara sauce and stir to combine; let it cook approximately 5 minutes. Transfer the onion/beef mixture to a buttered baking dish.

Spread double cream over the meat mixture.

Bake in the preheated oven at 390 degrees F for 15 minutes. Top with the Monterey Jack cheese and continue to bake for 6 minutes more or until nicely brown around edges. Bon appétit!

Per serving: 534 Calories; 43.5g Fat; 6.9g Carbs; 30.5g Protein; 1g Fiber

172. Festive Chuck Roast

(Ready in about 1 hour 35 minutes | Servings 5)

Ingredients

2 pounds chuck eye roast
1 tablespoon steak spice mix
1/3 cup cream of mushroom soup

1 tablespoon Dijon mustard
1/4 cup apple cider vinegar

Directions

Preheat your oven to 360 degrees F.

Spritz a large frying pan with cooking oil; preheat the frying pan over medium-high heat and sear the roast for about 4 minutes per each side until nicely brown. Lower the roast into a baking dish.

In a bowl, whisk the vinegar, cream of mushroom soup, mustards, and spices. Pour the sauce over the beef roast.

Cover with a piece of aluminum foil and roast for 1 hour 35 minutes. Let your roast sit for 10 minutes before slicing.

To serve, spoon the sauce over the chuck roast and enjoy!

Per serving: 267 Calories; 11.4g Fat; 2.4g Carbs; 37.8g Protein; 0.4g Fiber

173. Easy Short Loin

(Ready in about 30 minutes | Servings 3)

Ingredients

1 ½ pounds beef short loin
Sea salt and ground black pepper, to taste

1 teaspoon garlic powder
2 thyme sprigs, chopped
1 rosemary sprig, chopped

Directions

Place all ingredients in a re-sealable bag. Shake until the beef is well coated on all sides.

Grill for 10 minutes; turn over and cook for 10 minutes more.

Bon appétit!

Per serving: 313 Calories; 11.6g Fat; 0.1g Carbs; 52g Protein; 0.1g Fiber

174. Home-Style Burgers

(Ready in about 30 minutes | Servings 5)

Ingredients

1 tablespoon olive oil
1 ½ pounds ground beef
8 ounces cheddar cheese, shredded

Sea salt and freshly cracked black pepper, to season
1 egg, beaten

Directions

Mix ground beef, 4 ounces of cheese, salt, black pepper, and egg. Form the beef mixture into 5 patties.

Warm the olive oil in a frying pan over a moderate heat. Fry your burgers for 6 minutes.

Place the remaining cheddar cheese on top of your patties; fry them for a further 6 minutes.

Serve on lettuce leaves and enjoy!

Per serving: 297 Calories; 23.6g Fat; 0.7g Carbs; 20.2g Protein; 0.1g Fiber

175. Famous New York Steak

(Ready in about 15 minutes + marinating time | Servings 5)

Ingredients

2 pounds New York strip, cut into bite-sized chunks
1/2 cup steak marinade
2 cloves garlic, pressed

1 bell pepper, deseeded and sliced
1/2 pound Brussels sprouts, trimmed and halved

Directions

Place the New York strip and marinade in a large ceramic dish. Let it sit in your refrigerator for 2 hours.

Heat 1 tablespoon of the peanut oil in a frying pan. Brown the beef over moderate heat for 10 to 12 minutes; reserve.

Pour in a splash of the reserved marinade to deglaze the pan.

Heat 1 tablespoon of peanut oil. Now, cook the garlic, bell pepper and Brussels sprouts for 4 to 5 minutes until they have softened.

Season with salt and black pepper; return the beef to the frying pan and let it cook for about 3 minutes until cooked through. Bon appétit!

Per serving: 441 Calories; 23.1g Fat; 5.8g Carbs; 52.4g Protein; 1.9g Fiber

176. Mexican Taco Soup

(Ready in about 1 hour 10 minutes | Servings 4)

Ingredients

1 pound beef shoulder, cut into small chunks
1 cup celery, chopped
1 red bell pepper, chopped

1 cup tomato puree
1/2 (1.25-ounce) package taco seasoning mix

Directions

Melt 1 tablespoon of avocado oil in a large heavy-bottomed pot over medium-high heat. Brown the beef shoulder for about 5 minutes until nicely browned.

Add in the celery, pepper, tomato puree and taco seasoning mix. Reduce the temperature to medium-low. Pour in 4 cups of water or vegetable broth; stir to combine well.

Continue to simmer, partially covered, for 50 to 55 minutes. Enjoy!

Per serving: 201 Calories; 4.8g Fat; 8.9g Carbs; 26.4g Protein; 2.5g Fiber

177. Dad's Ragù with a Twist

(Ready in about 30 minutes | Servings 4)

Ingredients

1/2 cup shallots, chopped
2 cups button mushrooms, sliced
1 pound ground beef

1 cup tomato sauce with onion and garlic
1 cup cream of onion soup

Directions

Melt 1 tablespoon of lard in a pot over a moderate heat. Once hot, cook the shallots and mushrooms, stirring periodically, until just tender for 3 to 4 minutes.

Stir in the ground beef; continue to cook for 4 to 5 minutes, falling apart with a fork or spatula. Pour in tomato sauce and cream of onion soup.

Stir and partially cover. Allow it to simmer for 20 to 25 minutes more and serve warm. Bon appétit!

Per serving: 335 Calories; 23g Fat; 6.1g Carbs; 22.7g Protein; 1.1g Fiber

178. Aromatic Roast Beef with Herbs

(Ready in about 1 hour 10 minutes | Servings 2)

Ingredients

1 pound rump roast, boneless
1 tablespoon yellow mustard
1 tablespoon Mediterranean spice mix
1/2 cup beef bone broth
2 yellow onions, quartered

Directions

Pat the roast dry with kitchen towels. Then, place the roast, yellow mustard and spices in a resealable bag. Shake to coat your roast on all sides.

Place the roast in a baking pan and pour in the broth. Scatter the onions around the roast.

Roast in the preheated oven at 360 degrees F for 30 to 35 minutes. Then reduce the heat to 300 degrees F and cook the roast for 35 minutes longer. Enjoy !

Per serving: 316 Calories; 13.2g Fat; 2.6g Carbs; 47.2g Protein; 0.5g Fiber

179. Italian Meatloaf with Marinara Sauce

(Ready in about 1 hour 15 minutes | Servings 6)

Ingredients

1/2 cup leeks, chopped
1 ½ pounds ground chuck
1 egg, whisked
1/2 cup full-fat milk
1/2 cup low-carb marinara sauce

Directions

Preheat your oven to 330 degrees F.

Melt 1 teaspoon of tallow in a pan over moderate heat; cook the leeks and ground chuck for 5 to 6 minutes, stirring periodically.

Then, add in the egg and milk; season with the salt and black pepper to taste and mix to combine well.

Spoon the meat mixture in a lightly greased loaf pan. Bake in the preheated oven for 45 to 50 minutes.

Afterwards, top your meatloaf with the marinara sauce and continue to bake for another 8 to 10 minutes. Bon appétit!

Per serving: 342 Calories; 21.2g Fat; 5.9g Carbs; 30.4g Protein; 0.9g Fiber

180. Saucy Beef with Herbs

(Ready in about 50 minutes | Servings 4)

Ingredients

1 tablespoon olive oil
1 pound rib eye, cut into strips
1 tablespoon Italian herb mix
2 chipotle peppers in adobo sauce, chopped
1 cup tomato sauce with garlic and onions

Directions

Heat the oil in a saucepan over a moderate heat. Sear the beef for about 7 minutes or until no longer pink.

Add in the remaining ingredients along with 1/2 cup of beef bone broth. Then, reduce the temperature to medium-low; continue to simmer for 40 to 45 minutes.

Shred the beef with two forks and serve topped with cooking juice. Bon appétit!

Per serving: 421 Calories; 35.7g Fat; 5.9g Carbs; 19.7g Protein; 1g Fiber

181. Aromatic Beef Stew

(Ready in about 55 minutes | Servings 6)

Ingredients

1 ½ pounds top chuck, cut into bite-sized cubes
1/2 cup onions, chopped
2 Italian peppers, chopped
1 celery stalk, chopped
1 cup tomato sauce with garlic

Directions

In a heavy-bottomed pot, melt 1 teaspoon of lard over medium-high heat. Sear the top chuck for about 10 minutes until brown; reserve.

In the pan drippings, sauté the onion, Italian peppers, and celery for 5 to 6 minutes until they have softened.

Return the beef to the pot along with tomato sauce. Season with salt and black pepper.

Let it simmer, partially covered, for 35 to 40 minutes. Bon appétit!

Per serving: 277 Calories; 21.5g Fat; 2.7g Carbs; 17.4g Protein; 0.8g Fiber

182. Double-Cheese Meatloaf

(Ready in about 1 hour | Servings 4)

Ingredients

1 pound ground beef
2 teaspoons sunflower oil
1 egg, whisked
1 cup marinara sauce
1 Swiss cheese, grated

Directions

In a frying pan, heat the oil over medium-high heat. Cook ground beef until no longer pink or 4 to 5 minutes. Season with onion powder, salt, and black pepper to taste.

Add in the cheese and egg; mix until everything is well incorporated. Press the mixture into a lightly greased baking pan.

Bake in the preheated oven at 380 degrees F. for 40 minutes. Now, spoon marinara sauce over the meatloaf.

Continue to bake an additional 10 minutes or until cooked through. Enjoy!

Per serving: 361 Calories; 23.1g Fat; 5.6g Carbs; 32.2g Protein; 0.8g Fiber

183. Steak Salad with Avocado

(Ready in about 20 minutes | Servings 4)

Ingredients

8 ounces flank steak, salt-and-pepper-seasoned
1 ripe avocado, peeled and sliced
1 cucumber, sliced
2 medium-sized heirloom tomatoes, sliced
1/2 cup onions, finely sliced

Directions

Heat 1 tablespoon of olive oil in a frying pan over a moderate flame. Brown the flank steak for 5 to 7 minutes, turning periodically to ensure even cooking.

One the meat is cool enough to handle, slice it thinly across the grain. Place the meat in a serving bowl.

Add the remaining ingredients and toss with 1 tablespoon of olive oil and lemon juice.

Serve at room temperature or well chilled. Enjoy!

Per serving: 231 Calories; 17.1g Fat; 6g Carbs; 13.8g Protein; 3.4g Fiber

184. Harvest Vegetable and Hamburger Soup

(Ready in about 35 minutes | Servings 2)

Ingredients

1/2 pound lean ground beef
1 cup green cabbage, shredded
1/2 cup celery stalks, chopped
1 vine-ripe tomato, pureed
1/2 cup scallions, chopped

Directions

Heat 1 teaspoon of olive oil in a soup pot over medium-high heat. Now, cook the beef and celery for 4 to 5 minutes.

Add in scallions and continue to sauté an additional 2 to 3 minutes or until it is tender.

Then, stir in the cabbage and tomato; turn the temperature to simmer and continue to cook, partially covered, for 35 to 40 minutes longer. Bon appétit!

Per serving: 299 Calories; 15.1g Fat; 6.5g Carbs; 32g Protein; 2.7g Fiber

185. Italian Meatballs in Asiago Sauce

(Ready in about 15 minutes | Servings 3)

Ingredients

1 teaspoon Italian spice mix
1/2 pound ground beef
1 egg
3 ounces Asiago cheese, grated
1/4 cup mayonnaise

Directions

In a mixing bowl, thoroughly combine Italian slice mix, beef, and egg. Mix until everything is well combined. Roll the mixture into meatballs.

In another bowl, mix Asiago cheese and mayonnaise.

Heat 1 tablespoon of olive oil in a frying pan over a moderate heat. Then, sear the meatballs for about 5 minutes, turning them occasionally to ensure even cooking. Bon appétit!

Per serving: 458 Calories; 35.8g Fat; 4.3g Carbs; 28.2g Protein; 0.2g Fiber

186. Meatloaf with a Sweet Sticky Glaze

(Ready in about 1 hour | Servings 2)

Ingredients

3/4 pound ground chuck
1/4 cup flaxseed meal
2 eggs, beaten
1/2 cup tomato sauce with garlic and onion
1 teaspoon liquid monk fruit

Directions

In a mixing bowl, combine the ground chuck, flaxseed meal, and eggs; season with the salt and black pepper.

In a separate mixing bowl, combine the tomato sauce and liquid monk fruit; add 1 teaspoon of mustard and whisk until well combined.

Spoon the mixture into the foil-lined loaf pan and smooth the surface. Bake in the preheated oven at 365 degrees F for about 25 minutes.

Spoon the tomato mixture on top of the meatloaf and continue to bake for a further 25 minutes or until thoroughly cooked.

Allow your meatloaf to rest for 10 minutes before slicing and serving. Bon appétit!

Per serving: 517 Calories; 32.3g Fat; 8.4g Carbs; 48.5g Protein; 6.5g Fiber

EGGS & DAIRY

187. Classic Egg Salad

(Ready in about 20 minutes | Servings 5)

Ingredients

7 eggs
1/3 cup mayonnaise
1 cup radishes, thinly sliced

1 bell pepper, chopped
2 scallions, chopped

Directions

Add the eggs and water (1-inch above the eggs) to a saucepan and bring to a boil. Remove from heat and let it sit for 15 minutes.

Next, peel the eggs and rinse them under running water. Chop the eggs and place them in a serving bowl.

Stir in the scallions, radishes, and bell peppers. Season with salt and black pepper to taste. Add mayonnaise and 1 teaspoon of stone-ground mustard, if desired.

Stir to combine well and serve well chilled. Bon appétit!

Per serving: 172 Calories; 14.1g Fat; 2.5g Carbs; 8.1g Protein; 0.7g Fiber

188. Hard-Boiled Eggs with Avocado

(Ready in about 10 minutes | Servings 3)

Ingredients

1 avocado, pitted and sliced
6 eggs
1/2 teaspoon dried dill weed

1 tablespoon lemon juice
1/2 teaspoon kosher salt

Directions

Add the eggs and water (1-inch above the eggs) to a saucepan and bring to a boil. Remove from heat and let it sit for 15 minutes.

Peel the eggs and slice them into halves. Sprinkle the eggs with salt and dill. You can add black pepper and paprika, if desired.

Serve topped with avocado slices and fresh lemon juice. Enjoy!

Per serving: 222 Calories; 17.6g Fat; 5.7g Carbs; 12.2g Protein; 3.9g Fiber

189. Ande ki Curry

(Ready in about 20 minutes | Servings 4)

Ingredients

4 boiled egg, peeled
1/2 cup scallions, chopped
1/2 cup coconut milk

2 ripe tomatoes, pureed
1 teaspoon curry paste

Directions

Heat 2 tablespoons of rice bran oil in a deep saucepan over medium-high heat. Now, cook the scallions until aromatic or about 3 minutes.

Add in tomatoes and cook for 8 to 9 minutes more. Add in Kashmiri chili powder, if desired.

Pour in 1/2 cup of water (or chicken stock). Turn the heat to medium-low and let it cook for a further 3 to 4 minutes.

Add in the eggs, coconut milk, and curry paste. Continue to simmer for 8 to 10 minutes or until heated through. Garnish with curry leaves and enjoy!

Per serving: 305 Calories; 16.4g Fat; 5.7g Carbs; 32.2g Protein; 1.1g Fiber

190. Breakfast Sausage and Cheese Bites

(Ready in about 20 minutes | Servings 3)

Ingredients

1/2 pound breakfast sausage
1/2 cup almond flour
1/2 cup Colby cheese, shredded

4 tablespoons Romano cheese, freshly grated
1 egg

Directions

Preheat your oven to 365 degrees F.

Thoroughly combine all ingredients until everything is well mixed. Roll the mixture into balls; place the balls on a parchment-lined baking pan sheet.

Bake in the preheated oven for about 15 to 17 minutes. Bon appétit!

Per serving: 412 Calories; 34.6g Fat; 4.7g Carbs; 19.6g Protein; 0.1g Fiber

191. Famous Cheese Soup

(Ready in about 20 minutes | Servings 5)

Ingredients

1/2 stick butter, at room temperature
4 tablespoons almond meal

2 ½ cups canned milk
1 chicken bouillon cube
2 cups Swiss cheese, shredded

Directions

In a heavy-bottomed por, melt the butter over medium-high heat.

Add in the almond meal, canned milk, and chicken bouillon cube, Now, pour in 2 cups of warm water and let it simmer, partially covered, for 10 minutes.

Remove from the heat and fold in the cheese. Stir to combine, cover, and let it sit in the residual heat for 8 to 10 minutes.

Season with salt and black pepper, and serve in individual bowls. Bon appétit!

Per serving: 439 Calories; 37g Fat; 5.7g Carbs; 19.5g Protein; 2g Fiber

192. The Best Greek Aïoli Ever

(Ready in about 10 minutes | Servings 6)

Ingredients

2 egg yolks
1 teaspoon Greek seasoning mix

1 teaspoon garlic
1 tablespoon lemon juice
1/2 cup extra-virgin olive oil

Directions

Beat the egg yolks until pale and frothy.

Whisk in Greek seasoning mix, garlic, and lemon juice; season with salt and black pepper. Stir in 1 teaspoon of mustard, if desired.

Then, continue to mix until everything is well combined.

Gradually whisk in the oil in a steady stream. Mix until mixture is emulsified. Aioli will keep well in the refrigerator for up to 10 days.

Per serving: 94 Calories; 9.1g Fat; 1.3g Carbs; 1.5g Protein; 0.2g Fiber

193. Breakfast Egg Salad

(Ready in about 15 minutes | Servings 4)

Ingredients

4 eggs
1 Lebanese cucumber, sliced
4 cups lettuce, broken into pieces
1 avocado, pitted, peeled and sliced
8 ounces goat cheese, crumbled

Directions

Heat 2 tablespoons of canola oil in a frying pan over the highest heat. Then, crack the eggs into the oil and fry them for 1 to 2 minutes or until the yolks are set; set aside.

Mix Lebanese cucumber and lettuce in a serving bowl. Place fried eggs and avocado on top.

Garnish with crumbled cheese and serve.

Per serving: 474 Calories; 37.1g Fat; 6.8g Carbs; 28g Protein; 4g Fiber

194. Easy Eggs in a Mug

(Ready in about 5 minutes | Servings 1)

Ingredients

2 eggs
Flaky salt, to taste
1/4 teaspoon ground black pepper
2 tablespoons milk

Directions

In a microwave-safe mug, whisk the eggs lightly; add in the milk and whisk until well combined.

Cook the eggs in your microwave for about 1 ½ minutes.

Season with salt and black pepper to taste and serve immediately.

Per serving: 142 Calories; 9.4g Fat; 2.5g Carbs; 12.1g Protein; 0.1g Fiber

195. Soufflé with Sausage and Cheese

(Ready in about 55 minutes | Servings 8)

Ingredients

8 ounces Chorizo sausage, sliced
4 scallions, chopped
8 ounces cream cheese
10 eggs
1 cup Swiss cheese, grated

Directions

Preheat an oven-proof skillet over a moderate flame. Now, brown the sausage for 5 minutes, breaking apart it with a wide spatula.

Stir in the scallions and continue to sauté for a further 3 minutes. Season with salt and black pepper to your liking.

In a mixing dish, combine the cream cheese and eggs. Pour the egg mixture into the oven-proof skillet.

Transfer the skillet to the preheated oven. Bake at 365 degrees F for about 30 minutes.

Top with Swiss cheese and continue to bake for 7 minutes more or until the cheese is hot and bubbly. Bon appétit!

Per serving: 348 Calories; 28.7g Fat; 4.5g Carbs; 17.6g Protein; 0.3g Fiber

196. Bombay Masala Frittata

(Ready in about 40 minutes | Servings 5)

Ingredients

1 yellow onion, sliced
1 teaspoon Garam masala
8 eggs
2 tablespoons milk
8 ounces cream cheese

Directions

Grease a baking pan with 1 tablespoon of butter.

Melt 1 tablespoon of butter in a frying pan over medium-high heat. Sauté the onion until just tender and aromatic.

Add in the Garam masala and spoon the mixture into the prepared baking pan.

In a bowl, whisk the eggs, milk, and cream cheese. Spoon the egg mixture into the baking pan.

Bake in the preheated oven at 360 degrees F for 30 minutes or until cooked through. Enjoy!

Per serving: 306 Calories; 27g Fat; 4g Carbs; 12g Protein; 0.2g Fiber

197. Frittata with Mediterranean Herbs

(Ready in about 30 minutes | Servings 4)

Ingredients

6 eggs
2 ounces bacon, chopped
1 teaspoon Mediterranean herbs
1/2 cup red onions, peeled and sliced
8 ounces Feta cheese, crumbled

Directions

Start by preheating an oven to 365 degrees F. Brush a baking pan with a nonstick spray.

Mix the eggs, bacon, herbs and onion until well combined; season with the salt and black pepper.

Pour the mixture into the prepared baking dish.

Bake for 15 minutes until the eggs are set. Scatter feta cheese over the top and continue to bake for 5 minutes more. Enjoy!

Per serving: 394 Calories; 30.5g Fat; 6.1g Carbs; 23.1g Protein; ; 0.6g Fiber

198. Scrambled Eggs with Canadian Bacon

(Ready in about 15 minutes | Servings 2)

Ingredients

2 (1-ounce) slices Canadian bacon
8 cherry tomatoes, halves
4 eggs
Salt, to season
1/4 teaspoon ground black pepper

Directions

Cook Canadian bacon over medium-high heat until crisp-tender.

Then, fry the eggs in the bacon grease until the yolks are set. Season with the salt and pepper.

Serve with the reserved bacon and cherry tomatoes. Bon appétit!

Per serving: 326 Calories; 13.3g Fat; 5.2g Carbs; 46g Protein; 0.7g Fiber

199. Deviled Eggs with Tuna

(Ready in about 15 minutes | Servings 4)

Ingredients

4 eggs
1 (6-ounce) can tuna, drained
1/2 red onions, chopped

4 teaspoons cottage cheese, room temperature
1 tablespoon Dijon mustard

Directions

In a saucepan, bring the eggs and water to a boil; heat off. Let it sit for about 10 minutes.

Then, peel away the shells and separate the egg whites and yolks.

Mash the yolks with tuna, onions, cheese, and mustard. Sprinkle with the salt and black pepper, if desired.

Divide the mixture among egg whites and serve well chilled.

Per serving: 112 Calories; 4.7g Fat; 2.3g Carbs; 14.5g Protein; 0.5g Fiber

200. Keto Cauliflower Tots

(Ready in about 15 minutes | Servings 5)

Ingredients

3 tablespoons butter, softened
1/2 pound cauliflower florets
2 cups Romano cheese, grated

2 teaspoons psyllium husk powder
1 yellow onion, minced

Directions

Steam the cauliflower and process until it resembles mashed potatoes.

Then, mix the mashed cauliflower with yellow onion, cheese, and psyllium husk powder. Roll the mixture into balls.

Melt the butter in a frying pan over medium-high heat. Then, cook your tots until golden brown on all sides. Bon appétit!

Per serving: 285 Calories; 23.2g Fat; 4.6g Carbs; 14.2g Protein; 1.1g Fiber

201. Easy Home-Style Mayo

(Ready in about 10 minutes | Servings 8)

Ingredients

1/2 teaspoon stone-ground mustard
1 teaspoon garlic powder

1 cup olive oil
2 tablespoons lemon juice
2 egg yolks

Directions

Beat the egg yolks, mustard, and garlic powder with a hand mixer. Add in the salt, black pepper, and lemon juice and continue mixing until well combined.

Gradually pour in the oil, mixing continuously until the desired consistency is achieved.

Taste for seasoning, then add some extra salt or lemon juice if needed. Enjoy!

Per serving: 257 Calories; 28.1g Fat; 1.1g Carbs; 0.8g Protein; 0.1g Fiber

202. Cheesy Mexican Tortilla

(Ready in about 15 minutes | Servings 4)

Ingredients

2 tablespoons full-fat milk
2 eggs
4 ounces Cotija cheese, sliced

1/2 cup almond meal
1 teaspoons baking powder

Directions

Whisk the milk and eggs until frothy and pale.

In another bowl, combine the almond meal with baking powder; sprinkle with the salt to taste.

Add the egg mixture to the flour mixture and mix again.

Cook each tortilla for 2 minutes per side. Repeat until you run out of the batter. Top with Cotija cheese and serve. Devour!

Per serving: 205 Calories; 16.4g Fat; 3.2g Carbs; 11.5g Protein; 0.2g Fiber

203. Homemade Vanilla Blancmange

(Ready in about 15 minutes | Servings 5)

Ingredients

2 ½ cups double cream
1/2 cup whole milk
5 egg yolks

1/2 teaspoon vanilla extract
6 tablespoons Erythritol

Directions

Heat the cream and milk in a sauce pan, bringing the mixture to just below boiling point; remove from heat.

In a mixing bowl, whisk the egg yolks, vanilla and Erythritol. Gradually add the hot milk mixture to the egg mixture, stirring continuously with a wire whisk.

Reduce the heat to low. Pour the mixture into the saucepan and continue to simmer until the mixture has thickened and reduced slightly. Enjoy!

Per serving: 305 Calories; 28g Fat; 6.3g Carbs; 6.7g Protein; 0.1g Fiber

204. Deviled Eggs with Bacon

(Ready in about 15 minutes | Servings 6)

Ingredients

10 eggs
1 tablespoon Dijon mustard
1 roasted bell pepper, chopped

1/3 cup Cottage cheese
4 ounces bacon, diced

Directions

Cook the bacon in a nonstick skillet over medium-high flame; reserve.

Cook the eggs in a small saucepan and bring to a boil. Remove from heat and let it stand, covered, for about 10 minutes.

Then, peel the eggs and separate the egg whites and yolks.

Mix the egg yolks with the reserved bacon, bell pepper, mustard, and cheese. Season with the salt and black pepper to taste.

Divide the filling between egg whites and serve well-chilled. Devour!

Per serving: 293 Calories; 22.3g Fat; 4.8g Carbs; 18.6g Protein; 0.8g Fiber

205. Swiss Cheese and Onion Soup

(Ready in about 15 minutes | Servings 2)

Ingredients

2 tablespoons ghee, at room temperature
1/2 cup shallots, chopped
1/2 cup cream of onion soup
1 cup yogurt
4 ounces Swiss cheese, shredded

Directions

Melt the ghee in a heavy-bottomed pot over medium-high flame; sauté the shallots until tender or about 4 minutes.

Pour in the cream of onion soup along with 1/2 cup of water. Reduce the heat to simmer; then, let it cook for 10 to 12 minutes or until heated through.

Remove from heat and stir in in the yogurt and Swiss cheese. Mix until everything is thoroughly combined. Bon appétit!

Per serving: 365 Calories; 27.2g Fat; 6.6g Total Carbs; 21g Protein; 0.8g Fiber

206. Breakfast Bacon and Kale Muffins

(Ready in about 25 minutes | Servings 4)

Ingredients

1/2 cup bacon
1 cup kale
1 cup tomato paste with garlic and onion
6 eggs
1 cup Asiago cheese, shredded

Directions

Preheat your oven to 380 degrees F.

Then, cook the bacon for 3 to 4 minutes over the highest setting; reserve. Add in the kale, tomato paste, eggs and Asiago cheese. Add in the reserved bacon

Spoon the batter into lightly greased muffin cups; then, bake for 15 minutes or until the edges are golden brown. Bon appétit!

Per serving: 384 Calories; 29.8g Fat; 5.1g Carbs; 24g Protein; 1.1g Fiber

207. Easy Greek Omelet

(Ready in about 15 minutes | Servings 6)

Ingredients

8 eggs
1 medium-sized leek, chopped
2 cups broccoli florets
4 tablespoons sour cream
1/2 cup Greek feta cheese, crumbled

Directions

Melt 2 tablespoons of butter in a nonstick pan over medium-high heat. Now, sauté the leeks and broccoli until just tender.

Whisk the sour cream, and eggs, along with Greek seasoning mix. Spoon the cream/egg mixture into the pan.

Cook for 5 to 6 minutes until the eggs are fully set. Top with Greek feta cheese and serve warm!

Per serving: 266 Calories; 20.3g Fat; 5.7g Carbs; 14.8g Protein; 0.9g Fiber

208. Mediterranean Tomato Frittata

(Ready in about 35 minutes | Servings 4)

Ingredients

6 eggs
1/3 cup Greek-style yogurt
2 scallions, chopped
1 tomato, sliced
2/3 cup cheddar cheese, shredded

Directions

Preheat your oven to 360 degrees F. Butter a pie pan and set it aside.

Thoroughly combine Greek-style yogurt, and scallions. Spoon the mixture into the prepared pan. Top with the tomato slices.

Scatter the cheese over the top.

Bake for about 30 minutes or until the edges appear cooked. Slice into four wedges and serve.

Per serving: 299 Calories; 22.4g Fat; 3.4g Carbs; 19.6g Protein; 0.2g Fiber

209. Mom's Coconut Flan

(Ready in about 55 minutes | Servings 4)

Ingredients

2 eggs
1/2 cup granulated erythritol
1/2 tablespoon vanilla extract
20 ounces canned coconut milk
1/4 cup coconut, shredded, unsweetened

Directions

Preheat your oven to 335 degrees F; spritz 4 custard cups with nonstick cooking spray and place them in a large baking pan.

Then, whisk the eggs until pale and foamy.

Add in erythritol, vanilla, and coconut milk, add a pinch of coarse sea salt too; whisk until everything is well mixed and spoon into the prepared custard cups.

Pour boiling water into the baking pans around cups. Bake for 45 to 50 minutes or until a table knife inserted in the middle comes out clean.

Refrigerate until ready to serve. Gently, shake the mold to release and garnish with shredded coconut. Devour!

Per serving: 318 Calories; 32.3g Fat; 4.9g Carbs; 5.5g Protein; 0.2g Fiber

210. Cheesy Spanish Tortilla

(Ready in about 30 minutes | Servings 4)

Ingredients

1/2 cup leeks, chopped
1 Spanish pepper, chopped
1/4 cup milk
5 eggs, beaten
1 cup Manchego cheese, shredded

Directions

Melt 1 tablespoon of butter in a saucepan over medium-high flame. Now, cook the leeks and Spanish pepper until they have softened.

Season with salt and freshly ground black pepper. Spoon the sautéed mixture into a buttered baking pan.

In a bowl, whisk the milk and eggs until pale and frothy. Pour the mixture into the prepared baking pan.

Top with Manchego cheese and bake in the preheated oven at 365 degrees F for 23 to 25 minutes.

Let it cool on wired wrack for about 10 minutes before cutting and serving. Enjoy!

Per serving: 324 Calories; 24.2g Fat; 5.2g Carbs; 20.2g Protein; 0.5g Fiber

211. Russian Egg Salad

(Ready in about 15 minutes + chilling time | Servings 6)

Ingredients

6 medium-sized eggs
2 tablespoons mayonnaise
4 ounces cheddar cheese, shredded

1/2 cup sour cream
4 cups baby spinach

Directions

Cook the eggs in a small saucepan. Let it sit, covered, for about 10 minutes.

When they are cool enough to handle, peel away the shells; rinse, chop the eggs and place them in a serving bowl.

Stir in the remaining ingredients. Garnish with 4 tablespoons of green onions and serve well-chilled.

Per serving: 164 Calories; 11.5g Fat; 5.7g Carbs; 9.5g Protein; 0.9g Fiber

212. Cheesy Mini Frittatas with Sausage

(Ready in about 35 minutes | Servings 6)

Ingredients

5 eggs
1/3 cup double cream
6 ounces pork sausage, sliced

1 bell pepper, chopped
1 1/3 cups goat cheese, crumbled

Directions

Start by preheating your oven to 360 degrees F.

Cook the sausage and bell pepper in a preheated nonstick pan over a moderate heat.

In a mixing bowl, combine the eggs and double cream; stir in the pepper/sausage mixture. Season with salt and black pepper to your liking.

Spoon the mixture into foil-lined muffin cups and bake approximately 20 minutes.

Top with goat cheese and bake for about 6 minutes or until slightly browned around the edges. Bon appétit!

Per serving: 287 Calories; 23.7g Fat; 1.9g Carbs; 16.1g Protein; 0.2g Fiber

213. Creamy French Scrambled Eggs

(Ready in about 15 minutes | Servings 3)

Ingredients

1 tablespoon butter, at room temperature
6 large eggs
4 tablespoons crème fraîche

1/4 teaspoon ground black pepper
Sea salt, to taste

Directions

Beat the eggs with a wire whisk until foamy or the yolks and whites are fully incorporated into each other.

Then, melt the butter in a frying pan over medium-high flame. Pour the egg mixture into the skillet. Give it a quick swirl to distribute the eggs evenly across the frying pan.

Stir until just set or about 8 minutes. Season with black pepper and salt; fold in crème fraiche and immediately remove from the heat. Enjoy!

Per serving: 257 Calories; 21.1g Fat; 0.9g Carbs; 12.6g Protein; 0.1g Fiber

214. Wisconsin Beer Cheese Soup

(Ready in about 20 minutes | Servings 4)

Ingredients

1/2 cup beer
1 cup heavy cream
2 tablespoons butter

1/2 pound Pepper-Jack cheese, shredded
1/2 cup scallions, chopped

Directions

Melt the butter in a heavy-bottomed pot over medium-high heat. Sauté the scallions for about 4 minutes.

Pour in 2 ½ cups of beef bone broth and bring to a rapid boil. Add the garlic powder if desired and decrease the temperature to medium-low.

Add in beer and heavy cream and continue to simmer for 10 to 12 minutes more or until thoroughly cooked.

Afterwards, fold in Pepper-Jack cheese and stir well. Let it sit, covered, until the cheese is melted and incorporated. Enjoy!

Per serving: 391 Calories; 34.1g Fat; 3.9g Carbs; 14.8g Protein; 0.4g Fiber

215. Roasted Brussels Sprouts with Colby Cheese

(Ready in about 25 minutes | Servings 4)

Ingredients

2 tablespoons sesame oil
3/4 pound Brussels sprouts, cleaned and halved

6 ounces Colby cheese, shredded
1 teaspoon dried parsley flakes
1 sprig dried thyme

Directions

Preheat your oven to 395 degrees F. Brush a baking pan with a nonstick spray.

Place the Brussels sprouts on the baking pan and drizzle them with sesame oil.

Toss with parsley and thyme; sprinkle with salt and black pepper to your liking. Roast approximately 15 minutes or until tender and charred around the edges.

Top with shredded cheese and roast an additional 5 minutes. Devour!

Per serving: 202 Calories; 16.3g Fat; 5.8g Carbs; 8.8g Protein; 2.3g Fiber

216. Greek Tirokroketes

(Ready in about 1 hour 15 minutes | Servings 5)

Ingredients

3 eggs, lightly beaten
1/2 cup almond flour
1 teaspoon baking powder

4 ounces smoked gouda cheese, grated
3 ounces feta cheese, crumbled

Directions

Start by preheating your oven to 380 degrees F.

Thoroughly combine all ingredients in a mixing bowl.

Cover and place in your refrigerator for 1 hour. Then, shape the mixture into a ball using your hands.

Bake in the preheated F for 11 to 12 minutes. Serve and enjoy!

Per serving: 247 Calories; 19.3g Fat; 4.7g Carbs; 14.4g Protein; 2.9g Fiber

217. Easy Greek Scramble

(Ready in about 10 minutes | Servings 3)

Ingredients

2 tablespoons butter
1 teaspoon Mediterranean herbs
6 eggs

4 tablespoons Greek yogurt
3 ounces halloumi cheese, crumbled

Directions

In a frying pan, melt the butter over moderate heat.

In a mixing bowl, combine Mediterranean herbs, eggs, and Greek yogurt.

Pour the mixture into the pan and cook, stirring continuously, for 5 to 6 minutes until creamy curds form.

Garnish with halloumi cheese and serve warm!

Per serving: 313 Calories; 25.3g Fat; 2g Carbs; 18.8g Protein; 0.2g Fiber

218. Creamed Spicy Egg Salad

(Ready in about 15 minutes | Servings 2)

Ingredients

3 eggs
1/4 cup mayonnaise
1 teaspoon Dijon mustard

1/4 cup scallions, chopped
1 jalapeno pepper, deseeded and minced

Directions

Cook the eggs in a small saucepan and bring to a boil. Heat off and allow it to stand, covered, for 10 to 11 minutes.

When they are cool enough to handle, peel away the shells. Chop the eggs and place them in a nice serving bowl.

Add in the mayonnaise, Dijon mustard, scallions, and jalapeno pepper. Sprinkle paprika over the salad if desired. Devour!

Per serving: 398 Calories; 35.2g Fat; 5.5g Carbs; 14.6g Protein; 1g Fiber

219. Restaurant-Style Tortillas with Cheese

(Ready in about 10 minutes | Servings 2)

Ingredients

2 tablespoons flax seed meal
1 tablespoon almond meal
2 eggs

2 tablespoons full-fat milk
3 ounces cheddar cheese, sliced

Directions

Mix flax seed meal and almond meal; sprinkle with baking powder and mix to again.

In another bowl, whisk the eggs and milk until pale and frothy; add this wet mixture to the dry flour mixture. Mix until everything is well combined.

Cook your tortillas over a medium-high heat for 2 minutes per side.

Top with cheddar cheese, roll them up, and serve right away!

Per serving: 393 Calories; 31.7g Fat; 5.1g Carbs; 22.8g Protein; 1.6g Fiber

220. Greek Omelet with Scallions

(Ready in about 15 minutes | Servings 3)

Ingredients

1 tablespoon butter
2 scallions, chopped
6 eggs

2 tablespoons Greek-style yogurt
3 tablespoons feta cheese, crumbled

Directions

Melt the butter in a sauté pan over medium-high flame. Sauté the scallions until tender and fragrant.

In a mixing bowl, whisk the eggs and Greek yogurt.

Spoon the egg mixture into the sauté pan and cook until the eggs have set but the center jiggles just a bit. Flip on the other side and top with feta cheese.

Gently fold in half and serve warm. Bon appétit!

Per serving: 224 Calories; 16.3g Fat; 2.8g Carbs; 15.8g Protein; 0.3g Fiber

221. Cauliflower Fat Bombs

(Ready in about 35 minutes | Servings 4)

Ingredients

1/2 pound cauliflower, cut into florets
2 eggs, beaten

1/4 cup almond flour
1/2 cup Romano cheese, grated
1/2 cup pork rinds, crushed

Directions

Steam the cauliflower until it has softened and drain well. Then, mix the cauliflower with the remaining ingredients.

Roll the mixture into small balls and place them on a foil-lined baking sheet.

Bake in the preheated oven at 355 degrees F for about 25 minutes. Enjoy!

Per serving: 168 Calories; 10.9g Fat; 3.5g Carbs; 13.9g Protein; 1.1g Fiber

222. Cheese Stuffed Peppers

(Ready in about 25 minutes | Servings 4)

Ingredients

4 summer bell peppers, divined and halved

2 ounces mozzarella cheese, crumbled

2 tablespoons Greek-style yogurt

4 ounces cream cheese

1 clove garlic, minced

Directions

Boil the peppers until they are just tender.

Thoroughly combine the cheese, yogurt, and garlic. Stuff your peppers with this filling. Place the stuffed peppers in a foil-lined baking dish.

Bake in the preheated oven at 365 degrees F for about 10 minutes. Bon appétit!

Per serving: 140 Calories; 9.8g Fat; 6.4g Carbs; 7.8g Protein; 0.9g Fiber

223. Italian Zucchini Sandwiches

(Ready in about 10 minutes | Servings 2)

Ingredients

4 thin zucchini slices, cut lengthwise

2 eggs

4 slices Sopressata

2 slices provolone cheese

1 red bell pepper, sliced thinly

Directions

Melt 1 tablespoon of butter in a frying pan over medium-high flame. Then, fry the eggs for about 5 minutes.

Place one zucchini slice on each plate. Add the cheese, Sopressata, and peppers on top; season with salt and black pepper to taste.

Add fried eggs and top with the remaining zucchini slices. Bon appétit!

Per serving: 352 Calories; 26.5g Fat; 6.6g Total Carbs; 22.1g Protein; 0.6g Fiber

224. Creamy Dilled Egg Salad

(Ready in about 20 minutes + chilling time | Servings 3)

Ingredients

4 eggs, peeled and chopped

1 scallion, chopped

1 tablespoon fresh dill minced

1 teaspoon Dijon mustard

4 tablespoons mayonnaise

Directions

Add the eggs and water to a saucepan and bring to a boil; remove from heat. Allow the eggs to sit, covered, for about 11 minutes.

Peel and rinse the eggs under running water. Then, chop the eggs and transfer them to a nice salad bowl; stir in the scallions, dill, mustard, and mayonnaise.

Taste and season with salt and pepper. Enjoy!

Per serving: 212 Calories; 19.4g Fat; 0.9g Carbs; 7.6g Protein; 0.2g Fiber

225. Eggs with Goat Cheese

(Ready in about 10 minutes | Servings 2)

Ingredients

4 eggs, whisked

2 teaspoons ghee, room temperature

1 teaspoon paprika

Sea salt and ground black pepper, to taste

4 tablespoons goat cheese

Directions

In a frying pan, melt the ghee over a moderate heat. Then, cook the eggs, covered, for about 4 minutes.

Stir in goat cheese, paprika, salt, and black pepper; continue to cook for 2 to 3 minutes more or until cooked through.

Taste and adjust seasonings. Enjoy!

Per serving: 287 Calories; 22.6g Fat; 1.3g Carbs19.8g Protein; 0g Fiber

226. Dukkah Frittata with Cheese

(Ready in about 30 minutes | Servings 3)

Ingredients

3 tablespoons milk

1 tablespoon Dukkah spice mix

5 eggs

2 tablespoons olive oil

1 cup cheddar cheese, shredded

Directions

Preheat your oven to 360 degrees F.

Whisk the milk, spices mix and eggs until well mixed.

Grease the bottom of a small-sized baking pan with olive oil. Spoon the egg mixture into the pan and top with cheese.

Bake in the preheated oven for about 25 minutes until the eggs are set but the center jiggles just a bit. Bon appétit!

Per serving: 354 Calories; 29.2g Fat; 3.5g Carbs; 19.1g Protein; 0.5g Fiber

227. Classic Italian Omelet

(Ready in about 15 minutes | Servings 3)

Ingredients

3 ounces bacon, diced

1 Italian pepper, chopped

6 eggs, whisked

1 teaspoon Italian seasoning blend

1/2 cup goat cheese, shredded

Directions

Preheat a frying pan over a medium-high heat. Now, fry the bacon until crisp or 3 to 4 minutes; set aside.

Stir in Italian pepper and continue to sauté for 2 minutes more or until just tender and fragrant. Pour the eggs into the pan.

Sprinkle with the Italian seasoning blend; add the salt and black pepper to taste and cook until the eggs are ser. Top with the reserved bacon and goat cheese.

Slide your omelet onto serving plates and serve. Bon appétit!

Per serving: 481 Calories; 43.3g Fat; 4.8g Carbs; 17.2g Protein; 0.6g Fiber

228. Egg Salad with Anchovies

(Ready in about 15 minutes + chilling time | Servings 3)

Ingredients

3 ounces anchovies, flaked

5 eggs

2 tablespoons mayonnaise

1 teaspoon Dijon mustard

2 tablespoons Ricotta cheese

Directions

Add the eggs and water to a saucepan and bring to a boil; remove from heat. Allow the eggs to sit, covered, for about 11 minutes.

Then, peel the eggs and rinse them under running water. Then, transfer chopped eggs to a salad bowl.

Add in the remaining ingredients, gently stir to combine and enjoy!

Per serving: 329 Calories; 23.4g Fat; 2.6g Carbs; 25g Protein; 0.3g Fiber

229. Classic Keto Muffins

(Ready in about 20 minutes | Servings 4)

Ingredients

4 ounces cheddar cheese, shredded

6 tablespoons almond flour

2 tablespoons flaxseed meal

4 eggs

1/4 teaspoon baking soda

Directions

Start by preheating an oven at 355 degrees F

Thoroughly combine all of the above ingredients until well mixed.

Coat a muffin pan with cupcake liners. Spoon the batter into the muffin pan. Bake in the preheated oven for 16 minutes.

Place on a wire rack for 10 minutes before unmolding and serving. Enjoy!

Per serving: 292 Calories; 23.1g Fat; 5.4g Carbs; 16.4g Protein; 3.3g Fiber

230. Authentic Spanish Migas

(Ready in about 15 minutes | Servings 3)

Ingredients

6 eggs

6 lettuce leaves

1 white onion, chopped

1 tomato, chopped

1 Spanish pepper, chopped

Directions

Melt 1 tablespoon of butter in a cast-iron skillet over medium-high flame. Sauté the onion for about 4 minutes, stirring continuously to ensure even cooking.

Stir in the peppers and continue to sauté an additional 3 to 4 minutes. Whisk in the eggs. Continue to cook until the eggs are set.

Divide the egg mixture between lettuce leaves; top with tomatoes. Season with salt and black pepper and serve. Devour!

Per serving: 193 Calories; 12.3g Fat; 6g Carbs; 12g Protein; 1.7g Fiber

231. Double Cheese Fondue

(Ready in about 10 minutes | Servings 8)

Ingredients

4 ounces Ricotta cheese

1 cup double cream

Cayenne pepper, to taste

8 ounces Swiss cheese, shredded

4 tablespoons Greek-style yogurt

Directions

Warm Ricotta cheese and double cream and in a saucepan over medium-low flame.

Remove from the heat. Fold in cayenne pepper, Swiss cheese, and Greek-style yogurt. Stir until everything is well combined. Bon appétit!

Per serving: 196 Calories; 15.7g Fat; 3.4g Carbs; 10.1g Protein; 0g Fiber

232. Savory Rolls with Bacon and Cheese

(Ready in about 30 minutes | Servings 8)

Ingredients

1/2 cup goat cheese, crumbled

1/2 cup cream cheese

8 eggs

6 ounces bacon, diced

1/2 cup marinara sauce

Directions

In a nonstick skillet, fry the bacon over the highest heat until crisp; set aside.

Whisk the crema cheese and eggs until foamy. Add in the fried bacon along with salt and black pepper; whisk to combine well.

Spoon the mixture into greased muffin cups. Top each muffin with goat cheese. Bake in the preheated oven at 355 degrees F for about 14 minutes or until golden on the top.

Serve with marinara sauce and enjoy!

Per serving: 176 Calories; 15.8g Fat; 3g Carbs; 6g Protein; 0.6g Fiber

233. Broccoli Cheese Pie

(Ready in about 30 minutes | Servings 4)

Ingredients

6 eggs

1 red onion, sliced

6 tablespoons Greek yogurt

2 cups broccoli florets

1/2 cup cheddar cheese, shredded

Directions

Heat 2 teaspoon of olive oil in an oven-safe skillet over medium-high heat. Sweat red onion and broccoli until they have softened or about 4 minutes.

Season with salt and black pepper.

In a mixing bowl, whisk Greek yogurt and eggs until well mixed. Scrape the mixture into the pan.

Bake at 365 degrees F for 15 to 20 minutes or until a toothpick inserted into a muffin comes out dry and clean.

Top with cheddar cheese and bake for 5 to 6 minutes more. Bon appétit!

Per serving: 308 Calories; 23.2g Fat; 5.3g Carbs; 19.2g Protein; 0.9g Fiber

234. Herbed Cheese Ball

(Ready in about 10 minutes + chilling time | Servings 10)

Ingredients

1/2 cup sour cream

8 ounces extra-sharp cheddar cheese, shredded

6 ounces cream cheese, softened

2 tablespoons mayonnaise

1 tablespoon Moroccan herb mix

Directions

Thoroughly combine sour cream, cheddar cheese, cream cheese, and mayonnaise.

Cover the mixture with a plastic wrap and place in your refrigerator for about 3 hours.

Roll the mixture over Moroccan herb mix until well coated. Serve with assorted keto veggies. Enjoy!

Per serving: 176 Calories; 15.7g Fat; 2g Carbs; 7.2g Protein; 0.9g Fiber

235. Mexican Eggs with Vegetables

(Ready in about 15 minutes | Servings 2)

Ingredients

1/2 cup cauliflower florets

2 ounces Cotija cheese, crumbled

2 scallion stalks, chopped

2 bell peppers, chopped

3 eggs

Directions

Warm 2 teaspoons of olive oil in a frying pan over medium-high heat. Sauté the cauliflower, scallions and peppers until tender and aromatic about 3 minutes.

In the meantime, beat the eggs with salt and black pepper. Add in Mexican oregano, if desired.

Pour the egg mixture over the vegetables in the frying pan. Continue to cook for about 5 minutes.

Top with Cotija cheese and cook for 2 minutes longer. Serve immediately.

Per serving: 287 Calories; 20.5g Fat; 7.2g Total Carbs; 17.4g Protein; 2.9g Fiber

236. Masala Eggs with Brown Mushrooms

(Ready in about 15 minutes | Servings 2)

Ingredients

4 eggs, whisked

1/2 pound brown mushrooms, sliced

1/2 brown onion, thinly sliced

1 garlic clove, thinly sliced

1/2 teaspoon garam masala

Directions

Heat 1 tablespoon of oil in a frying pan over medium-high heat. Sauté the onion, garlic, and mushrooms for 3 to 4 minutes until tender and aromatic. Set aside.

Add the eggs and garam masala to the pan. Give it a quick swirl and cook for about 3 minutes.

Turn the omelet over and cook for a further 2 minutes. Add the mushroom mixture, fold your omelet and serve. Enjoy!

Per serving: 217 Calories; 15.6g Fat; 5g Carbs; 14.4g Protein; 1.2g Fiber

237. Easy Keto Quesadillas

(Ready in about 15 minutes | Servings 2)

Ingredients

4 tablespoons sour cream

4 eggs

1 white onion, chopped

1/2 cup Monterey-Jack cheese, shredded

1 cup kale, torn into pieces

Directions

Heat 1 tablespoon of olive oil in an oven-proof skillet over medium-high heat. Cook the onion until tender and translucent about 3 minutes.

Fold in the kale leaves and stir for a minute or so.

Then, thoroughly combine the sour cream with eggs; season with the salt and black pepper to taste. Spoon the mixture into the skillet and tilt to distribute evenly.

Top with Monterey-Jack cheese.

Bake in the preheated oven at 380 degrees F for 10 minutes until the eggs are golden brown. Slice into wedges and serve.

Per serving: 417 Calories; 34.5g Fat; 5.3g Carbs; 20.6g Protein; 1.1g Fiber

238. Ham and Cheese Muffins

(Ready in about 30 minutes | Servings 2)

Ingredients

1/4 cup mozzarella cheese, shredded

4 eggs

1/4 cup double cream

2 ounces ham, chopped

1 cup broccoli florets

Directions

In a frying pan, melt 1 teaspoon of butter. Cook the broccoli until crisp tender about 3 minutes.

In a mixing bowl, combine the eggs and double cream. Stir in the sautéed broccoli and ham; divide the mixture between muffin cups.

Top with shredded mozzarella cheese.

Bake in the preheated oven at 365 degrees F for 12 minutes or until a knife inserted into a muffin comes out clean. Bon appétit!

Per serving: 249 Calories; 15.3g Fat; 5.5g Carbs; 22.5g Protein; 1.4g Fiber

239. Aleppo Pepper Deviled Eggs

(Ready in about 15 minutes | Servings 4)

Ingredients

4 eggs

1 teaspoon Aleppo chili pepper

2 slices bacon, diced

1/3 cup Asiago cheese, grated

1 tablespoon Dijon mustard

Directions

Place the eggs and water in a saucepan and bring to a boil. Let them sit, covered, for 9 minutes; then, place the eggs in the ice bath.

Peel the eggs and cut them in half. Then, fry the bacon in the preheated skillet for about 4 minutes.

Mash the yolks with fried bacon, mustard, Aleppo chili pepper, and Asiago cheese; mix to combine well.

Stuff the egg whites with this filling and serve.

Per serving: 163 Calories; 12.7g Fat; 1.7g Carbs; 10.1g Protein; 0.3g Fiber

240. Skinny Eggs with Spinach

(Ready in about 10 minutes | Servings 2)

Ingredients

4 eggs, well whisked
2 teaspoons olive oil
1/2 teaspoon garlic powder

Sea salt cayenne pepper, to taste, to taste
4 cups baby spinach

Directions

Heat the olive oil in a cast-iron skillet over medium-high heat.

Add in the baby spinach and garlic powder; season with salt and cayenne pepper and cook for 1 to 2 minutes or until wilted.

Fold in the eggs, and continue to cook, stirring continuously with a spatula. Enjoy!

Per serving: 183 Calories; 13.1g Fat; 3.3g Carbs; 12.9g Protein; 1.4g Fiber

241. Oven-Baked Eggs with Ham

(Ready in about 35 minutes | Servings 5)

Ingredients

8 eggs
2 tablespoons bacon drippings
1 shallot, chopped

6 ounces cooked ham, diced
3 tablespoons cream of celery soup

Directions

In an oven-safe skillet, warm the bacon drippings over medium-high heat.

Sweat the shallot until tender and caramelized or about 10 minutes.

Mix the eggs with the celery soup. Stir in the cooked ham and pour the egg mixture into the skillet.

Bake in the preheated oven at 380 degrees F for 20 to 23 minutes. Bon appétit!

Per serving: 258 Calories; 17.3g Fat; 2.8g Carbs; 20.5g Protein; 0.2g Fiber

242. Famous Double-Cheese Chips

(Ready in about 10 minutes | Servings 6)

Ingredients

3/4 cup Romano cheese, shredded

1 tablespoon Italian seasoning blend
1 cup Asiago cheese, shredded

Directions

Start by preheating your oven to 360 degrees F.

Mix the ingredients together in a bowl. Spoon tablespoon-sized heaps of the mixture onto foil-lined baking sheets.

Bake in the preheated oven approximately 7 minutes until they are browned around the edges.

Transfer the cheese chips to paper towels and allow them to cool until crisp. Enjoy!

Per serving: 148 Calories; 11.7g Fat; 1.1g Carbs; 9.4g Protein; 0.2g Fiber

243. Fast and Simple Spicy Eggs

(Ready in about 15 minutes | Servings 3)

Ingredients

2 scallions, chopped
1 tablespoon olive oil
1/2 teaspoon chili powder

1/3 cup full-fat milk
6 eggs

Directions

Heat the olive oil in a frying pan over medium-high flame. Cook the scallions until tender and aromatic about 3 minutes.

In a mixing dish, whisk the milk, eggs, and chili powder. Season with the salt and black pepper to your liking.

Spoon the egg mixture into the pan; shake the pan to spread the mixture evenly.

Cook the eggs for about 5 minutes. Taste, adjust the seasonings, and serve immediately.

Per serving: 317 Calories; 24.3g Fat; 4.2g Carbs; 19g Protein; 0.4g Fiber

244. Favorite Breakfast Tabbouleh

(Ready in about 20 minutes | Servings 3)

Ingredients

6 eggs, beaten
1 shallot, sliced
2 cups cauliflower rice

1 bell pepper, deseeded and sliced
1/2 cup cherry tomatoes, halved

Directions

Melt 1 tablespoon of butter in an oven-safe skillet over medium-high heat.

Cook the cauliflower rice for 5 to 6 minutes or until it has softened. Stir in shallot and bell pepper and continue to cook for 4 minutes more.

Pour the beaten eggs over vegetables and cook until the eggs are set; do not overcook eggs.

Top with cherry tomatoes and place under the preheated broiler for 5 minutes. Taste and adjust seasonings. Bon appétit!

Per serving: 204 Calories; 8.6g Fat; 8.6g Carbs; 13.7g Protein; 2.8g Fiber

245. Egg Cups with Ham

(Ready in about 30 minutes | Servings 6)

Ingredients

6 thin slices ham
6 eggs
4 ounces cream cheese

1 teaspoon mustard
6 ounces Colby cheese, shredded

Directions

Line muffin cups with cupcake liners. Add a ham slice to each muffin cup and gently press down.

In a mixing dish, whisk the eggs, cream cheese, and mustard; season with salt and pepper to taste.

Spoon the egg mixture into the cups. Top with the shredded cheese. Bake in the preheated oven at 355 degrees F approximately 27 minutes.

Garnish with 2 tablespoons of green onions just before serving and enjoy!

Per serving: 258 Calories; 19.1g Fat; 2.8g Carbs; 17.5g Protein; 0.2g Fiber

VEGETABLES & SIDE DISHES

246. Broccoli and Sardine Salad

(Ready in about 10 minutes | Servings 4)

Ingredients

2 (4-ounce) cans sardines in oil, drained

1/2 white onion, thinly sliced

1 teaspoon stone-ground mustard

2 tablespoons fresh lime juice

1 pound broccoli florets

Directions

In a nonstick skillet, cook the broccoli over medium-high heat for about 6 minutes; work in batches.

Place the charred broccoli in a serving bowl along with sardines and onions.

Toss your salad with the mustard and lime juice. Bon appétit!

Per serving: 159 Calories; 7.1g Fat; 5.7g Carbs; 17.8g Protein; 3g Fiber

247. Creamed Spinach with Cheese

(Ready in about 10 minutes | Servings 4)

Ingredients

10 ounces spinach

1 tablespoon butter, room temperature

1/2 cup double cream

3 ounces cream cheese

1 clove garlic, minced

Directions

Melt the butter in a sauté pan over medium-high heat. Then, sauté the garlic until fragrant for 30 seconds or so.

Fold in spinach leaves, cover and let it simmer for 2 to 3 minutes or until spinach wilts. Season with salt and black pepper to taste.

Fold in double cream and cheese and gently stir until everything is well incorporated. Enjoy!

Per serving: 166 Calories; 15.1g Fat; 5g Carbs; 4.4g Protein; 1.7g Fiber

248. Vegan Mushroom Stroganoff

(Ready in about 15 minutes | Servings 3)

Ingredients

2 tablespoons olive oil

1/2 shallot, diced

3 cloves garlic, chopped

12 ounces brown mushrooms, thinly sliced

2 cups tomato sauce

Directions

In a heavy-bottomed pot, heat the oil until sizzling. Sauté the shallot for 2 to 3 minutes until just tender.

Then, cook the garlic and mushrooms for 1 to 2 minutes until they are just tender and fragrant.

Stir in the tomato sauce and bring to a rolling boil; reduce the heat to simmer, cover, and continue to cook for about 10 minutes.

Taste and adjust seasonings. Enjoy!

Per serving: 138 Calories; 9.2g Fat; 7.1g Carbs; 3.4g Protein; 1.8g Fiber

249. Easy Insalata Caprese

(Ready in about 20 minutes | Servings 2)

Ingredients

1/2 pound asparagus spears, trimmed

1 garlic clove, pressed

1-2 drops liquid stevia

1 cup grape tomatoes, halved

1/2 cup mozzarella, grated

Directions

Toss your asparagus with the 1 tablespoon of oil and garlic; drizzle with fresh lemon juice.

Cook the asparagus spears on the hot grill until charred.

Slice the asparagus into small pieces and transfer to a serving bowl. Add in stevia and tomatoes; toss to combine well.

Top with mozzarella and serve at room temperature.

Per serving: 187 Calories; 13.3g Fat; 7.4g Carbs; 9.5g Protein; 3.4g Fiber

250. Cabbage Stir-Fry

(Ready in about 25 minutes | Servings 2)

Ingredients

3/4 pound green cabbage, sliced

2 tablespoons olive oil

1 shallot, chopped

1/2 cup chicken stock

1 teaspoon ginger-garlic paste

Directions

In a wok, heat the olive oil until sizzling; then, sauté the ginger-garlic paste until fragrant.

Then, cook the shallot for 3 to 4 minutes. Pour in the chicken stock to scrape up the browned bits that stick to the bottom of the pot.

Add in the cabbage along with salt and pepper. Continue to cook, covered, for about 16 minutes or until cooked through. Enjoy!

Per serving: 168 Calories; 13g Fat; 7g Carbs; 2.6g Protein; 4.1g Fiber

251. Cheesy Eggplant Casserole with Kale

(Ready in about 2 hours 45 minutes | Servings 6)

Ingredients

1 (3/4-pound) eggplant, cut into 1/2-inch slices

14 ounces garlic-and-tomato pasta sauce, without sugar

1 1/2 cups Gorgonzola cheese, grated

1/3 cup cream cheese

8 ounces kale leaves, torn into pieces

Directions

Sprinkle eggplant slices with coarse salt and allow it to sit for 1 hour. Rinse the eggplant slices and brush them with 2 tablespoons of olive oil

Cook the eggplant in a grill pan for 4 to 5 minutes until golden brown on each side; reserve.

Place the kale leaves in the pan and cook until wilted. Mix cream cheese with Gorgonzola cheese.

Place the grilled eggplant slices on the bottom of a lightly greased casserole dish. Top with the kale. Place 1/2 of cheese blend on top.

Spoon the tomato sauce over the cheese layer. Top with the remaining cheese blend. Bake in the preheated oven at 360 degrees F for 30 to 35 minutes. Enjoy!

Per serving: 230 Calories; 18.5g Fat; 6.7g Carbs; 10.6g Protein; 2.4g Fiber

252. Buttery and Garlicky Cauliflower Rice

(Ready in about 10 minutes | Servings 4)

Ingredients

1 tablespoon butter
1 pound cauliflower florets
1 tablespoon smoked paprika
Flaky salt, to taste
2 cloves garlic, minced

Directions

In a saucepan, melt the butter over a moderate heat.

Pulse the cauliflower in your blender or food processor until it has broken down into rice-sized pieces.

Cook the cauliflower rice in hot butter for 5 to 6 minutes. Stir in the paprika, salt, and garlic, and continue to cook for 30 seconds more.

Bon appétit!

Per serving: 56 Calories; 3.2g Fat; 6.1g Carbs; 2.3g Protein; 2.3g Fiber

253. Herby Roasted Portobellos

(Ready in about 45 minutes | Servings 2)

Ingredients

1 pound white portobello mushrooms, cleaned and sliced
3 ounces edam cheese, shredded
2 tablespoons ghee, melted
1 tablespoon fresh cilantro, chopped
1 tablespoon Mediterranean herb mix

Directions

Brush portobello mushrooms with the melted ghee. Sprinkle the mushrooms with Mediterranean herb mix.

Roast in the preheated oven at 365 degrees F for about 30 minutes or until they are tender.

Top your mushrooms with the edam cheese and continue to roast for 5 minutes longer. Garnish with fresh cilantro and enjoy!

Per serving: 308 Calories; 24.1g Fat; 6.1g Carbs; 17.9g Protein; 2.8g Fiber

254. Classic Zucchini Soup

(Ready in about 20 minutes | Servings 3)

Ingredients

2 teaspoons extra-virgin olive oil
1/2 pound zucchini, peeled and diced
1/2 shallot, chopped
1/2 cup celery, chopped
2 cups vegetable broth

Directions

Heat 1 teaspoon of the olive oil in a heavy-bottomed pot over a moderate heat; sauté the zucchini for about 2 minutes and reserve.

Heat the remaining teaspoon of olive oil until sizzling; sauté the shallot until softened.

Add in celery and vegetable broth along with the reserved zucchini; bring to a boil. Turn the heat to simmer, let it cook, partially covered, for 15 to 18 minutes.

Taste and adjust the seasonings. Bon appétit!

Per serving: 58 Calories; 3.3g Fat; 3.5g Carbs; 2.3g Protein; 1.2g Fiber

255. Autumn Butternut Squash Stew

(Ready in about 35 minutes | Servings 4)

Ingredients

1 Spanish onion, peeled and diced
1/2 pound butternut squash, diced
1 celery stalk, chopped
4 cups baby spinach
4 tablespoons sour cream

Directions

Heat 2 tablespoons of olive oil in a stock pot over medium-high flame. Sauté Spanish onion until tender and fragrant.

Stir in the butternut squash and celery; pour in 3 cups of water or vegetable broth. Reduce the temperature to medium-low and continue to cook for 25 to 30 minutes.

Fold in spinach, cover, and let it stand in the residual heat until the spinach leaves wilt. Season with salt and black pepper to taste. Serve with cold sour cream. Bon appétit!

Per serving: 148 Calories; 11.5g Fat; 6.8g Carbs; 2.5g Protein; 2.3g Fiber

256. Zucchini Muffins with Romano Cheese

(Ready in about 40 minutes | Servings 4)

Ingredients

1 (1/2-pound) zucchini, grated
1 teaspoon sea salt
1 cup Romano cheese, grated
2 eggs, beaten
1/2 cup almond flour

Directions

Place zucchini and salt in a bowl and let it stand for 30 minutes; then, squeeze using a cheesecloth.

Add in cheese, eggs, and almond flour; stir to combine well. Brush a muffin pan with cooking spray. Spoon the mixture into the pan.

Bake in the preheated oven at 330 degrees F for 20 minutes. Bon appétit!

Per serving: 224 Calories; 18g Fat; 3g Carbs; 13.4g Protein; 1.5g Fiber

257. Braised Kale with Wine Sauce

(Ready in about 15 minutes | Servings 5)

Ingredients

6 cups kale, torn into pieces
1 shallot, chopped
1/2 cup double cream
1/2 teaspoon fresh garlic, minced
2 tablespoons dry white wine

Directions

Heat 2 tablespoons of olive oil in a saucepan over a moderate flame. Sauté the shallot until tender and aromatic about 4 minutes.

Stir in kale leaves and continue to cook for 1 to 2 minutes or until kale wilts completely. Add in the garlic and wine. Continue cooking for 2 minutes more.

Add in double cream and reduce the heat to simmer. Continue to cook, partially covered, for a further 5 minutes or until the sauce has reduced slightly. Serve warm.

Per serving: 130 Calories; 10.5g Fat; 6.1g Carbs; 3.7g Protein; 3g Fiber

258. Brussels Sprouts with Bacon and Dijon Sauce

(Ready in about 15 minutes | Servings 3)

Ingredients

12 Brussels sprouts, trimmed and halved
6 ounces smoked bacon, diced
1/2 cup dry white wine
1 teaspoon Dijon mustard
1 teaspoon Herbes de Provence

Directions

In a saucepan, cook the bacon for 2 minutes.

Add the Brussels sprouts and Herbes de Provence; continue to cook, adding wine periodically.

Cook until the Brussels sprouts are tender or about 10 minutes.

Lastly, stir in Dijon mustard and remove from the heat. Enjoy!

Per serving: 297 Calories; 22.5g Fat; 6.3g Carbs; 9.7g Protein; 3g Fiber

259. Ensalada de Pimientos Rojos

(Ready in about 15 minutes | Servings 2)

Ingredients

2 red peppers, deveined and sliced
2 tablespoons herb infused olive oil
1 garlic clove, minced
1 jarred piquillo pepper, sliced
1/2 Spanish onion, chopped

Directions

Start by preheating your oven to 390 degrees F.

Toss all ingredients in a lightly oiled baking pan. Bake in the preheated oven for about 9 minutes or until your vegetables are tender and slightly charred.

Drizzle 2 tablespoons of wine vinegar over vegetables and serve at room temperature. Enjoy!

Per serving: 195 Calories; 18.1g Fat; 8.1g Carbs; 1.5g Protein; 2.5g Fiber

260. Keto Mushroom Chili

(Ready in about 20 minutes | Servings 3)

Ingredients

3 ounces bacon, diced
3/4 pound brown mushrooms, sliced
2 cloves garlic, minced
1 brown onion, chopped
3 tablespoons dry red wine

Directions

In a preheated soup pot, fry the bacon until crisp or about 4 minutes; reserve.

In the pan drippings, sauté the brown mushrooms, garlic, and brown onion and until they have softened. Pour in red wine and deglaze the pot with a wide spatula. Add in 1 teaspoon of chili powder.

Reduce the heat to simmer; stir in the remaining ingredients and continue cooking for 10 to 15 minutes or until the sauce has thickened.

Garnish with the reserved bacon and serve warm.

Per serving: 159 Calories; 11.3g Fat; 6g Carbs; 6.9g Protein; 1.3g Fiber

261. Authentic German Cabbage

(Ready in about 20 minutes | Servings 3)

Ingredients

4 ounces bacon, diced
1 medium-sized onion, chopped
2 cloves garlic, minced
1 cup beef bone broth
1 pound red cabbage, shredded

Directions

Cook the bacon in a preheated skillet over medium-high heat; reserve.

Then, cook the onion in the same skillet for about 3 minutes or until it is tender and aromatic. After that, cook the garlic until fragrant for 30 seconds or so.

Add in broth and cabbage. Stir fry for 10 to 15 minutes more.

Garnish with the reserved bacon and serve warm.

Per serving: 243 Calories; 22.2g Fat; 6.8g Carbs; 6.5g Protein; 1.9g Fiber

262. Easy Cheesy Broccoli Fritters

(Ready in about 15 minutes | Servings 5)

Ingredients

1 pound broccoli florets
1 cup Romano cheese, preferably freshly grated
3 eggs
2 tablespoons olive oil
5 ounces Swiss cheese, sliced

Directions

Pulse the broccoli in your food processor using 1 second intervals to chop it into "rice".

Mix the broccoli florets with Romano cheese and eggs; add in salt and black pepper. Using oiled hands, form the mixture into balls and flatten them slightly.

Heat 2 tablespoons of olive oil in a frying pan over medium-high heat.

Cook for 3 minutes, turn them over and top with Swiss cheese. Let it cook on the other side for 3 minutes more or until cheese melts. Serve warm and enjoy!

Per serving: 323 Calories; 24.1g Fat; 5.9g Carbs; 19.8g Protein; 2.4g Fiber

263. Eggplant and Goat Cheese Bake

(Ready in about 35 minutes | Servings 3)

Ingredients

2 bell peppers, deveined and quartered
1 (1-pound) eggplant, cut into rounds
1/2 cup sour cream
1 ½ cups goat cheese
2 vine-ripe tomatoes, sliced
1 teaspoon Asian spice mix

Directions

Start by preheating your oven to 410 degrees F. Lightly oil a baking dish with nonstick spray.

Place the peppers and eggplant in the baking dish; place the sliced tomatoes on top. Drizzle 2 tablespoons of olive oil all over the vegetables.

Season with Asian spice mix. Bake in the preheated oven for 15 to 17 minutes. Rotate the pan and continue to bake for a further 7 to 9 minutes.

Top with sour cream and cheese. Garnish with 2 tablespoons of green onions just before serving, if desired. Bon appétit!

Per serving: 477 Calories; 41.4g Fat; 7.2g Carbs; 18.4g Protein; 3.6g Fiber

264. Kid-Friendly Celery Boats

(Ready in about 35 minutes | Servings 2)

Ingredients

2 ounces Gruyère cheese
3 tablespoons scallions, minced
1 teaspoon Mediterranean herb blend

1 jalapeno pepper, deveined and minced
3 celery stalks, halved

Directions

In a mixing dish, combine Gruyère cheese, scallions, herbs, and jalapeno pepper; mix to combine well.

Divide the mixture between the celery stalks. Then, arrange them on a parchment-lined baking tray.

Roast in the preheated oven at 360 degrees F for 35 minutes or until cooked through.

Per serving: 194 Calories; 17.1g Fat; 7g Carbs; 2.5g Protein; 5g Fiber

265. Cream of Broccoli Soup

(Ready in about 25 minutes | Servings 4)

Ingredients

1 (1-pound) head broccoli, broken into florets
1/2 white onion, finely chopped
1 celery rib, chopped

1/2 cup double cream
1 ½ cups Monterey Jack cheese, grated

Directions

Heat 3 tablespoons of olive oil in a heavy-bottomed pot over medium-high heat. Sauté the broccoli, onion, and celery rib until they have softened.

Pour in 4 cups of water or vegetable broth and bring to boil. Decrease the heat to medium-low. Continue to cook for 15 minutes or until the broccoli is thoroughly cooked.

Fold in the cream; heat off. Spoon the soup into four ramekins; top each ramekin with Monterey Jack cheese.

Place under the preheated broiler for 5 to 6 minutes. Bon appétit!

Per serving: 323 Calories; 28.2g Fat; 4.4g Carbs; 13.4g Protein; 0.6g Fiber

266. Baked Eggplant Rounds

(Ready in about 40 minutes | Servings 6)

Ingredients

1 pound eggplant, peeled and sliced
1 ½ cups marinara sauce
1 cup mozzarella cheese

2 tablespoons fresh basil leaves, snipped
2 teaspoons Italian seasoning blend

Directions

Preheat your oven to 370 degrees F. Coat a baking sheet with a piece of parchment paper.

Toss the eggplant rounds with the Italian seasoning blend and place on the baking sheet.

Bake for 25 minutes, flipping them over half-way through cooking time.

Top with marinara sauce and mozzarella cheese. Continue to bake for a further 7 minutes until mozzarella is hot and bubbling. Garnish with fresh basil leaves and enjoy!

Per serving: 91 Calories; 4.8g Fat; 5.3g Carbs; 5.3g Protein; 2.9g Fiber

267. Mexican Guacamole with Queso Fresco

(Ready in about 5 minutes | Servings 4)

Ingredients

1 tablespoon extra-virgin olive oil
2 ripe avocados, peeled, pitted and diced

1 poblano pepper, chopped
2 tomatoes, diced
1/4 cup queso fresco, crumbled

Directions

Combine the oil, avocados, poblano pepper, and tomatoes in a serving bowl. Add in 1 tablespoon of olive oil and lime juice and stir to combine.

Season with salt and black pepper to taste.

Garnish with crumbled queso fresco and serve immediately!

Per serving: 188 Calories; 16g Fat; 6.9g Carbs; 3.6g Protein; 4.2g Fiber

268. Italian Roasted Peppers with Cheese

(Ready in about 20 minutes | Servings 4)

Ingredients

4 Italian sweet peppers, deveined and halved
2 teaspoons olive oil

1/4 teaspoon red pepper flakes
Sat and black pepper, to taste
8 ounces mozzarella cheese

Directions

Drizzle olive oil over your peppers. Season the peppers with red pepper, salt, and black pepper.

Top the peppers with mozzarella cheese.

Bake for about 13 minutes until the peppers are tender and blistered. Enjoy!

Per serving: 214 Calories; 15.1g Fat; 6.7g Carbs; 13.5g Protein; 2g Fiber

269. Avocado with Parmigiano-Reggiano

(Ready in about 15 minutes | Servings 6)

Ingredients

3 tablespoons extra-virgin olive oil
3 avocados, pitted
6 tablespoons Parmigiano-Reggiano cheese, grated

1/2 teaspoon Himalayan salt
1/2 teaspoon red pepper flakes, crushed

Directions

Slice avocados into halves. Using a sharp knife, cut a crisscross pattern about 3/4 of the way through on each avocado half.

Season them with Himalayan salt and red pepper. Brush with olive oil and top with Parmigiano-Reggiano cheese.

Transfer your avocados to a roasting pan and place under the preheated broiler for 4 to 5 minutes or until hot and bubbly. Bon appétit!

Per serving: 196 Calories; 18.8g Fat; 6.5g Carbs; 2.7g Protein; 4.6g Fiber

270. Party Romaine Boats

(Ready in about 15 minutes | Servings 4)

Ingredients

1 head romaine lettuce, separated into leaves
1/2 pound pork sausage, sliced
1/2 cup tomato puree
1 green bell pepper, deveined and chopped
2 scallions, chopped

Directions

In a preheated frying pan, cook pork sausage for 3 to 4 minutes, breaking apart with a fork.

Add in the bell pepper and continue sautéing for 2 minutes more.

Fold in the tomato puree. Season with salt and black pepper and continue to cook for 2 to 3 minutes longer.

Place the lettuce boats on a serving platter. Divide the sausage mixture between lettuce boats. Garnish with scallions just before serving. Bon appétit!

Per serving: 230 Calories; 18.1g Fat; 5.6g Carbs; 10.2g Protein; 2.1g Fiber

271. Middle Eastern-Style Shakshuka

(Ready in about 35 minutes | Servings 6)

Ingredients

6 eggs
3 bell peppers, sliced
1 large-sized zucchini, sliced
3 tomatoes, sliced
1 shallot, sliced

Directions

Preheat your oven to 390 degrees F. Spritz the sides and bottom of a baking pan with nonstick spray.

Place the vegetables in the prepared pan and cover with a piece of foil. Pour in 1 cup of water or vegetable broth. Season with Baharat if desired.

Transfer to the preheated oven and bake for 20 to 25 minutes.

Create six indentations with a spoon and crack the egg directly into it. Bake until the egg whites are opaque white and the yolks are a bit soft. Enjoy!

Per serving: 439 Calories; 45g Fat; 5.5g Carbs; 6.5g Protein; 1g Fiber

272. Italian Peppers with Mozzarella di Bufala

(Ready in about 20 minutes | Servings 5)

Ingredients

4 tablespoons canola oil
1 teaspoon Italian seasoning mix
1 1/3 pounds Italian peppers, deveined and sliced
2 balls buffalo mozzarella, drained and halved
1 yellow onion, sliced

Directions

Heat the canola oil in until sizzling. Once hot, sauté the peppers and onions until tender and fragrant.

Add a splash of water to deglaze the pan along with Italian seasoning mix; cook for a further 10 minutes, stirring continuously.

Top with cheese and serve. Bon appétit!

Per serving: 183 Calories; 13.1g Fat; 7g Carbs; 5.4g Protein; 1.9g Fiber

273. Roasted Asparagus Salad

(Ready in about 20 minutes | Servings 5)

Ingredients

2 tablespoons olive oil
14 ounces asparagus spears, trimmed
1 cup cherry tomatoes, halved
3 tablespoons sour cream
5 tablespoons mayonnaise

Directions

Toss the asparagus with olive oil and Italian seasoning mix. Transfer to a roasting pan and roast at 420 degrees F for about 15 minutes until crisp-tender and lightly charred.

In a mixing dish, combine sour cream and mayonnaise. Toss asparagus with this mixture and top with cherry tomatoes. Bon appétit!

Per serving: 179 Calories; 11.5g Fat; 7.7g Carbs; 3.5g Protein; 2.4g Fiber

274. Greek-Style Salad

(Ready in about 20 minutes | Servings 4)

Ingredients

4 tablespoons extra-virgin olive oil
1/2 cup Kalamata olives, pitted and sliced
1/2 pound zucchini, sliced
1/2 pound tomatoes, sliced
4 ounces feta cheese, cubed

Directions

Start by preheating your oven to 365 degrees F.

Toss the zucchini slices and tomatoes with extra-virgin olive oil; transfer them to a roasting pan.

Bake in the preheated oven for about 7 minutes.

Add in olives and serve topped with feta cheese. Enjoy!

Per serving: 175 Calories; 14.7g Fat; 6.1g Carbs; 6.5g Protein; 1.8g Fiber

275. Sriracha-Spiced Eggplant

(Ready in about 20 minutes | Servings 2)

Ingredients

1 large-sized eggplant, cut into slices lengthwise
1/2 teaspoon Sriracha sauce
1 tablespoon olive oil
1 teaspoon balsamic vinegar
1/4 cup fresh chives, chopped

Directions

Toss your eggplant with salt and black pepper and transfer it to a foil-lined baking sheet. Roast in the preheated oven at 410 degrees F for 13 to 15 minutes.

In the meantime, combine Sriracha sauce, olive oil, and balsamic vinegar. Drizzle the mixture over the eggplant slices.

Place under the preheated broil for about 4 minutes. Garnish with fresh chives an enjoy.

Per serving: 102 Calories; 7g Fat; 8g Carbs; 1.6g Protein; 4.7g Fiber

276. Tuscan-Style Asparagus

(Ready in about 10 minutes | Servings 2)

Ingredients

1/2 pound asparagus spears, trimmed, cut into bite-sized pieces
1/2 tablespoon lemon juice
1 tablespoon extra-virgin olive oil
1 teaspoon Italian spice blend
4 tablespoons Romano cheese, freshly grated

Directions

Boil asparagus in a saucepan of lightly salted water for 3 to 4 minutes. Drain and place in a bowl.

Toss your asparagus with lemon juice, extra-virgin olive oil, and Italian spice blend.

Top with Romano cheese and serve!

Per serving: 193 Calories; 14.1g Fat; 5.6g Carbs; 11.5g Protein; 2.4g Fiber

277. Easy Moroccan Tajine

(Ready in about 50 minutes | Servings 4)

Ingredients

2 tablespoons leeks, sliced
2 cups zucchini, thinly sliced
1/2 cup cheddar cheese, grated
1/4 cup heavy cream
1 tablespoon Moroccan spice mix

Directions

Brush the sides and bottom of a baking dish with 1 tablespoon of melted butter.

Place 1 cup of the zucchini slices in the bottom of the baking dish; add 1 tablespoon of leeks; sprinkle with Moroccan spice mix. Top with 1/4 cup of Cheddar cheese.

Repeat the layers of zucchini and leeks.

In a mixing bowl, thoroughly combine cheddar cheese and heavy cream. Spoon the mixture over the vegetable layer.

Bake in the preheated oven at 370 degrees F approximately 45 minutes until the top is nicely browned. Bon appétit!

Per serving: 155 Calories; 12.9g Fat; 3.5g Carbs; 7.6g Protein; 0.8g Fiber

278. Chorizo and Ricotta Stuffed Peppers

(Ready in about 25 minutes | Servings 4)

Ingredients

4 red peppers, deveined and halved
1 Spanish onion, chopped
1 ripe tomato, chopped
4 ounces Ricotta cheese
8 ounces Chorizo sausage, chopped into small chunks

Directions

In a saucepan, heat 1 tablespoon of olive oil over a moderate heat. Sauté Spanish onion until tender and translucent.

Add a splash of Spanish wine to deglaze the pan. Stir in Chorizo sausage, tomato, and Ricotta cheese.

Microwave the peppers for about 7 minutes or until they have softened.

Stuff the peppers with the prepared filling and place them in a lightly-oiled baking dish. Season with salt and black pepper.

Pour 2 cups of broth around the peppers.

Bake in the preheated oven at 430 degrees F for 13 to 15 minutes. Serve warm or at room temperature. Enjoy!

Per serving: 340 Calories; 27.2g Fat; 5.2g Carbs; 14.7g Protein; 1.5g Fiber

279. Japanese Tamago Gohan

(Ready in about 15 minutes | Servings 3)

Ingredients

1 tablespoon sesame oil
1/2 pound fresh cauliflower
3 eggs
1/2 cup leeks, chopped
1 garlic, pressed

Directions

Pulse the cauliflower in your blender or food processor until it has broken down into rice-sized pieces.

In a saucepan, heat sesame oil over medium-high heat; sauté the leeks and garlic until just tender and fragrant for 2 minutes.

Add the cauliflower rice to the saucepan; add Japanese 7 spice blend if desired if desired. Continue to cook, stirring periodically, until the cauliflower is just tender, about 6 minutes.

Stir the eggs into the saucepan and continue to cook for 3 minutes more. Serve warm.

Per serving: 131 Calories; 8.9g Fat; 6.2g Carbs; 7.2g Protein; 1.8g Fiber

280. Balkan Traditional Satarash

(Ready in about 20 minutes | Servings 3)

Ingredients

3 teaspoons olive oil
1 onion, chopped
2 garlic cloves, minced
3 bell peppers, deveined and sliced
1 cup tomato sauce with onion and garlic

Directions

In a saucepan, heat olive oil until sizzling. Then, cook the onion until just tender and translucent.

Add in the garlic and bell peppers; continue to sauté for 2 to 3 minutes more or until they are tender and fragrant. After that, fold in tomato sauce.

Cover, decrease the temperature to simmer and continue to cook for 11 to 13 minutes or until cooked through.

Season with salt and black pepper to taste and serve warm!

Per serving: 83 Calories; 4.7g Fat; 6.4g Carbs; 1.7g Protein; 1.8g Fiber

281. Easy Zucchini Slaw

(Ready in about 10 minutes | Servings 3)

Ingredients

2 tablespoons extra-virgin olive oil
1 zucchini, shredded

1 teaspoon Dijon mustard
1 yellow bell pepper, sliced
1 red onion, thinly sliced

Directions

Combine all ingredients in a salad bowl. Season with the salt and black pepper to taste.

Let it sit in your refrigerator for about 1 hour before serving. Bon appétit!

Per serving: 96 Calories; 9.4g Fat; 2.8g Carbs; 0.7g Protein; 0.4g Fiber

282. Broc n' Cheese

(Ready in about 25 minutes | Servings 5)

Ingredients

1 ½ pounds broccoli florets
3 tablespoons olive oil
1/2 cup cream of mushrooms soup

1 teaspoon garlic, minced
6 ounces Swiss cheese, shredded

Directions

Start by preheating your oven to 380 degrees F. Brush the sides and bottom of a baking dish with 1 tablespoon of olive oil.

In a small nonstick skillet, heat 1 tablespoon of the olive oil over a moderate heat. Sauté the garlic for 30 seconds or until just beginning to brown.

In a soup pot, parboil the broccoli until crisp-tender; place the rinsed broccoli in the prepared baking dish. Place the sautéed garlic on top. Drizzle the remaining tablespoon of olive oil over everything.

Season with the salt and black pepper. Pour in the cream of mushroom soup. Top with the Swiss cheese.

Bake for 20 minutes until the cheese is hot and bubbly. Enjoy!

Per serving: 179 Calories; 10.3g Fat; 7.6g Carbs; 13.5g Protein; 3.6g Fiber

283. Greek Avgolemono Soup

(Ready in about 25 minutes | Servings 6)

Ingredients

1 pound fennel bulbs, sliced
1 celery stalk, chopped
1 tablespoon freshly squeezed lemon juice

2 eggs
5 cups chicken stock

Directions

Heat 2 tablespoons of olive oil in a soup pot over medium-high heat. Sauté the fennel and celery until tender but not browned, approximately 7 minutes.

Add in Mediterranean seasoning mix and continue to sauté until they are fragrant.

Add in the chicken stock and bring to a rapid boil. Turn the temperature to medium-low; let it simmer for 10 to 13 minutes.

Puree your soup using a food processor or an immersion blender.

Thoroughly whisk the eggs and lemon juice until well combined; pour 2 cups of the hot soup into the egg mixture, whisking continuously.

Return the mixture to the pot; continue cooking for 2 to 3 minutes more until cooked through. Spoon into individual bowls and enjoy!

Per serving: 86 Calories; 6.1g Fat; 6g Carbs; 2.8g Protein; 2.4g Fiber

284. Italian Zuppa Di Pomodoro

(Ready in about 35 minutes | Servings 4)

Ingredients

1/2 cup scallions, chopped
1 ½ pounds Roma tomatoes, diced
2 cups Brodo di Pollo (Italian broth)

2 tablespoons tomato paste
2 cups mustard greens, torn into pieces

Directions

Heat 2 teaspoon of olive oil in a large pot over medium-high heat. Sauté the scallions for 2 to 3 minutes until tender.

Add in Roma tomatoes, Italian broth, and tomato paste and bring to a boil. Reduce the temperature to medium-low and continue to simmer, partially covered, for about 25 minutes.

Puree the soup with an immersion blender and return it to the pot. Add in the mustard greens and continue to cook until the greens wilt.

Taste, adjust seasonings and serve immediately.

Per serving: 104 Calories; 7.2g Fat; 6.2g Carbs; 2.6g Protein; 3.1g Fiber

285. Easy Zucchini Croquets

(Ready in about 40 minutes | Servings 6)

Ingredients

1 egg
1/2 cup almond meal
1 pound zucchini, grated and drained
1/2 cup goat cheese, crumbled
2 tablespoons olive oil

Directions

Combine the egg, almond milk, zucchini and cheese in a mixing bowl. Refrigerate the mixture for 20 to 30 minutes.

Heat the oil in a frying pan over medium-high heat. Scoop the heaped tablespoons of the mixture into the hot oil.

Cook for about 4 minutes per side; cook in batches. Serve warm.

Per serving: 111 Calories; 8.9g Fat; 3.2g Carbs; 5.8g Protein; 1g Fiber

286. Pork and Cheese Stuffed Peppers

(Ready in about 30 minutes | Servings 2)

Ingredients

2 sweet Italian peppers, deveined and halved
1/2 Spanish onion, finely chopped
1 cup marinara sauce
1/2 cup cheddar cheese, grated
4 ounces pork, ground

Directions

Heat 1 tablespoon of canola oil in a saucepan over a moderate heat. Then, sauté the onion for 3 to 4 minutes until tender and fragrant.

Add in the ground pork; cook for 3 to 4 minutes more. Add in Italian seasoning mix. Spoon the mixture into the pepper halves.

Spoon the marinara sauce into a lightly greased baking dish. Arrange the stuffed peppers in the baking dish.

Bake in the preheated oven at 395 degrees F for 17 to 20 minutes. Top with cheddar cheese and continue to bake for about 5 minutes or until the top is golden brown. Bon appétit!

Per serving: 313 Calories; 21.3g Fat; 5.7g Carbs; 20.2g Protein; 1.9g Fiber

287. Stewed Cabbage with Goan Chorizo Sausage

(Ready in about 30 minutes | Servings 3)

Ingredients

6 ounces Goan chorizo sausage, sliced
3/4 cup cream of celery soup
1 pound white cabbage, outer leaves removed and finely shredded
2 cloves garlic, finely chopped
1 teaspoon Indian spice blend

Directions

In a large frying pan, sear the sausage until no longer pink; set aside.

Then, sauté the garlic and Indian spice blend until they are aromatic. Add in the cabbage and cream of celery soup.

Turn the heat to simmer; continue to simmer, partially covered, for about 20 minutes or until cooked through.

Top with the reserved Goan chorizo sausage and serve.

Per serving: 235 Calories; 17.7g Fat; 6.1g Carbs; 9.8g Protein; 2.4g Fiber

288. Cauliflower and Ham Casserole

(Ready in about 10 minutes | Servings 6)

Ingredients

1 ½ pounds cauliflower, broken into small florets
6 ounces ham, diced
4 eggs, beaten
1/2 cup Greek-Style yogurt
1 cup Swiss cheese, preferably freshly grated

Directions

Parboil the cauliflower in a saucepan for about 10 minutes or until tender. Drain and puree in your food processor.

Add in the ham, eggs, and Greek-Style yogurt; stir to combine well.

Spoon the mixture into a lightly buttered baking dish. Top with the Swiss cheese and bake in the preheated oven at 385 degrees F for about 20 minutes. Enjoy!

Per serving: 236 Calories; 13.8g Fat; 7.2g Carbs; 20.3g Protein; 2.3g Fiber

289. Stuffed Spaghetti Squash

(Ready in about 1 hour | Servings 4)

Ingredients

1/2 pound spaghetti squash, halved, scoop out seeds
1 garlic clove, minced
1 cup cream cheese
2 eggs
1/2 cup Mozzarella cheese, shredded

Directions

Drizzle the insides of each squash with 1 teaspoon of olive oil. Bake in the preheated oven at 380 degrees F for 45 minutes.

Scrape out the spaghetti squash "noodles" from the skin. Fold in the remaining ingredients; stir to combine well.

Spoon the cheese mixture into squash halves. Bake at 360 degrees F for about 9 minutes, until the cheese is hot and bubbly. Enjoy!

Per serving: 219 Calories; 17.5g Fat; 6.9g Carbs; 9g Protein; 0.9g Fiber

290. Spicy and Warm Coleslaw

(Ready in about 45 minutes | Servings 4)

Ingredients

1 medium-sized leek, chopped
1 tablespoon balsamic vinegar
1 teaspoon yellow mustard
1/2 pound green cabbage, shredded
1/2 teaspoon Sriracha sauce

Directions

Drizzle 2 tablespoons of the olive oil over the leek and cabbage; sprinkle with salt and black pepper.

Bake in the preheated oven at 410 degrees F for about 40 minutes. Transfer the mixture to a salad bowl.

Toss with 1 tablespoon of olive oil, mustard, balsamic vinegar, and Sriracha sauce. Serve warm!

Per serving: 118 Calories; 10.2g Fat; 6.6g Carbs; 1.1g Protein; 1.9g Fiber

291. Easy Mediterranean Croquettes

(Ready in about 40minutes | Servings 2)

Ingredients

1/2 pound zucchini, grated
1/2 cup Swiss cheese, shredded
3 eggs, whisked Mediterranean
1/3 cup almond meal
2 tablespoons pork rinds

Directions

Place the grated zucchini in a colander, sprinkle with 1/2 teaspoon of salt, and let it stand for 30 minutes. Drain the zucchini well and discard any excess water.

Heat 2 tablespoons of olive oil in a frying pan over medium-high heat. Mix the zucchini with the remaining ingredients until well combined.

Shape the mixture into croquettes and cook for 2 to 3 minutes per side. Enjoy!

Per serving: 463 Calories; 36g Fat; 7.6g Carbs; 27.5g Protein; 2.8g Fiber

292. Tuscan Asparagus with Cheese

(Ready in about 20 minutes | Servings 5)

Ingredients

1 ½ pounds asparagus, trimmed
1 tablespoon Sriracha sauce
1 tablespoon fresh cilantro, roughly chopped
4 tablespoons Pecorino Romano cheese, grated
4 tablespoons butter, melted

Directions

Toss the asparagus with the cheese, melted butter, and Sriracha sauce; season with Italian spice mix, if desired.

Arrange your asparagus on a baking sheet and roast in the preheated oven at 410 degrees F for 12 to 15 minutes.

Garnish with fresh cilantro and enjoy!

Per serving: 140 Calories; 11.5g Fat; 5.5g Carbs; 5.6g Protein; 2.9g Fiber

293. Brown Mushroom Stew

(Ready in about 20 minutes | Servings 6)

Ingredients

2 pounds brown mushrooms, sliced
1 bell pepper, sliced
2 cups chicken broth
1/2 cup leeks, finely diced
1 cup herb-infused tomato sauce

Directions

Heat 4 tablespoons of oil in a soup pot over a moderate flame. Sauté the pepper and leeks for about 4 to 5 minutes.

Stir in the mushrooms and continue to sauté for about 2 minutes. Pour in a splash of broth to deglaze the bottom of the pan.

After that, add in the tomato sauce and the remaining broth; bring to a boil. Turn the heat to simmer.

Continue to cook, partially covered, for about 10 minutes or until the mushrooms are tender and thoroughly cooked.

Ladle into soup bowls and serve. Bon appétit!

Per serving: 123 Calories; 9.2g Fat; 5.8g Carbs; 4.7g Protein; 1.4g Fiber

294. Wax Beans in Wine Sauce

(Ready in about 15 minutes | Servings 4)

Ingredients

1/2 pound wax beans, trimmed
2 tablespoons dry white wine
1 tablespoon butter
1/2 teaspoon mustard seeds
1/2 cup tomato sauce with garlic and onions

Directions

Melt the butter in a soup pot over medium-high heat. Then, fry wax beans in hot butter for 2 to 3 minutes.

Add in tomato sauce, wine, and mustard seeds; season with salt and black pepper.

Turn the temperature to medium-low and continue to simmer for about 8 longer or until wax beans are tender and the sauce has thickened slightly. Bon appétit!

Per serving: 56 Calories; 3.5g Fat; 6g Carbs; 1.5g Protein; 2.2g Fiber

295. Lebanese Mushroom Stew with Za'atar

(Ready in about 1 hour 50 minutes | Servings 4)

Ingredients

8 ounces Chanterelle mushroom, sliced
1 cup tomato sauce with onion and garlic
4 tablespoons olive oil
2 bell peppers, chopped
1/2 teaspoon Za'atar spice

Directions

Heat olive oil in a heavy-bottomed pot over medium-high heat. Once hot, sauté the peppers until tender or about 3 minutes.

Stir in the mushrooms and continue to sauté until they have softened.

Add in Za'atar spice and tomato sauce; bring to a rapid boil. Immediately, turn the heat to medium-low.

Continue to simmer for about 35 minutes until cooked through. Bon appétit!

Per serving: 155 Calories; 13.9g Fat; 6g Carbs; 1.4g Protein; 2.9g Fiber

296. Skinny Cucumber Noodles with Sauce

(Ready in about 35 minutes | Servings 2)

Ingredients

1 cucumber, spiralized
1/2 teaspoon sea salt
1 tablespoon olive oil
1 tablespoon fresh lime juice
1 California avocado, pitted, peeled and mashed

Directions

Sprinkle your cucumber with salt; let it stand for 30 minutes; after that, discard the excess water and pat the cucumber dry with kitchen towels.

In the meantime, combine olive oil, lime juice, and avocado. Season with salt and black pepper.

Toss the cucumber noodles with sauce and serve. Bon appétit!

Per serving: 194 Calories; 17.1g Fat; 7.6g Carbs; 2.5g Protein; 4.6g Fiber

297. Balkan-Style Stir-Fry

(Ready in about 25 minutes | Servings 5)

Ingredients

8 bell peppers, deveined and cut into strips
1 tomato, chopped
2 eggs
1 yellow onion, sliced
3 garlic cloves, halved

Directions

Heat 2 tablespoons of olive oil in a saucepan over medium-low flame. Sweat the onion for about 4 minutes or until tender and translucent.

Stir in the garlic and peppers and continue to sauté for 5 to 6 minutes. Fold in chopped tomato along with salt and black pepper.

Stir fry for a further 7 minutes. Stir in the eggs and continue to cook for 4 to 5 minutes longer. Serve immediately.

Per serving: 114 Calories; 7.6g Fat; 6g Carbs; 3.4g Protein; 1.5g Fiber

298. Italian Zoodles with Romano Cheese

(Ready in about 15 minutes | Servings 3)

Ingredients

1 ½ tablespoons olive oil
3 cups button mushrooms, chopped
1 cup tomato sauce with garlic and herbs
1 pound zucchini, spiralized
1/3 cup Pecorino Romano cheese, preferably freshly grated

Directions

In a saucepan, heat the olive oil over a moderate heat. Once hot, cook the mushrooms for about 4 minutes until they have softened.

Stir in the tomato sauce and zucchini, bringing to a boil.

Immediately reduce temperature to simmer. Continue to cook, partially covered, for about 7 minutes or until cooked through. Season with salt and black pepper.

Top with Pecorino Romano cheese and serve. Bon appétit!

Per serving: 160 Calories; 10.6g Fat; 7.4g Carbs; 10g Protein; 3.4g Fiber

299. Garden Vegetable Mash

(Ready in about 15 minutes | Servings 3)

Per serving: 162 Calories; 12.8g Fat; 7.2g Carbs; 4.7g Protein; 3.5g Fiber

Ingredients

1 ½ tablespoons butter
4 tablespoons cream cheese
1/2 pound cauliflower florets
1/2 pound broccoli florets
1/2 teaspoon garlic powder

Directions

Parboil the broccoli and cauliflower for about 10 minutes until they have softened. Mash them with a potato masher.

Add in garlic powder, cream cheese, and butter; mix to combine well.

Season with salt and black pepper to taste. Bon appétit!

300. Spicy and Cheesy Roasted Artichokes

(Ready in about 1 hour 10 minutes | Servings 2)

Per serving: 368 Calories; 33g Fat; 7.2g Carbs; 10.6g Protein; 3.8g Fiber

Ingredients

2 small-sized globe artichokes, cut off the stalks
2 tablespoons butter, melted
2 tablespoons fresh lime juice
1/2 cup Romano cheese, grated
2 tablespoons mayonnaise

Directions

Start by preheating your oven to 420 degrees F.

To prepare your artichokes, discard the tough outer layers; cut off about 3/4 inches from the top. Slice them in half lengthwise.

Toss your artichokes with butter and fresh lime juice; season with the salt and pepper to taste.

Top with the grated Romano cheese; wrap your artichokes in foil and roast them in the preheated oven for about 1 hour.

Serve with mayonnaise and enjoy!

301. Cheesy Stuffed Peppers with Cauliflower Rice

(Ready in about 45 minutes | Servings 6)

Per serving: 244 Calories; 12.9g Fat; 3.2g Carbs; 1g Fiber; 16.5g Protein;

Ingredients

6 medium-sized bell peppers, deveined and cleaned
1 cup cauliflower rice
1/2 cup tomato sauce with garlic and onion
1 pound ground turkey
1/2 cup Cheddar cheese, shredded

Directions

Heat 2 tablespoons of olive oil in a frying pan over medium-high heat. Then, cook ground turkey until nicely browned or about 5 minutes.

Add in cauliflower rice and season with salt and black pepper. Continue to cook for 3 to 4 minutes more.

Add in tomato sauce. Stuff the peppers with this filling and cover with a piece of aluminum foil.

Bake in the preheated oven at 390 degrees F for 17 to 20 minutes. Remove the foil, top with cheese, and bake for a further 10 to 13 minutes. Bon appétit!

302. Broccoli and Bacon Soup

(Ready in about 20 minutes | Servings 4)

Per serving: 95 Calories; 7.6g Fat; 4.1g Carbs; 3g Protein; 1g Fiber

Ingredients

1 head broccoli, broken into small florets
1 carrot, chopped
1 celery, chopped
1/2 cup full-fat yogurt
2 slices bacon, chopped

Directions

Fry the bacon in a soup pot over a moderate flame; reserve.

Then, cook the carrots, celery and broccoli in the bacon fat. Season with salt and pepper to taste.

Pour in 4 cups of water or vegetable stock, bringing to a boil. Turn the temperature to a simmer and continue to cook, partially covered, for 10 to 15 minutes longer.

Add in yogurt and remove from heat. Puree your soup with an immersion blender until your desired consistency is reached.

Garnish with the reserved bacon and serve.

303. Aromatic Kale with Garlic

(Ready in about 20 minutes | Servings 3)

Per serving: 93 Calories; 4.4g Fat; 6.1g Carbs; 7.1g Protein; 2.7g Fiber

Ingredients

1/2 tablespoon olive oil
1/2 cup cottage cheese, creamed
1/2 teaspoon sea salt
1 teaspoon fresh garlic, chopped
9 ounces kale, torn into pieces

Directions

Heat the olive oil in a pot over medium-high flame. Once hot, fry the garlic until just tender and fragrant or about 30 seconds.

Add in kale and continue to cook for 8 to 10 minutes until all liquid evaporates.

Add in cottage cheese and sea salt, remove from heat, and stir until everything is combined. Bon appétit!

304. Spanish-Style Keto Slaw

(Ready in about 10 minutes | Servings 4)

Per serving: 122 Calories; 9.1g Fat; 5.9g Carbs; 4.5g Protein; 3g Fiber

Ingredients

1 teaspoon fresh garlic, minced
4 tablespoons tahini (sesame paste)
1/2 pound Napa cabbage, shredded
2 cups arugula, torn into pieces
1 Spanish onion, thinly sliced into rings

Directions

Make a dressing by whisking the garlic and tahini; add in 2 teaspoons of balsamic vinegar along with salt and black pepper.

In a salad bowl, combine Napa cabbage, arugula, and Spanish onion. Toss the salad with dressing.

Garnish with sesame seeds if desired and serve.

305. Cheesy Breakfast Broccoli Casserole

(Ready in about 40 minutes | Servings 4)

Per serving: 188 Calories; 11.3g Fat; 5.7g Carbs; 14.9g Protein; 1.1g Fiber

Ingredients

1 (1/2-pound) head broccoli, broken into florets
1 cup cooked ham, chopped
1/2 cup Greek-style yogurt
1 cup Mexican cheese, shredded
1/2 teaspoon butter, melted

Directions

Begin by preheating an oven to 350 degrees F. Now, butter the bottom and sides of a casserole dish with melted butter.

Cook broccoli for 6 to 7 minutes until it is "mashable". Mash the broccoli with a potato masher.

Now, stir in Greek-style yogurt, Mexican cheese, and cooked ham. Season with Mexican spice blend, if desired.

Press the cheese/broccoli mixture in the buttered casserole dish. Bake in the preheated oven for 20 to 23 minutes. Serve and enjoy!

FISH & SEAFOOD

306. Traditional Gambas al Ajillo

(Ready in about 15 minutes | Servings 5)

Ingredients

2 tablespoons butter
2 cloves garlic, minced
2 small cayenne pepper pods

2 pounds shrimp, peeled and deveined
1/4 cup Manzanilla

Directions

In a frying pan, melt the butter over medium-high heat. Then, sauté the garlic with cayenne peppers for about 30 seconds or until fragrant.

Stir in the shrimp and continue to cook for a further 1 to 2 minutes. Pour in the Manzanilla; season with salt and black pepper.

Continue to cook until everything is cooked through. Garnish with lemon slices, if desired. Enjoy!

Per serving: 203 Calories; 5.5g Fat; 1.8g Carbs; 36.6g Protein; 0.4g Fiber

307. Restaurant-Style Fish Masala

(Ready in about 25 minutes | Servings 6)

Ingredients

1 ½ pounds white fish fillets, skinless, boneless
1/2 cup Indian onion masala
1 cup coconut milk

2 tablespoons sesame oil
2 bell peppers, deveined and sliced

Directions

Ina wok, heat sesame oil over medium-high heat; sauté the peppers until tender for 3 to 4 minutes.

Add in white fish fillets and Indian onion masala; pour in 1/2 cup of haddi ka shorba and coconut milk. Season with salt and black pepper to taste.

Turn the heat to a simmer and let it cook for 5 minutes longer or until everything is cooked through. Enjoy!

Per serving: 349 Calories; 24.9g Fat; 6.2g Carbs; 22.7g Protein; 2.5g Fiber

308. Anchovies with Caesar Dressing

(Ready in about 15 minutes | Servings 3)

Ingredients

6 anchovies, cleaned and deboned
2 egg yolks

1 teaspoon Dijon mustard
1 fresh garlic clove, peeled
1/3 cup extra-virgin olive oil

Directions

Rinse the anchovies and pat dry.

Grill the anchovies in a lightly greased grill pan just until golden.

Then, blend egg yolks, Dijon mustard, garlic, and extra-virgin olive oil until smooth and creamy.

Serve warm anchovies with the Caesar dressing and enjoy!

Per serving: 449 Calories; 34.3g Fat; 1g Carbs; 32.6g Protein; 0.1g Fiber

309. Fish and Egg Salad

(Ready in about 20 minutes | Servings 4)

Ingredients

1 pound red snapper fillets
4 cups lettuce salad
1 bell pepper, deseeded and sliced

1 tomato, sliced
5 eggs

Directions

Steam the red snapper fillets for 8 to 10 minutes or until fork-tender. Cut the fish into small strips.

Boil the eggs in a saucepan for about 9 minutes; peel the eggs and carefully slice them.

Place bell peppers, tomato, and lettuce leaves in a salad bowl; add in 4 tablespoons of olive oil and 4 tablespoons of apple cider vinegar; toss to combine well.

Top with the reserved fish and eggs. Salt to taste. Serve well-chilled and enjoy!

Per serving: 300 Calories; 19.3g Fat; 3.5g Carbs; 26.5g Protein; 1g Fiber

310. Italian Haddock Fillets with Marinara Sauce

(Ready in about 15 minutes | Servings 6)

Ingredients

2 pounds haddock fillets
1/2 cup marinara sauce
2 tablespoons olive oil

Sea salt and freshly ground black pepper, to taste
1 tablespoon Italian spice mix

Directions

Brush the haddock fillets with 1/4 cup of marinara sauce and olive oil.

Cook haddock fillets on a grill pan over a moderate heat for about 6 minutes per side. Season with salt, black pepper, and Italian spice mix.

Serve with the remaining 1/4 cup of marinara sauce. Bon appétit!

Per serving: 226 Calories; 5.9g Fat; 2.2g Carbs; 38.3g Protein; 0.6g Fiber

311. Swordfish with Greek Sauce

(Ready in about 30 minutes | Servings 6)

Ingredients

4 swordfish steaks
1 cup Greek yogurt
4 tablespoons mayonnaise
1 teaspoon garlic, minced
1 yellow onion, sliced

Directions

Start by preheating your oven to 380 degrees F.

Grease the sides and bottom of a casserole dish with 2 tablespoons of melted butter. Toss the swordfish steaks with the Mediterranean spice mix.

Place the swordfish steaks in the buttered casserole dish.

Place the onion and garlic around the swordfish. Bake in the preheated oven for about 20 to 25 minutes.

In the meantime, whisk the Greek yogurt with mayonnaise; add in garlic powder if desired. Serve swordfish steaks with the sauce on the side. Enjoy!

Per serving: 346 Calories; 22.5g Fat; 3.2g Carbs; 31.5g Protein; 0.3g Fiber

312. Cod Fillets with Sesame Sauce

(Ready in about 15 minutes | Servings 6)

Ingredients

3 tablespoons olive oil
6 cod fillets, skin-on
3 tablespoons toasted sesame seeds
3 tablespoons toasted sesame oil
1 lemon, freshly squeezed

Directions

Season cod fillets with salt and black pepper.

Heat 1 tablespoon of olive oil in grill pan over moderate flame. Once hot, cook the cod fillets for about 8 minutes until it is lightly charred on top.

In a mixing bowl, whisk the remaining olive oil, lemon, sesame seeds and sesame oil; add in minced garlic, salt and black pepper, if desired.

Spoon the sauce over cod fillets and serve immediately.

Per serving: 341 Calories; 17g Fat; 3.2g Carbs; 42.1g Protein; 0.9g Fiber

313. Favorite Monkfish Salad

(Ready in about 20 minutes | Servings 5)

Ingredients

2 pounds monkfish
1 bell pepper, sliced
1/2 cup radishes, sliced
1 red onion, chopped
1/2 cup mayonnaise

Directions

Brush monkfish with nonstick cooking oil. Cook over medium-high heat for about 10 minutes until opaque.

Flake the fish with a fork and transfer to a salad bowl; add in bell peppers, radishes, and onion; afterwards, fold in mayo and stir until everything is well combined.

Salt to taste. Bon appétit!

Per serving: 306 Calories; 19.4g Fat; 3.8g Carbs; 27g Protein; 0.6g Fiber

314. Omelet with Tilapia and Goat Cheese

(Ready in about 20 minutes | Servings 4)

Ingredients

1/2 cup leeks, sliced
1 pound tilapia fillets
8 medium-sized eggs
1 cup milk
12 ounces goat cheese, crumbled

Directions

Heat 1 tablespoon of the olive oil in a nonstick skillet over medium-high heat. Once hot, sauté the leeks for 4 minutes, stirring occasionally.

Then, cook tilapia fish for 5 to 6 minutes on each side; flake your tilapia using a fork and set it aside.

Season with salt and black pepper to taste.

In a mixing bowl, whisk the eggs with milk until well combined. Heat the remaining tablespoon of olive oil and cook your omelet until eggs are set.

Spoon the fish mixture on one side of your omelet; top with goat cheese and fold your omelet over the filling. Bon appétit!

Per serving: 558 Calories; 38g Fat; 6.5g Carbs; 45.5g Protein; 0.2g Fiber

315. Cod with Mustard Greens

(Ready in about 20 minutes | Servings 2)

Ingredients

1 tablespoon olive oil
2 stalks green onions, sliced
1 bell pepper, seeded and sliced
2 cod fish fillets
1 cup mustard greens, torn into bite-sized pieces

Directions

Heat the oil in a saucepan over a moderate heat. Then, sauté green onions and peppers for about 4 minutes until they have softened.

Pour in 1/2 cup of vegetable broth. Add in fish fillets along with salt and pepper to taste. Fold in mustard greens.

Turn the temperature to simmer, cover, and continue to cook for about 12 minutes or until cooked through. Bon appétit!

Per serving: 171 Calories; 7.8g Fat; 4.8g Carbs; 20.3g Protein; 1.6g Fiber

316. Keto Tacos with Anchovies

(Ready in about 10 minutes | Servings 4)

Ingredients

12 lettuce leaves
1 red onion, chopped
1 large-sized tomato, diced
2 (2-ounce) can anchovies in olive oil, drained
4 tablespoons mayonnaise

Directions

In a mixing bowl, combine red onion, tomato, anchovies, and mayonnaise. Season with salt and black pepper to taste.

Spoon the anchovy mixture into the center of lettuce leaves. Wrap lettuce leaves in taco-style and serve immediately.

Per serving: 170 Calories; 9.3g Fat; 4.9g Carbs; 14g Protein; 1.2g Fiber

317. Grilled Fish Salad

(Ready in about 15 minutes + chilling time | Servings 2)

Ingredients

3/4 pound tuna fillets, skinless
1 teaspoon Dijon mustard
8 Niçoise olives, pitted and sliced

1 white onion, sliced
1/2 teaspoon anchovy paste

Directions

Brush tuna fillets with nonstick cooking oil and season with salt and black pepper. Grill your tuna for about 3 minutes on each side until slightly pink in the center.

Flake the fish into bite-sized strips and place them in a serving bowl.

Toss your tuna with Dijon mustard, Niçoise olives, white onion, and anchovy paste. Taste and adjust seasonings. Enjoy!

Per serving: 194 Calories; 3.4g Fat; 0.9g Carbs; 37.1g Protein; 0.5g Fiber

318. Garlicky Mackerel Fillets

(Ready in about 15 minutes | Servings 2)

Ingredients

2 mackerel fillets
1 tablespoon olive oil
1/2 teaspoon thyme

1 teaspoon rosemary
2 garlic cloves, minced

Directions

In a frying pan, heat the oil over medium-high heat.

Sear the fish fillets for about 5 minutes per side until crisp.

Add in the garlic, thyme, and rosemary and continue to cook for 30 seconds more. Enjoy!

Per serving: 481 Calories; 14.5g Fat; 1.1g Carbs; 80g Protein; 0.1g Fiber

319. Fisherman's Tilapia Burgers

(Ready in about 50 minutes | Servings 5)

Ingredients

1 ½ pounds tilapia fish, broken into chunks
1 tablespoon Cajun seasoning mix

1/2 cup shallots, chopped
1/2 cup almond flour
2 eggs, whisked

Directions

In a mixing bowl, thoroughly combine all ingredients. Form the mixture into 10 patties; refrigerate for 30 to 35 minutes.

Spritz a nonstick skillet and place it over medium-high flame. Fry your burgers for about 4 minutes per side until golden brown.

Garnish with lemon slices and enjoy!

Per serving: 238 Calories; 10.9g Fat; 2.6g Carbs; 32.9g Protein; 1.2g Fiber

320. Hearty Fisherman's Stew

(Ready in about 30 minutes | Servings 4)

Ingredients

1 pound halibut, cut into bite-sized chunks
1 ripe fresh tomato, pureed

1 tablespoon tallow, room temperature
1 red onion, chopped
2 garlic cloves, smashed

Directions

Melt the tallow in a soup pot over medium-high heat. Then, sauté the onion for 3 to 4 minutes until just tender and fragrant; stir in the garlic and continue to sauté for 30 seconds more until fragrant.

Add in tomato and continue to cook for 7 to 8 minutes, stirring periodically. Pour in 3 cups of shellfish stock or water. Add in halibut and season with the salt and black pepper to taste.

Reduce temperature to a simmer and continue to cook, partially covered, for 15 to 18 minutes longer. Ladle into individual bowls and serve hot.

Per serving: 271 Calories; 19.5g Fat; 4.8g Carbs; 18.5g Protein; 1g Fiber

321. Thai Salmon Curry

(Ready in about 20 minutes | Servings 4)

Ingredients

3/4 pound salmon, cut into bite-sized chunks
6 ounces full-fat coconut milk, canned

1 tablespoon coconut oil
1/2 cup leeks, chopped
1 teaspoon turmeric powder

Directions

Melt coconut oil in a heavy-bottomed pot over medium-high flame. Sauté the leeks for about 3 minutes or until tender and fragrant.

Add in turmeric powder and coconut milk; pour in 2 cups of water or fish stock. Fold in salmon chunks.

Reduce temperature to medium-low and continue to simmer for 10 to 12 minutes more. Serve hot!

Per serving: 246 Calories; 16.2g Fat; 4.9g Carbs; 20.3g Protein; 0.6g Fiber

322. Bay Shrimp and Mushrooms

(Ready in about 35 minutes | Servings 6)

Ingredients

1 ½ pounds large-sized button mushroom cups
6 tablespoons mayonnaise
8 ounces ricotta cheese, softened

1 cup cheddar cheese, shredded
16 ounces fresh Bay shrimp, chopped

Directions

Bake the mushrooms in the preheated oven at 380 degrees F for 15 minutes until they are just tender.

Melt 1 tablespoon of butter in a saucepan over medium-high heat. Cook Bay shrimp for 1 to 2 minutes.

Add in mayonnaise and ricotta cheese; stir to combine well.

Divide the shrimp mixture between mushroom cups; bake for about 10 minutes. Top with cheddar cheese and continue to bake for 7 to 8 minutes until hot and bubbly. Enjoy!

Per serving: 297 Calories; 18.3g Fat; 5.5g Carbs; 28g Protein; 1.3g Fiber

323. Catfish and Cauliflower Bake

(Ready in about 30 minutes | Servings 4)

Ingredients

24 ounces catfish, cut into
pieces
2 ounces butter, cold

11 ounces cauliflower
1 cup cream cheese
1 egg

Directions

Begin by preheating your oven to 385 degrees F. Then, spritz a
baking dish with a nonstick cooking spray.

Heat 1 tablespoon of sesame oil in a saucepan over medium-high
flame; cook the cauliflower for about 5 minutes.

Place the cauliflower in the prepared baking dish. Sprinkle with salt
and black pepper. Place catfish on top.

In a bowl, combine cream cheese and egg. Spread this mixture on
the cauliflower.

Top with butter and bake for about 20 minutes or until heated
through. Bon appétit!

Per serving: 510 Calories; 40g Fat; 5.5g Carbs; 1.6g Fiber; 31.3g
Protein;

324. Snapper and Vegetable Mélange

(Ready in about 20 minutes | Servings 4)

Ingredients

1 teaspoon sesame oil
1/2 cup scallions, thinly sliced
1/2 teaspoon garlic, crushed

1 pound snapper, cut into bite-
sized pieces
2 ripe tomatoes, crushed

Directions

Heat sesame oil in a heavy-bottomed pot over medium-high heat.
Sauté the scallions until they have softened or about 3 minutes.

Now, sauté the garlic for 30 seconds more.

Add in snapper and tomatoes and reduce the heat to simmer.
Continue to cook for 13 to 15 minutes or until the fish flakes easily
and the sauce has thickened slightly. Bon appétit!

Per serving: 151 Calories; 3g Fat; 5.8g Carbs; 1.5g Fiber; 24.4g
Protein;

325. Tuna and Ham Wraps

(Ready in about 10 minutes + chilling time | Servings 3)

Ingredients

1/2 pound ahi tuna steak
1/2 Hass avocado, peeled,
pitted and sliced

6 slices of ham
6 lettuce leaves
1/2 cup dry white wine

Directions

Pour 1/2 cup of water into a saucepan; add in wine and bring to a
boil. Add in tuna steak and simmer for 3 to 5 minutes.

Cut tuna into bite-sized chunks. Place tuna pieces on the ham.

Top with avocado; drizzle with fresh lemon juice, if desired. Roll
them up and serve on lettuce leaves. Enjoy!

Per serving: 308 Calories; 19.9g Fat; 4.3g Carbs; 27.8g Protein;
2.5g Fiber

326. Tuna with Sriracha Sauce

(Ready in about 25 minutes | Servings 4)

Ingredients

4 tuna fillets
4 tablespoons mayonnaise
1/2 cup sour cream

1 teaspoon Sriracha sauce
2 scallions, chopped

Directions

Start by preheating your oven to 380 degrees F. Brush tuna fillets
with 1 tablespoon of peanut oil and season with salt and pepper. Top
with chopped scallions.

Wrap tuna fillets in foil, making the packet.

Bake for 18 to 20 minutes or until opaque and fork-tender.

Mix mayonnaise, sour cream, and Sriracha sauce in a bowl. Serve
warm tuna with the sauce on the side and enjoy!

Per serving: 389 Calories; 17.9g Fat; 3.5g Carbs; 50.3g Protein;
0.3g Fiber

327. Asian-Style Scallops and Mushrooms

(Ready in about 15 minutes | Servings 4)

Ingredients

1 pound bay scallops
1/2 cup enoki mushrooms
1/2 cup yellow onion, sliced

1 cup asparagus spears, sliced
1/2 cup dry roasted peanuts,
roughly chopped

Directions

In a wok, warm 1 teaspoon of the sesame oil over medium-high
heat. Cook the onion until tender and fragrant; set aside.

In the same wok, warm another teaspoon of the sesame oil; fry your
asparagus for 2 to 3 minutes until crisp-tender; set aside.

Heat another teaspoon of the sesame oil and sauté enoki mushrooms
for 1 to 2 minutes until they begin to soften; reserve.

Heat the remaining teaspoon of sesame oil and cook bay scallops
until they are opaque.

Stir all ingredients into the wok and serve with roasted peanuts.
Enjoy!

Per serving: 236 Calories; 12.5g Fat; 5.9g Carbs; 27g Protein;
2.4g Fiber

328. Classic Louisiana-Style Gumbo

(Ready in about 30 minutes | Servings 6)

Ingredients

1 pound andouille sausage,
sliced
1 red onion, chopped
2 tomatoes, pureed

2 pounds halibut, cut into bite-
sized chunks
1 pound lump crabmeat

Directions

Melt 1 teaspoon of the butter in a stockpot over moderate heat. Cook andouille sausage for about 3 minutes; set aside.

Melt the 2 teaspoons of butter and sauté the onion until tender and fragrant or about 3 to 4 minutes.

Now, stir in tomatoes and halibut' pour in 4 cups of water or beef broth; bring to a rapid boil. Turn the heat to simmer, partially covered, and continue to cook for 13 to 15 minutes.

Add in the Cajun seasoning blend if desired; return the reserved sausage to the stockpot.

Continue to cook for about 5 minutes or until thoroughly cooked. Enjoy!

Per serving: 530 Calories; 40.5g Fat; 5.1g Carbs; 31.8g Protein; 1g Fiber

329. One-Skillet Mackerel with Clam

(Ready in about 15 minutes | Servings 3)

Ingredients

2 mackerel fillets, patted dry
9 littleneck clams, scrubbed
1/2 cup dry white wine

1 shallot, finely chopped
2 cloves garlic, minced

Directions

In a cast-iron skillet, heat 1 teaspoon of the olive oil and swirl to coat well. Cook your fish for about 6 minutes; reserve.

Heat another teaspoon of olive oil and sauté the shallot and garlic until tender and fragrant about 2 minutes.

Add in the wine to scrape up the browned bits that stick to the bottom of the skillet. Add in Cajun seasoning blend and cook for 4 to 5 minutes more.

Stir in the clams and continue to cook for about 6 minutes or until they open. Add the fish back to the skillet, gently stir and serve warm.

Per serving: 379 Calories; 8.7g Fat; 3.7g Carbs; 60.1g Protein; 0.1g Fiber

330. Sea Bass in Dijon Sauce

(Ready in about 20 minutes | Servings 3)

Ingredients

3 sea bass fillets
2 tablespoons olive oil
3 tablespoons butter

2 cloves garlic, minced
1 tablespoon Dijon mustard

Directions

Pat dry the sea bass fillets. Heat olive oil in a frying pan over medium-high flame.

Cook the fish fillets for 4 to 5 minutes on each side until they are opaque. Season with red pepper and salt to taste.

In another saucepan, melt the butter over low flame; sauté the garlic for 30 seconds. Add in mustard and continue to simmer for 2 to 3 minutes.

Serve warm fish fillets with Dijon sauce and enjoy!

Per serving: 314 Calories; 23.2g Fat; 1.4g Carbs; 24.2g Protein; 0.3g Fiber

331. Spicy Tiger Prawns

(Ready in about 15 minutes | Servings 6)

Ingredients

2 ½ pounds tiger prawns, deveined
2 bell peppers, chopped

2 scallions, chopped
1/2 cup Marsala wine
3 tablespoons olive oil

Directions

In a saucepan, heat olive oil until sizzling. Cook the peppers and scallions for about 4 minutes or until tender and fragrant.

Stir in tiger prawns and cook for 2 minutes or until they are cooked all the way through.

Pour in wine, reduce the heat to simmer, and continue to cook for 5 to 6 minutes. Bon appétit!

Per serving: 219 Calories; 6.5g Fat; 2.7g Carbs; 39g Protein; 0.6g Fiber

332. Creole Fish Stew

(Ready in about 20 minutes | Servings 4)

Ingredients

16 ounces haddock steak, cut into bite-sized chunks
4 ounces turkey smoked sausage, sliced

1 onion, chopped
2 tomatoes, pureed
1 celery stalk, chopped

Directions

Melt 2 tablespoons of butter in a stockpot over medium-high heat. Sauté the onion and celery for 2 to 3 minutes until they have softened.

Add in the sausage and pureed tomatoes; season with Creole seasoning blend.

Add in 2 cups of water or fish broth and bring to a rolling boil. Turn the heat to medium-low.

Stir in haddock steak, partially cover, and continue to cook for 13 to 15 minutes. Serve in individual bowls and enjoy!

Per serving: 216 Calories; 9.4g Fat; 8.1g Carbs; 24.2g Protein; 1.4g Fiber

333. Shrimp and Sea Scallop Medley

(Ready in about 15 minutes | Servings 2)

Ingredients

1/2 pound shrimp, deveined
1/2 pound sea scallops
1/2 cup scallions, chopped

1/2 cup fish broth
1 garlic clove, minced

Directions

In a saucepan, heat 1 tablespoon of olive oil. Once hot, cook the scallions and garlic for 2 to 3 minutes or until they are fragrant.

Cook the shrimp and sea scallops for about 3 minutes or until they are opaque. You can add a splash of rum to deglaze the pan.

Pour in the fish broth; season with Cajun spice mix. Serve in individual bowls and enjoy!

Per serving: 305 Calories; 8.8g Fat; 2.7g Carbs; 47.3g Protein; 0.7g Fiber

334. Halibut Steaks with Herbs

(Ready in about 20 minutes | Servings 2)

Ingredients

2 halibut steaks
2 tablespoons olive oil
1 teaspoon fish seasoning mix
1 red bell pepper, sliced
1 yellow onion, sliced

Directions

Begin by preheating an oven to 380 degrees F.

Brush the halibut steaks with olive oil and transfer them to a lightly-greased baking dish.

Top with the bell peppers and onion. Sprinkle fish seasoning mix over everything. Bake in the preheated oven for about 15 minutes. Bon appétit!

Per serving: 502 Calories; 19.1g Fat; 5.7g Carbs; 72g Protein; 1g Fiber

335. Warm Shrimp and Vegetable Salad

(Ready in about 10 minutes | Servings 4)

Ingredients

2 pounds large shrimp, peeled and deveined
1 red onion, sliced
2 garlic cloves, sliced
2 Italian peppers, sliced
1 cup arugula

Directions

Pat the shrimp dry with a kitchen towel. In a preheated grill, cook the shrimp for 3 to 4 minutes until they are cooked all the way through.

Place the prepared shrimp in a salad bowl. Stir in the onion, garlic, Italian peppers, and arugula.

Then, toss the ingredients with 2 tablespoons of olive oil and fresh lime juice. Serve and enjoy!

Per serving: 268 Calories; 8g Fat; 3.5g Carbs; 46.3g Protein; 0.6g Fiber

336. White Sea Bass Chowder

(Ready in about 20 minutes | Servings 4)

Ingredients

3/4 pound sea bass, broken into chunks
2 teaspoons butter, at room temperature
1 cup double cream
1/2 white onion, chopped
1 tablespoon Old Bay seasoning

Directions

In a soup pot, melt the butter over medium-high heat. Sauté the onion until just tender.

Stir in Old Bay seasoning along with 3 cups of water; bring to a boil. Turn the heat to medium-low and allow it to simmer for about 10 minutes.

Now, stir in the sea bass and double cream; continue to simmer for about 5 minutes until cooked through. Serve in individual bowls.

Per serving: 257 Calories; 17.8g Fat; 3.8g Carbs; 21.3g Protein; 0.4g Fiber

337. Sardine Burgers with Romano Cheese

(Ready in about 15 minutes | Servings 3)

Ingredients

2 tablespoons butter
1 egg, beaten
1/2 onion, chopped
2 (5.5-ounces) canned sardines, drained
2 ounces Romano cheese, preferably freshly grated

Directions

In a mixing dish, combine sardines, cheese, egg, and onion; season with Italian spice blend.

Shape the mixture into six equal patties.

Melt the butter in a nonstick skillet over medium-high heat. Once hot, cook your burgers for about 5 minutes per side. Bon appétit!

Per serving: 267 Calories; 21.3g Fat; 6.1g Carbs; 13.5g Protein; 3.3g Fiber

338. Creamed Shrimp Chowder

(Ready in about 30 minutes | Servings 4)

Ingredients

1 cup broccoli, broken into small florets
12 ounces shrimp, peeled and deveined
2 tablespoons coconut oil
1 shallot, chopped
1 cup double cream

Directions

Melt the coconut oil in a stockpot over medium-high flame. Cook the shallot for about 3 minutes or until tender and translucent.

Stir in the broccoli florets along with 4 cups of water or fish broth; bring to a boil. Reduce the heat to medium-low, partially cover, and let it simmer for about 10 minutes.

Fold in shrimp and double cream. Continue to simmer an additional 4 minutes just until the shrimp are done.

Taste and adjust the seasonings. Bon appétit!

Per serving: 253 Calories; 18.8g Fat; 2.9g Carbs; 19g Protein; 0.4g Fiber

339. Cod Fillets with Greek Mustard Sauce

(Ready in about 10 minutes | Servings 4)

Ingredients

4 Alaskan cod fillets
1/2 cup Greek-style yogurt
3 tablespoons cream cheese
1 garlic clove, minced
1 teaspoon yellow mustard

Directions

Heat 1 tablespoon of coconut oil in a saucepan over a moderate heat. Sear cod fillets for about 3 minutes; flip them over and cook an additional 3 minutes on the other side.

Season with salt and ground black pepper to your liking.

To make the sauce, whisk yellow mustard, cream cheese, Greek yogurt, and garlic until well combined.

Top cod fillets with the sauce and serve immediately!

Per serving: 166 Calories; 8.2g Fat; 2.6g Carbs; 19.8g Protein; 0.3g Fiber

340. One-Pan Scallops and Veggies

(Ready in about 15 minutes | Servings 5)

Ingredients

2 medium Italian peppers, deveined and sliced
1 teaspoon garlic, minced
2 pounds sea scallops
1 cup chicken broth
2 cups cauliflower florets

Directions

Melt 1 tablespoon of butter in a frying pan over a moderate heat.

Once hot, sauté Italian peppers, cauliflower, and garlic for 3 to 4 minutes or until the vegetables are tender.

Stir in the sea scallops and continue to cook for 3 minutes; stir to coat.

Pour in chicken broth and let it simmer, partially covered, for 4 minutes more. Bon appétit!

Per serving: 217 Calories; 3.5g Fat; 4.8g Carbs; 23.5g Protein; 1.2g Fiber

341. Monkfish Fillets in Cheddar Sauce

(Ready in about 20 minutes | Servings 6)

Ingredients

6 monkfish fillets
1/2 cup cheddar cheese, shredded
2 green onions, sliced
1/2 cup sour cream
2 tablespoons olive oil

Directions

Heat the olive oil in a saucepan over medium-high heat. Then, sear the monkfish for 3 to 4 minutes per side or until it is golden brown.

Season with salt and black pepper to taste.

Place the monkfish fillets in a lightly greased baking dish. Add in the green onions.

Then, thoroughly combine the sour cream and cheddar cheese; add in Cajun seasoning mix.

Spoon the cheese mixture into the baking dish. Bake in the preheated oven at 365 degrees F for about 15 minutes until cooked through.

Bon appétit!

Per serving: 229 Calories; 12.5g Fat; 2.2g Carbs; 25.9g Protein; 0.1g Fiber

342. Traditional Hungarian Halászlé

(Ready in about 20 minutes | Servings 2)

Ingredients

1 red onion, chopped
2 bell peppers, chopped
2 vine-ripe tomatoes, pureed
1/2 pound tilapia, cut into bite-sized pieces
2 tablespoons sour cream

Directions

Heat 1 tablespoon of canola oil in a soup pot over medium-high flame. Now, sauté the peppers and onion until tender and fragrant.

Stir in tomatoes and tilapia. Turn the heat to medium-low and let it simmer, partially covered, for about 10 minutes.

Serve in soup bowls, garnished with well-chilled sour cream.

Per serving: 252 Calories; 12.6g Fat; 5g Carbs; 28.2g Protein; 1.9g Fiber

343. Salmon Fillets in Marsala Sauce

(Ready in about 20 minutes | Servings 6)

Ingredients

2 ½ pounds salmon fillets
4 tablespoons Marsala wine
2 bell peppers, deseeded and sliced
1/2 cup scallions, chopped
2 cups marinara sauce

Directions

In a Dutch oven, heat 2 tablespoons of peanut oil over a moderate heat. Sauté the bell peppers and scallions for 3 to 4 minutes until they have softened.

Add a splash of wine to deglaze the pan. Stir in marinara sauce and salmon.

Reduce the heat to medium-low and let it simmer for 15 to 20 minutes or until the salmon easily flakes with a fork. Enjoy!

Per serving: 347 Calories; 18.5g Fat; 4g Carbs; 39.9g Protein; 1g Fiber

344. Old Bay Prawns with Sour Cream

(Ready in about 20 minutes | Servings 2)

Ingredients

3/4 pound prawns, peeled and deveined
1 teaspoon Old Bay seasoning mix
1 bell pepper, deveined and minced
1 cup pound broccoli florets
2 dollops of sour cream, for garnish

Directions

Begin by preheating your oven to 380 dergees F. Toss the prawns with the Old Bay seasoning mix.

Place them on a parchment-lined roasting pan. Scatter the bell peppers and broccoli florets around them.

Drizzle 2 teaspoon of olive oil over everything.

Roast in the preheated oven for about 10 minutes or until the prawns are pink, rotating the pan periodically to ensure even cooking.

Serve with sour cream and enjoy!

Per serving: 269 Calories; 9.6g Fat; 7.2g Carbs; 38.2g Protein; 2.5g Fiber

345. Dad's Fish Jambalaya

(Ready in about 15 minutes | Servings 2)

Ingredients

1 teaspoon canola oil
1 small-sized leek, chopped
1 cup marinara sauce

1 pound sole fish fillets, cut into bite-sized strips
1 cup spinach, torn into pieces

Directions

Heat canola oil in a heavy-bottomed pot over a moderate heat. Sauté the leeks until they have softened.

Stir in the fish fillets, marinara sauce, and 1 cup of water (clam juice). Reduce the temperature to medium-low.

Let it simmer, covered, for about 5 minutes or until the cooking liquid has reduced and thickened slightly.

Stir in the spinach and continue to simmer for 2 to 3 minutes more. Serve in individual bowls. Bon appétit!

Per serving: 232 Calories; 3.6g Fat; 6.7g Carbs; 38.1g Protein; 2.1g Fiber

346. Mediterranean Haddock with Cheese Sauce

(Ready in about 30 minutes | Servings 4)

Ingredients

1 pound haddock fillets
2 scallions, chopped
1/4 cup mayonnaise

1/4 cup cream cheese, at room temperature
1 tablespoon olive oil

Directions

Begin by preheating an oven to 365 degrees F. Toss the haddock with the olive oil, salt, and black pepper.

Wrap your fish with foil and bake for about 25 minutes.

Then, prepare the sauce by whisking the scallions, cream cheese and mayo. Serve and enjoy!

Per serving: 260 Calories; 19.1g Fat; 1.3g Carbs; 19.6g Protein; 0.3g Fiber

347. Fish Cakes with Classic Horseradish Sauce

(Ready in about 20 minutes | Servings 4)

Ingredients

1 pound cod fillets
8 tablespoons Ricotta cheese
4 tablespoons parmesan cheese, grated

1 teaspoon creamed horseradish
2 eggs, beaten

Directions

Steam the cod fillets for about 10 minutes or until easily flakes with a fork. Chop your fish and mix with eggs and parmesan cheese.

Form the mixture into 4 fish cakes. Heat 2 tablespoons of olive oil in a frying skillet. Once hot, cook the fish cakes over medium-high heat for 3 to 4 minutes on each side.

Make the sauce by whisking Ricotta cheese and creamed horseradish. Bon appétit!

Per serving: 206 Calories; 8.3g Fat; 1.9g Carbs; 27.3g Protein; 0.1g Fiber

348. Classic Fish Curry

(Ready in about 20 minutes | Servings 4)

Ingredients

1 ½ pounds tilapia
1 tablespoon peanut oil
1 shallot, chopped

1 tablespoon curry paste
1 cup tomato onion masala sauce

Directions

Heat the peanut oil in a wok over medium-high heat. Cook the shallot for 2 to 3 minutes until tender and fragrant.

Pour in tomato onion masala sauce along with 1 cup of chicken broth. Bring to a boil.

Reduce the heat to a simmer and stir in the curry paste and tilapia; season with the salt and pepper to your liking.

Continue to simmer, partially covered, for 10 to 12 minutes until heated through. Serve hot and enjoy!

Per serving: 226 Calories; 6.9g Fat; 3.1g Carbs; 34.8g Protein; 1.8g Fiber

349. Sea Bass with Dill Sauce

(Ready in about 25 minutes | Servings 2)

Ingredients

1/4 cup Greek yogurt
1 tablespoon fresh dill, chopped
1 pound sea bass fillets

1 cup red onions, sliced
2 bell peppers, deveined and sliced

Directions

Start by preheating your oven to 390 degrees F.

Toss sea bass fillets, bell peppers, and the onions with 1 tablespoon of olive oil; season with the salt and pepper.

Place the fish and vegetables in a lightly greased baking dish. Bake for 20 to 22 minutes, rotating the pan once or twice

Make the sauce by whisking Greek yogurt and chopped dill. Serve warm fish and vegetables with the sauce on the side and enjoy!

Per serving: 374 Calories; 17g Fat; 6.2g Carbs; 43.2g Protein; 2.2g Fiber

350. Salmon Lettuce Tacos

(Ready in about 20 minutes | Servings 5)

Ingredients

10 lettuce leaves
2 pounds salmon
1 tomato, halved

1 avocado, pitted and peeled
4 tablespoons green onions

Directions

Toss the salmon with salt and black pepper to your liking.

Drizzle the salmon with 2 tablespoons of olive oil and grill over medium-high heat for about 15 minutes. Flake the fish with two forks.

Divide the fish among the lettuce leaves.

Puree avocado, tomato, and green onions in your blender until your desired consistency is reached; add 1 tablespoon of olive oil to your blender, if desired.

Top each taco with the avocado sauce, drizzle with fresh lemon juice and serve.

Per serving: 304 Calories; 14.1g Fat; 5.3g Carbs; 38.6g Protein; 3.4g Fiber

351. Traditional Mahi Mahi Ceviche

(Ready in about 15 minutes | Servings 4)

Ingredients

1 ½ pounds mahi-mahi fish, cut into bite-sized cubes
2 Roma tomatoes, sliced
1 bell pepper, sliced
2 garlic cloves, minced
4 scallions, chopped

Directions

Season mahi-mahi fish with salt and black pepper to taste. Brush them with nonstick cooking oil.

In a preheated grill pan, cook mahi-mahi fish for about 10 minutes until golden-brown on edges.

Toss mahi-mahi fish with the garlic, scallions, tomatoes, and bell pepper. Toss with 4 tablespoons of extra-virgin olive oil and 2 tablespoons of fresh lemon juice.

Divide between individual bowls and serve.

Per serving: 424 Calories; 29.8g Fat; 5.8g Carbs; 32.5g Protein; 1.6g Fiber

352. Fried Cod Fillets

(Ready in about 15 minutes | Servings 3)

Ingredients

2 tablespoons butter
3 cod fillets
1 cup Romano cheese, preferably freshly grated
1 teaspoon dried rosemary, crushed
1/2 cup almond meal

Directions

Place the fish, almond meal, salt, black pepper, and rosemary in a resealable bag; shake to coat well. Press cod fillets into the grated Romano cheese.

Melt the butter in a nonstick skillet over medium-high heat.

Cook the fish until it is nearly opaque, about 5 minutes on each side. Bon appétit!

Per serving: 406 Calories; 29.5g Fat; 4.1g Carbs; 31.9g Protein; 2.2g Fiber

353. Shrimp and Ham Jambalaya

(Ready in about 25 minutes | Servings 4)

Ingredients

1 shallot, chopped
1 ½ cups vegetable broth
1 ½ cups tomatoes, crushed
1 cup ham, cut into 1/2-inch cubes
3/4 pound shrimp

Directions

Heat up a lightly oiled stockpot over medium-high heat. Sweat the shallot for about 4 minutes until tender and fragrant.

Add in vegetable broth, tomatoes, and ham, and bring to a boil. Reduce heat to medium-low, cover and continue to simmer for 12 minutes more.

Stir in the shrimp and continue to simmer until they are pink and thoroughly cooked about 5 minutes.

Serve warm and enjoy!

Per serving: 170 Calories; 4.8g Fat; 5.6g Carbs; 25.9g Protein; 1.4g Fiber

354. Herring and Spinach Salad

(Ready in about 10 minutes | Servings 3)

Ingredients

1/2 cup baby spinach
6 ounces pickled herring pieces, drained and flaked
1 teaspoon garlic, minced
1 red onion, chopped
1 bell pepper, chopped

Directions

In a salad bowl, combine the spinach, herring, garlic, red onion, and bell pepper.

Toss your salad with 2 tablespoons of fresh lime juice. Season with the salt and pepper to your liking.

Serve immediately and enjoy!

Per serving: 134 Calories; 7.9g Fat; 5.4g Carbs; 1g Fiber; 10.2g Protein;

355. Haddock and Parmesan Fish Burgers

(Ready in about 20 minutes | Servings 4)

Ingredients

8 ounces smoked haddock
4 lemon wedges
1 egg
1/4 cup scallions, chopped
1/4 cup Parmesan cheese, grated

Directions

Heat 1 tablespoon of olive oil in a frying pan over medium-high flame. Once hot, cook the haddock for 5 to 6 minutes; flake the fish with a fork, discarding the skin and bones

Add in cheese, eggs, and scallions; season with sea salt and pepper to taste.

Heat 1 tablespoon of olive oil until sizzling. Now, fry your burgers for 5 to 6 minutes until they are thoroughly cooked. Garnish with lemon wedges and enjoy!

Per serving: 174 Calories; 11.4g Fat; 1.5g Carbs; 0.2g Fiber; 15.4g Protein;

356. Greek-Style Halibut Fillets

(Ready in about 35 minutes | Servings 4)

Ingredients

1 ½ pounds halibut fillets
1 tablespoon Greek seasoning blend
2 tablespoons fresh lemon juice
2 tablespoons olive oil
1/2 cup Kalamata olives, pitted and sliced

Directions

Begin by preheating your oven to 385 degrees F.

Toss the halibut fillets with Greek seasoning blend, lemon juice, and olive oil. Place the halibut fillets in a lightly-greased baking dish.

Bake for about 15 minutes, flip the fillets over and bake an additional 15 minutes.

Garnish with Kalamata olives and serve immediately!

Per serving: 397 Calories; 32.1g Fat; 1.5g Carbs; 24.6g Protein; 0.6g Fiber

357. Cod Fish à La Nage

(Ready in about 20 minutes | Servings 5)

Ingredients

1 ½ pounds cod fish fillets
2 tablespoons olive oil
1 medium-sized zucchini, diced

2 vine-ripe tomatoes, pureed
1 Spanish onion, chopped

Directions

Heat the olive oil in a Dutch oven over medium-high heat. Cook the Spanish onion until softened.

Add in zucchini and pureed tomatoes; pour in 2 cups of water and bring to a boil. Turn the heat to medium-low. Allow it to simmer for about 12 minutes.

Stir in cod fish and continue to cook, covered, for about 6 minutes (an instant-read thermometer should register 140 degrees F).

Serve the fish with cooking juice. Bon appétit!

Per serving: 177 Calories; 6.4g Fat; 4g Carbs; 24.9g Protein; 1g Fiber

358. Tilapia in Garlic Butter Sauce

(Ready in about 15 minutes | Servings 6)

Ingredients

6 tilapia fillets, patted dry
1 teaspoon fresh lime juice
1 teaspoon garlic, minced

1 tablespoon parsley, chopped
6 tablespoons butter

Directions

Spritz a frying pan skillet with nonstick cooking oil. Preheat the frying pan over medium-high flame.

Once hot, fry the tilapia for 5 to 6 minutes; flip it over using a wide spatula and continue to cook for 5 minutes more.

Season with salt and black pepper to taste.

In a mixing bowl, whisk the butter, garlic, parsley, and lime juice. Serve warm fish with a dollop of chilled butter sauce. Bon appétit!

Per serving: 215 Calories; 13.5g Fat; 0.4g Carbs; 23.5g Protein; 0.1g Fiber

359. Chinese Fish Salad

(Ready in about 15 minutes | Servings 2)

Ingredients

1/2 pound salmon fillets
2 tablespoons low-carb salad dressing
1 tomato, sliced

1 medium-sized white onion, sliced
1 cup Chinese cabbage, sliced

Directions

Place 1/2 cup of water and in a saucepan over a moderate flame.

Now, cook the salmon fillets for about 7 minutes and reserve.

Place the Chinese cabbage, tomato, and onion in a serving bowl. Toss the salad with low-carb dressing. Top with reserved salmon fillets and serve!

Per serving: 277 Calories; 15.1g Fat; 4.9g Carbs; 24.4g Protein; 0.9g Fiber

360. Indian Fish Fry

(Ready in about 15 minutes | Servings 3)

Ingredients

3 carp fillets
1/2 teaspoon garam masala
3 tablespoons full-fat coconut milk

1 egg
2 tablespoons olive oil

Directions

Pat the fish fillets dry with pepper towels. Toss fish fillets with garam masala along with sea salt and black pepper.

In a mixing dish, beat the coconut milk and egg until pale and frothy. Dip the fillets into the milk/egg mixture.

Heat olive oil in a frying pan over medium-high heat. Fry the fish fillets until they begin to flake when tested with a fork.

Serve with curry leaves if desired and enjoy!

Per serving: 443 Calories; 28.3g Fat; 2.6g Carbs; 42.5g Protein; 1g Fiber

361. Tilapia and Shrimp Soup

(Ready in about 25 minutes | Servings 5)

Ingredients

1 cup celery, chopped
2 cups cauliflower, grated
2 cups tomato sauce with onion and garlic

1 pound tilapia, skinless and chopped into small chunks
1/2 pound medium shrimp, deveined

Directions

Melt 2 tablespoons of butter in a soup pot over medium-high flame. Once hot, cook celery and cauliflower for 4 to 5 minutes or until tender.

Add in tomato sauce along with 4 cups of chicken broth and bring to a boil. Now, turn the heat to medium-low.

Stir in the tilapia and continue to cook, partially covered, for about 10 minutes. Stir in the shrimp and continue to simmer for 3 to 4 minutes or until shrimp is pink.

Ladle into soup bowls and serve hot!

Per serving: 215 Calories; 7g Fat; 5.6g Carbs; 26.4g Protein; 2.6g Fiber

362. Provençal Fish and Prawn Stew

(Ready in about 20 minutes | Servings 5)

Ingredients

1/3 pound prawns
1 pound grouper fish
1/3 pound cockles, scrubbed

1 shallot, sliced
1 cup tomato sauce with onion and garlic

Directions

Heat 2 tablespoons of olive oil in a heavy-bottomed pot over medium-high heat. Sauté the shallot for 3 to 4 minutes or until it has softened.

Stir in tomato sauce along with 5 cups of white fish stock. When the stew reaches boiling, add in salt and black pepper.

Reduce the heat to medium-low and stir in the grouper and cockles; continue to simmer for 2 to 3 minutes.

Fold in the prawns and continue to simmer approximately 3 minutes or until they are pink.

Garnish each serving with fresh lemon juice if desired and enjoy!

Per serving: 176 Calories; 6.5g Fat; 5.1g Carbs; 23.8g Protein; 0.8g Fiber

363. Mexican-Style Grilled Salmon

(Ready in about 1 hour | Servings 4)

Ingredients

2 cloves garlic, pressed
1 tablespoon Taco seasoning mix

2 tablespoons fresh lemon juice
4 (5-ounce) salmon steaks
4 tablespoons olive oil

Directions

Place all ingredients in a ceramic dish. Cover and allow it to marinate in your refrigerator for 35 to 40 minutes.

Grill the salmon steaks for about 6 minutes per side, basting with the reserved marinade. Serve warm and enjoy!

Per serving: 331 Calories; 21.4g Fat; 2.2g Carbs; 30.4g Protein; 0.4g Fiber

364. Portuguese Caldeirada De Peixe

(Ready in about 25 minutes | Servings 3)

Ingredients

3/4 pound sole fillets, cut into 1-inch pieces
1 shallot, chopped
1 cup tomatoes, pureed

1 teaspoon curry paste
1 tablespoon butter, at room temperature

Directions

In a heavy-bottomed pot, melt the butter a moderate flame. Sauté the shallot until tender and translucent.

Add in pureed tomatoes and curry paste and along with 2 cups of water. When your stew reaches boiling, immediately reduce the temperature to a simmer.

Continue to simmer, covered, for 10 to 15 minutes, stirring periodically.

Stir in sole fillets and continue to simmer for about 7 minutes or until the internal temperature of your fish reaches 145 degrees F. Enjoy!

Per serving: 191 Calories; 9.1g Fat; 2.8g Carbs; 23.9g Protein; 1.1g Fiber

365. Sea Bass with Peppers

(Ready in about 20 minutes | Servings 6)

Ingredients

2 pounds sea bass fillets, chopped into small chunks
2 cups marinara sauce, low-carb

1 leek, chopped
1 bell pepper, chopped
1 serrano pepper, chopped

Directions

Melt 2 tablespoons of butter in a soup pot over medium-high heat. Sauté the leek and peppers for about 4 to 5 minutes or until they have softened.

Add in marinara sauce and sea bass along with 4 cups fish stock. Turn the heat to a simmer.

Let it cook, partially covered, for 10 to 12 minutes. Bon appétit!

Per serving: 218 Calories; 7.3g Fat; 7g Carbs; 29.3g Protein; 2g Fiber

366. Cod Fish Salad (Insalata di Baccalà)

(Ready in about 15 minutes | Servings 5)

Ingredients

5 cod fillets
2 cups lettuce, cut into small pieces
1/4 cup balsamic vinegar

1 red onion, sliced
1/2 pound green cabbage, shredded

Directions

Heat 1 tablespoon of the olive oil in a large saucepan over a moderate flame.

Once hot, cook the fish for about 10 minutes or until it is golden brown on top. Flake the fish and reserve.

Then, whisk 3 tablespoons of olive oil and balsamic vinegar; season with salt and black pepper; stir in 1 tablespoon of stone-ground mustard, if desired.

Combine the lettuce, green cabbage, and onion in a serving bowl. Dress the salad and top with cod fish. Enjoy!

Per serving: 276 Calories; 6.9g Fat; 6.4g Carbs; 42.7g Protein; 1.7g Fiber

SNACKS & APPETIZERS

367. Walnut and Chocolate Bites

(Ready in about 10 minutes + chilling time | Servings 10)

Ingredients

5 ounces butter
3 ounces walnut butter
1/4 cup Erythritol

2 tablespoons keto chocolate protein powder
10 whole walnuts, halved

Directions

In a saucepan, melt the butter, walnut butter, Erythritol, and chocolate protein powder over low heat.

Place the butter mixture into a piping bag and pipe into mini cupcake liners. Add the walnut halves to the cupcakes.

Let it cool in your refrigerator for 2 to 3 hours. Enjoy!

Per serving: 260 Calories; 26.4g Fat; 3.2g Carbs; 4.8g Protein; 1.6g Fiber

368. Turkey Roll-Ups with Avocado and Cheese

(Ready in about 10 minutes | Servings 8)

Ingredients

16 slices cooked turkey breasts, deli-sliced
1/2 fresh lemon, juiced
Salt and black pepper, to taste

16 slices Swiss cheese
2 avocados, pitted, peeled and diced

Directions

Drizzle fresh lemon juice over diced avocado. Divide avocado pieces among turkey slices.

Season with salt and black pepper.

Add the slice of Swiss cheese to each roll. Roll them up and serve immediately!

Per serving: 332 Calories; 23.9g Fat; 7g Carbs; 22.4g Protein; 3.6g Fiber

369. Spicy Chicken Drumettes

(Ready in about 25 minutes | Servings 6)

Ingredients

2 pounds chicken drumettes
1/3 cup hot sauce
1 teaspoon garlic powder

1 teaspoon dried oregano
1 tablespoon stone-ground mustard

Directions

Start by preheating your oven to 420 degrees F.

Sprinkle chicken drumettes with oregano; season with the salt and black pepper.

Brush chicken drumettes with a nonstick cooking oil and bake in the preheated oven for about 20 minutes.

Toss chicken drumettes with the hot sauce, mustard and garlic powder. Place them under the preheated broiler for 5 to 6 minutes or until they are golden brown. Bon appétit!

Per serving: 179 Calories; 2.5g Fat; 2.3g Carbs; 34.2g Protein; 0.7g Fiber

370. Mexican Taco Wings

(Ready in about 1 hour | Servings 5)

Ingredients

2 tablespoons extra-virgin olive oil
2 pounds chicken wings

1 tablespoon Taco seasoning mix
1 tablespoon whiskey
1 cup tomato sauce

Directions

Begin by preheating your oven to 400 degrees F. Toss chicken wings with extra-virgin olive oil, Taco seasoning mix, whiskey, and tomato sauce.

Lower the wings onto a rack in the roasting pan.

Bake the wings at the lowest oven rack setting for about 55 minutes until they are nicely browned and crispy.

Serve with a keto dipping sauce of choice. Enjoy!

Per serving: 293 Calories; 12.1g Fat; 3.4g Carbs; 40.6g Protein; 0.9g Fiber

371. Greek-Style Mini Muffins

(Ready in about 40 minutes | Servings 6)

Ingredients

4 eggs, well whisked
4 tablespoons Greek yogurt
1/2 cup scallions, chopped

1 cup kale, torn into small pieces
2 slices cooked bacon, chopped

Directions

Coat a mini muffin tin with cupcake liners. Then, whisk the eggs and Greek yogurt until pale and frothy.

Stir in the scallions, kale, and bacon. Mix until everything is well combined.

Salt to taste and spoon the mixture into the prepared muffin tin.

Bake in the preheated oven at 370 degrees F for 25 to 30 minutes or until a toothpick inserted in the center of your muffin comes out dry and clean.

Serve at room temperature.

Per serving: 88 Calories; 6.5g Fat; 1.7g Carbs; 5.4g Protein; 0.3g Fiber

372. Beef-Stuffed Mini Peppers

(Ready in about 25 minutes | Servings 6)

Ingredients

12 mini peppers, deveined
3/4 pound ground beef
2 garlic cloves, minced

1/2 cup onion, chopped
1/2 cup cheddar cheese, shredded

Directions

Parboil the peppers for about 6 minutes or until they are just tender.

Heat a lightly oiled frying pan over medium-high flame. Now, cook the ground beef for 3 to 4 minutes, breaking apart with a spatula.

Stir in the garlic and onions and continue to sauté for 1 to 2 minutes more or until they are just tender.

Stuff mini peppers with the beef mixture. Top with cheddar cheese and place them in a foil-lined baking dish.

Bake in the preheated oven at 370 degrees F approximately 15 minutes. Bon appétit!

Per serving: 207 Calories; 10.2g Fat; 6.8g Carbs; 19.7g Protein; 1.6g Fiber

373. Meatballs with Romano Cheese

(Ready in about 25 minutes | Servings 10)

Ingredients

1 1/2 ground turkey
4 ounces pork rinds
1/4 cup full-fat milk
1 shallot, chopped
1/2 cup Romano cheese, grated

Directions

Combine all ingredients in a mixing bowl; form the mixture into small meatballs.

Arrange your meatballs on a foil-lined baking pan; spritz them with nonstick cooking oil.

Bake your meatballs for about 20 minutes, rotating the pan to ensure even cooking. Serve and enjoy!

Per serving: 247 Calories; 18g Fat; 1.1g Carbs; 19.1g Protein; 0.1g Fiber

374. Deviled Eggs with Mustard Cream Cheese

(Ready in about 20 minutes + chilling time | Servings 8)

Ingredients

1 teaspoon Dijon mustard
8 eggs
1 tablespoon mayonnaise
1 tablespoon tomato puree, no sugar added
2 tablespoons cream cheese

Directions

Cook the eggs in a saucepan and bring to a boil. Remove from the heat and let the eggs sit, covered, for 15 minutes.

Peel the eggs and slice them into halves lengthwise; combine the yolks with cream cheese, Dijon mustard, mayonnaise, and tomato puree; season with the salt and black pepper to taste.

Spoon the yolk mixture into egg whites. Garnish with fresh chives just before serving.

Per serving: 149 Calories; 11.3g Fat; 1.6g Carbs; 9.4g Protein; 0.1g Fiber

375. Italian Paprika Cheese Sauce

(Ready in about 10 minutes | Servings 10)

Ingredients

1 cup double cream
4 ounces feta cheese
1 cup Asiago cheese, shredded
1 tablespoon paprika

Directions

Melt double cream and cheese in a saucepan over medium-low flame.

Place the sauce in a serving bowl and top with paprika.

Bon appétit!

Per serving: 126 Calories; 11g Fat; 1.4g Carbs; 5.4g Protein; 0g Fiber

376. Herby Cheese Chips

(Ready in about 30 minutes | Servings 5)

Ingredients

1/2 teaspoon dried oregano
1 teaspoon paprika
1/2 teaspoon garlic powder
1 teaspoon dried dill
6 ounces provolone cheese, grated

Directions

Start by preheating your oven to 390 degrees F.

Arrange the grated cheese in small heaps on a parchment-lined roasting pan.

Sprinkle the spices over them.

Bake in the preheated oven for about 10 minutes. Place on a cooling rack for about 30 minutes. Enjoy!

Per serving: 119 Calories; 9g Fat; 0.7g Carbs; 8.7g Protein; 0.2g Fiber

377. Saucy St. Louis-style Spareribs

(Ready in about 2 hours 35 minutes | Servings 4)

Ingredients

2 pounds St. Louis-style spareribs
2 cloves garlic, pressed
1/2 cup chicken bone broth
1 tablespoon Fajita seasoning mix
1 cup tomato sauce

Directions

Begin by preheating your oven to 280 degrees F.

Toss St. Louis-style spareribs with garlic, chicken bone broth, Fajita seasoning mix, and tomato sauce until they are coated on all sides.

Place the spare ribs on a foil-lined baking sheet.

Bake in the preheated oven for 2 hours and 40 minutes. You can broil them for the last 10 minutes if desired. Bon appétit!

Per serving: 344 Calories; 13.6g Fat; 4.9g Carbs; 49.5g Protein; 1.2g Fiber

378. Dijon Anchovies Fat Bombs

(Ready in about 5 minutes | Servings 2)

Ingredients

1 tablespoon Dijon mustard
2 (2-ounce) cans anchovies, drained
1/3 cup cheddar cheese, shredded
2 scallions, chopped
1/3 cup cream cheese, chilled

Directions

Combine all ingredients in a mixing bowl. Form the mixture into small balls.

Serve well chilled. Bon appétit!

Per serving: 391 Calories; 26.6g Fat; 3.1g Carbs; 33.8g Protein; 0.7g Fiber

379. Cucumber and Pepper Bites

(Ready in about 10 minutes | Servings 3)

Ingredients

1 cucumber, cut into rounds
1 bell pepper, deveined and cut into 4 pieces lengthwise
1/4 cup mayonnaise
1 teaspoon Dijon mustard
1/2 cup cream cheese

Directions

Arrange the cucumber and bell peppers on a serving platter.

Mix mayonnaise, mustard, and cream cheese until everything is well combined.

Divide the mayo/cheese mixture between cucumbers and peppers. Serve and enjoy!

Per serving: 164 Calories; 16.3g Fat; 3g Carbs; 2g Protein; 0.6g Fiber

380. Cheesy Chicken Rolls

(Ready in about 30 minutes | Servings 5)

Ingredients

5 slices ham
5 chicken fillets, about ¼-inch thin
3 ounces Ricotta cheese
1/3 cup Colby cheese, grated
1/2 cup spicy tomato sauce

Directions

Begin by preheating your oven to 380 degrees F.

Lay a slice of ham on each chicken fillet. Then, mix Ricotta cheese and Colby until well combined.

Spoon the cheese mixture onto the chicken fillets. Roll them up, wrap in a piece of foil and place them in a lightly greased baking pan.

Bake in the preheated oven approximately 15 minutes; flip them over, pour in tomato sauce and bake another 15 minutes.

Bon appétit!

Per serving: 289 Calories; 11.1g Fat; 7.2g Carbs; 36.8g Protein; 2g Fiber

381. Cheese and Prosciutto Fat Bombs

(Ready in about 10 minutes | Servings 4)

Ingredients

1 red bell pepper, deveined and finely chopped
2 tablespoons sesame seeds, toasted
3 ounces prosciutto, chopped
2 ounces goat cheese, crumbled
2 ounces feta cheese crumbled

Directions

Combine the prosciutto, cheese, and pepper in a mixing bowl. Form the mixture into bite-sized balls.

Roll the keto balls over toasted sesame seeds and serve well-chilled.

Per serving: 176 Calories; 12.9g Fat; 2.3g Carbs; 12.8g Protein; 0.6g Fiber

382. Deviled Eggs with Roasted Peppers

(Ready in about 15 minutes | Servings 10)

Ingredients

2 tablespoons olive oil
1/4 cup sour cream
1/4 cup red roasted pepper, chopped
1 garlic clove, minced
10 eggs

Directions

Place the eggs in a saucepan. Pour in water and bring to a boil. Remove from heat and let it sit, covered, for about 10 minutes.

Then, peel the eggs and separate egg whites and yolks.

Mix the egg yolks with the sour cream, roasted pepper, olive oil, and garlic; season with sea salt to taste.

Stuff the eggs with this filling and serve well-chilled.

Per serving: 97 Calories; 7.5g Fat; 1.1g Carbs; 5.8g Protein; 0.1g Fiber

383. Ranch Blue Cheese Sauce

(Ready in about 10 minutes | Servings 10)

Ingredients

1 cup blue cheese, crumbled
2 tablespoons ranch seasoning
1/2 cup mayonnaise
1 tablespoon lime juice
1/2 cup Greek-style yogurt

Directions

Mix all ingredients until well combined.

Serve well chilled with your favorite keto dippers. Enjoy!

Per serving: 94 Calories; 8.1g Fat; 1.3g Carbs; 4.1g Protein; 0.1g Fiber

384. Prawn Cocktail Skewers

(Ready in about 15 minutes | Servings 4)

Ingredients

1 pound king prawns, deveined and cleaned
2 tablespoons fresh lime juice
1 cup cherry tomatoes
2 bell peppers, diced
2 tablespoons olive oil

Directions

In a large saucepan, heat olive oil over medium-high heat.

Sauté the prawns for 3 to 4 minutes until they are pink. Stir in Cajun seasoning mix.

Now, toss king prawns with the lime juice. Tread the prawns, cherry tomatoes and peppers onto bamboo skewers.

Bon appétit!

Per serving: 179 Calories; 8.3g Fat; 5.1g Carbs; 20.4g Protein; 0.7g Fiber

385. Mozzarella Stuffed Meatballs

(Ready in about 25 minutes | Servings 8)

Ingredients

1 1/2 pound ground pork
4 ounces mozzarella string cheese, cubed

1 ripe tomato, pureed
1 garlic clove, minced
2 tablespoons shallots, chopped

Directions

Mix ground pork, garlic, shallots, and tomato until well combined.

Take a tablespoon of the meat mixture and place a piece of the cheese inside. Shape the meat around the cheese in a ball. Repeat with remaining ingredients.

Bake the meatballs in the preheated oven at 360 degrees F for about 20 minutes. Bon appétit!

Per serving: 389 Calories; 31.3g Fat; 1.6g Carbs; 23.8g Protein; 0.5g Fiber

386. Chorizo and Cheese Stuffed Mushrooms

(Ready in about 30 minutes | Servings 6)

Ingredients

10 ounces goat cheese, crumbled
8 ounces Chorizo sausage, crumbled

2 scallions, chopped
2 green garlic stalks, chopped
30 button mushrooms, stalks removed and cleaned

Directions

Begin by preheating your oven to 350 degrees F.

Arrange the mushroom caps on a foil-lined roasting pan.

In a mixing bowl, combine the sausage, scallions, garlic, and cheese. Divide the filling between prepared mushroom caps.

Bake in the preheated oven for 25 to 30 minutes or until they are tender and cooked through. Bon appétit!

Per serving: 324 Calories; 23.7g Fat; 5g Carbs; 23.1g Protein; 1.1g Fiber

387. Dad's Hamburger Dipping Sauce

(Ready in about 1 hour 10 minutes | Servings 6)

Ingredients

1/2 pound ground pork
1/2 cup Provolone cheese, grated

2 ounces tomato paste
1/2 red onion, chopped
2 ounces sour cream

Directions

Cook ground pork, onion, and tomato paste in your slow cooker for 1 hour at Low setting.

Stir in in sour cream and cheese.

Serve with your favorite keto dippers. Bon appétit!

Per serving: 156 Calories; 11.9g Fat; 2.1g Carbs; 9.7g Protein; 0.2g Fiber

388. Spicy Bacon-Wrapped Shrimp

(Ready in about 15 minutes | Servings 8)

Ingredients

24 medium shrimp, deveined
8 slices of thick-cut bacon, cut into thirds
1 teaspoon onion powder

1/2 teaspoon granulated garlic
1/2 teaspoon red pepper flakes, crushed

Directions

Preheat your oven to 390 degrees F. Line a baking pan with a piece of aluminum foil.

Wrap each shrimp with a piece of bacon, roll them up, and secure with a toothpick. Place them on the prepared baking sheet.

Season these rolls with onion powder, garlic and red pepper.

Bake in the preheated oven for about 12 minutes or until everything is cooked through. Bon appétit!

Per serving: 119 Calories; 10.3g Fat; 0.3g Carbs; 5.7g Protein; 0g Fiber

389. Ham and Avocado Stuffed Eggs

(Ready in about 20 minutes | Servings 4)

Ingredients

4 large eggs
2 ounces cooked ham, chopped
1/2 teaspoon yellow mustard

1/2 avocado, mashed
1 garlic clove, minced

Directions

Add the eggs to a saucepan; fill with enough water and bring it to a boil; remove from heat. Let the eggs sit, covered, for about 10 minutes.

Slice cooled eggs into halves and separate egg whites and yolks.

Then, mix the yolks with the mustard, avocado, and garlic.

Divide the filling between egg whites and top with the chopped ham. Serve and enjoy!

Per serving: 128 Calories; 8.9g Fat; 2.9g Carbs; 9.2g Protein; 1.7g Fiber

390. Cocktail Franks with Mustard

(Ready in about 25 minutes | Servings 10)

Ingredients

2 tablespoons olive oil
18 ounces cocktail franks
Sea salt and red pepper flakes, to taste

2 tablespoons wholegrain mustard
1/2 cup vegetable broth

Directions

Preheat your oven to 370 degrees F. Then, brush the sides and bottom a baking pan with olive oil. Arrange the cocktail franks on the prepared baking pan.

Sprinkle them with the salt and red pepper flakes; stir in the mustard and broth.

Bake for about 15 minutes until they are golden brown. Enjoy!

Per serving: 155 Calories; 11.9g Fat; 5g Carbs; 9.4g Protein; 1.4g Fiber

391. Greek-Style Dip

(Ready in about 15 minutes + chilling time | Servings 8)

Ingredients

4 tablespoons Greek yogurt
4 tablespoons olives, sliced
10 ounces ricotta cheese

1/2 teaspoon garlic salt
4 tablespoons cilantro, minced

Directions

In a mixing bowl, combine the Greek yogurt, olives, ricotta cheese, and garlic salt.

Place the mixture in a serving bowl.

Garnish with cilantro and enjoy!

Per serving: 72 Calories; 5.5g Fat; 1.9g Carbs; 4.3g Protein; 0.2g Fiber

392. Ranch Tangy Wings

(Ready in about 55 minutes | Servings 6)

Ingredients

2 pounds chicken wings
1 clove garlic, minced
1/2 cup sour cream

2 tablespoons onion, finely chopped
1/2 cup mayonnaise

Directions

Pat chicken wings dry with a paper towel. Preheat your oven to 410 degrees F.

Brush the chicken wings with a nonstick cooking spray. Season the chicken wings with salt and pepper. Place the chicken wings in a foil-lined roasting pan.

Bake in the preheated oven for 45 to 50 minutes or until the skin is golden-brown and crispy.

Make the sauce by whisking sour cream, mayo, garlic, and onion. Serve warm wings with the sauce on the side. Enjoy!

Per serving: 466 Calories; 37.2g Fat; 1.9g Carbs; 28.6g Protein; 0.1g Fiber

393. Cheese Chips with Spicy Sauce

(Ready in about 30 minutes | Servings 8)

Ingredients

2 ripe tomatoes, peeled
1 teaspoon Mediterranean seasoning mix

1/2 teaspoon chili powder
1/2 cup Asiago cheese, grated
1 ¼ cups Romano cheese, grated

Directions

Begin by preheating your oven to 390 degrees F.

Combine the cheese in a mixing bowl and place tablespoon-sized heaps of the mixture onto foil-lined baking pan.

Bake in the preheated oven for 7 to 8 minutes until they are golden brown around the edges. Let them cool for 15 to 20 minutes.

In the meantime, puree the tomatoes and cook for 30 minutes or until it has reduced by half. Add in Mediterranean seasoning mix and chili powder.

Serve your chips with the spicy sauce on the side. Enjoy!

Per serving: 109 Calories; 7.6g Fat; 1.9g Carbs; 8.3g Protein; 0.4g Fiber

394. Favorite BLT Cups

(Ready in about 15 minutes | Servings 10)

Ingredients

10 pieces lettuce
10 tomatoes cherry tomatoes, discard the insides
2 tablespoons mayonnaise

5 tablespoons Parmigiano-Reggiano cheese, grated
5 ounces bacon, chopped

Directions

Cook the bacon in the preheated frying pan for about 6 minutes and reserve.

In a mixing bowl, combine the mayonnaise and cheese; season with the salt and black pepper to taste. Divide the mixture between cherry tomatoes.

Top with the reserved bacon. Place on lettuce leaves and serve on a nice serving platter.

Per serving: 92 Calories; 8.3g Fat; 1.6g Carbs; 2.7g Protein; 0.3g Fiber

395. Kid-Friendly Boats with Sardines

(Ready in about 15 minutes | Servings 2)

Ingredients

3 bell peppers, deveined and halved
2 ounces canned boneless sardines, drained and chopped

2 eggs
1/2 cup tomatoes, chopped
1/3 cup Ricotta cheese

Directions

Place the eggs and water in a saucepan and bring to a boil; remove from the heat and let it sit, covered, approximately 10 minutes.

Peel the eggs, rinse, and chop them.

Add in sardines, tomatoes, and Ricotta cheese. Season with garlic salt and pepper to taste.

Stuff the pepper halves with this mixture and serve chilled. Enjoy!

Per serving: 371 Calories; 31.1g Fat; 6g Carbs; 16.2g Protein; 1.3g Fiber

396. Summer Turkey Meatballs

(Ready in about 15 minutes | Servings 2)

Ingredients

1/2 pound ground turkey
1/2 cup cheddar cheese, shredded

1 ounce bacon, chopped
1 egg, beaten
1/4 cup flaxseed meal

Directions

Begin by preheating your oven to 390 degrees F.

In a mixing bowl, stir all ingredients until well combined. Then, roll the mixture into bite-sized meatballs.

Place the meatballs in a foil-lined baking sheet. Bake in the preheated oven for about 20 minutes, flipping them and rotating the pan to ensure even cooking.

Serve with cocktail sticks and enjoy!

Per serving: 569 Calories; 42.2g Fat; 6.5g Carbs; 40.1g Protein; 5.7g Fiber

397. Paprika Zucchini Parmesan Crisps

(Ready in about 25 minutes | Servings 2)

Ingredients

1/2 pound zucchini, sliced into rounds

2 tablespoons Parmesan cheese, grated

1 tablespoon extra-virgin olive oil

1 teaspoon hot paprika

1/4 teaspoon sea salt

Directions

Start by preheating your oven to 390 degrees F.

Toss the zucchini rounds with extra-virgin olive oil, paprika, and salt. Arrange them on a parchment-lined baking pan.

Scater Parmesan cheese over each zucchini round.

Bake in the preheated oven for about 20 minutes or until your crisps are golden-brown around the edges. Bon appétit!

Per serving: 52 Calories; 4.6g Fat; 1.4g Carbs; 1.7g Protein; 0.5g Fiber

398. Hot Bacon Chips

(Ready in about 15 minutes | Servings 12)

Ingredients

1 ½ pounds bacon, cut into 1-inch squares

1 teaspoon Ranch seasoning mix

1 tablespoon hot sauce

1/4 cup lemon juice

Directions

Preheat your oven to 370 degrees F.

Toss the bacon with the Ranch seasoning mix, hot sauce, and lemon juice. Place the bacon squares on a foil-lined baking pan.

Roast in the preheated oven for 10 to 12 minutes or until crisp. Let it cool completely and serve!

Per serving: 232 Calories; 22.4g Fat; 0.8g Carbs; 7.1g Protein; 0g Fiber

399. Double-Cheese Biscuits

(Ready in about 25 minutes | Servings 10)

Ingredients

1 cup Romano cheese, grated

1 ½ cups Colby cheese, grated

3 cups almond meal

1 stick butter

2 eggs

Directions

Mix almond meal with 1 teaspoon of baking powder; season with salt and paprika. In another mixing bowl, beat the butter and eggs until pale and frothy.

Stir the butter/egg mixture into the almond meal mixture. Fold in the grated cheese and stir until everything is well combined.

Shape the batter into 16 balls; arrange balls on a lightly oiled baking sheet. Flatten them slightly and bake at 355 degrees F approximately 15 minutes. Bon appétit!

Per serving: 377 Calories; 33.7g Fat; 6.5g Carbs; 13.9g Protein; 4.9g Fiber

400. Restaurant-Style Onions Rings

(Ready in about 20 minutes | Servings 4)

Ingredients

1/2 cup coconut flour

3 eggs

2 onions, cut into 1/2-inch thick rings

4 ounces pork rinds

3 ounces parmesan cheese, grated

Directions

Place the coconut flour in a shallow bowl. In a separate shallow bowl, mix the eggs and gradually add in 4 tablespoons of water.

In the third bowl, mix the pork rinds and parmesan.

Dip the onion rings into the coconut flour; then, dredge them into the egg mixture. Press the onion rings in the parmesan mixture.

Place the onion rings on a lightly greased baking rack and bake at 410 degrees F for about 15 minutes. Enjoy!

Per serving: 322 Calories; 27.8g Fat; 5.7g Carbs; 10.1g Protein; 1g Fiber

401. Double Cheese Fat Bombs

(Ready in about 1 hour 5 minutes | Servings 8)

Ingredients

8 ounces cottage cheese, at room temperature

8 ounces mozzarella cheese, crumbled

1/2 stick butter, at room temperature

1 teaspoon Italian seasoning blend

2 ounces bacon bits

Directions

Thoroughly combine cheese, butter, and Italian seasoning until everything is well blended.

Refrigerate for about 1 hour.

Shape the mixture into bite-sized balls and roll them over bacon bits. Bon appétit!

Per serving: 149 Calories; 9.3g Fat; 2.2g Carbs; 13.1g Protein; 0.6g Fiber

402. Hot Saucy Ribs

(Ready in about 2 hours 10 minutes | Servings 2)

Ingredients

1 pound spare ribs

1 teaspoon Dijon mustard

1 tablespoon rice wine

1 tablespoon avocado oil

1 cup spicy tomato sauce with garlic, no sugar added

Directions

Start by prehating your oven to 365 degrees F.

Toss the ribs with mustard, rice wine, and avocado oil; season with salt and pepper to taste. Place the spare ribs on a foil-lined baking pan.

Bake in the preheated oven for 55 to 60 minutes. Flip them over and roast for a further 55 minutes.

After that, pour the hot sauce over the ribs. Place under the broiler for about 8 minutes (an internal temperature should reach 145 degrees F).

Brush hot sauce onto each rib and serve immediately!

Per serving: 472 Calories; 27g Fat; 6.5g Carbs; 48.7g Protein; 2g Fiber

403. Ranch Kale Chips

(Ready in about 15 minutes | Servings 2)

Ingredients

1 tablespoons olive oil
2 cups kale, torn into pieces
Sea salt, to taste

1 teaspoon Ranch seasoning mix

Directions

Begin by preheating your oven to 300 degrees F.

Toss the kale leaves with olive oil, salt, and Ranch seasoning mix until well coated.

Bake for about 12 minutes and let it cool before storing. Enjoy!

Per serving: 68 Calories; 6.6g Fat; 1.4g Carbs; 0.6g Protein; 0.6g Fiber

404. Exotic Chicken Wings

(Ready in about 50 minutes | Servings 2)

Ingredients

2 tablespoons sesame seeds
4 chicken wings
1 tablespoon coconut aminos

2 tablespoons rum
2 tablespoons butter

Directions

Start by preheating your oven to 410 degrees F.

Pat dry the chicken wings with kitchen towels. Toss the chicken wings with the remaining ingredients until well coated. Arrange the wings on a foil-lined roasting pan.

Bake in the preheated oven for 40 to 45 minutes until skin is crisp and golden brown.

Bon appétit!

Per serving: 286 Calories; 18.5g Fat; 5.2g Carbs; 15.6g Protein; 1.9g Fiber

405. Greek-Style Souvlaki

(Ready in about 15 minutes + marinating time | Servings 2)

Ingredients

1/2 cup Greek-style yogurt
1/4 cup dry red wine
1/2 pound pork loin, cut into bite-sized pieces

1/2 Lebanese cucumber, grated
1 scallion stalk, chopped

Directions

Place the pork loin, scallion, and red wine in a ceramic dish; add in 1 teaspoon of garlic and 1 tablespoon of olive oil. Let it marinate in your refrigerator for about 3 hours.

Thread the marinated pork pieces onto bamboo skewers and grill them for 10 to 12 minutes.

Whisk Greek-style yogurt with cucumber. Serve the pork skewers with the sauce on the side enjoy!

Per serving: 312 Calories; 19.7g Fat; 2.3g Carbs; 29.3g Protein; 0.7g Fiber

406. Stuffed Jalapeños with Bacon and Cheese

(Ready in about 35 minutes | Servings 10)

Ingredients

20 jalapeno peppers, deveined and halved lengthwise
2 ounces bacon, chopped
1 pound ground beef

4 ounces parmesan cheese, preferably freshly grated
1/2 cup tomato sauce with onion and garlic

Directions

Cook the bacon and beef in a preheated frying pan until no longer pink for 4 to 5 minutes.

Season with salt and black pepper to taste. Fold in tomato sauce and stir to combine.

Reduce the heat to medium-low and cook 4 to 5 minutes. Spoon the mixture into jalapeno peppers.

Bake in the preheated oven at 380 degrees F for 18 to 20 minutes. Top with parmesan cheese and bake an additional 7 minutes or until cheese is hot and bubbly. Bon appétit!

Per serving: 189 Calories; 13.2g Fat; 4.9g Carbs; 12.7g Protein; 1.1g Fiber

407. Italian Cheddar Crisps

(Ready in about 10 minutes | Servings 4)

Ingredients

1 teaspoon Italian seasoning
1 cup sharp Cheddar cheese, grated

1/4 teaspoon ground black pepper
1/2 teaspoon cayenne pepper

Directions

Combine all ingredients in a mixing bowl.

Then, place tablespoon-sized heaps of the mixture onto a parchment-lined baking sheet.

Bake in the preheated oven at 390 degrees F for 10 minutes, until the edges start to brown. Enjoy!

Per serving: 134 Calories; 11.1g Fat; 0.4g Carbs; 4.9g Protein; 0g Fiber

408. Mediterranean-Style Zucchini Rounds

(Ready in about 20 minutes | Servings 6)

Ingredients

2 eggs
2 tablespoons olive oil
1/2 teaspoon smoked paprika

1/2 cup Romano cheese, shredded
2 pounds zucchini, sliced into rounds

Directions

Start by preheating your oven to 410 degrees F. Line a baking sheet with parchment paper.

Then, whisk the eggs, olive oil, and paprika; sprinkle with salt and black pepper. Place shredded Romano cheese in another shallow bowl.

Dip the zucchini rounds into the egg mixture; press them onto the shredded cheese.

Bake for 13 to 15 minutes until they are golden-brown around edges. Enjoy!

Per serving: 137 Calories; 9.8g Fat; 5.7g Carbs; 8.8g Protein; 1.8g Fiber

409. Home-Style Seed Crackers

(Ready in about 2 hours | Servings 12)

Ingredients

4 tablespoons coconut oil, melted

1 cup sunflower seeds

1/4 cup pumpkin seeds

1 teaspoon psyllium husk powder

1/4 cup almond meal

Directions

Start by preheating your oven to 320 degrees F.

Thoroughly combine the almond meal, seeds, and psyllium husk; season with salt and pepper to taste.

Pour 3/4 cup of boiling water into the seed mixture; add in the melted coconut oil.

Spread out the batter on a parchment-lined baking pan. Bake in the preheated oven for about 1 hour, rotating the pan halfway through cooking.

Let the crackers dry for another 50 minutes in the warm oven. Enjoy!

Per serving: 128 Calories; 12.3g Fat; 3.1g Carbs; 3.3g Protein; 1.9g Fiber

410. The Best Keto Sushi Ever

(Ready in about 15 minutes | Servings 8)

Ingredients

8 bacon slices

2 scallions, finely chopped

1 avocado, mashed

2 tablespoons fresh lemon juice

4 ounces cream cheese, softened

Directions

Thoroughly combine the scallions, cream cheese, avocado, and fresh lemon juice.

Divide the mixture between the bacon slices.

Roll them up, secure with toothpicks, and garnish with sesame seeds, if desired. Enjoy!

Per serving: 350 Calories; 37.2g Fat; 3.4g Carbs; 1.5g Protein; 1.9g Fiber

411. Breakfast Egg Cups

(Ready in about 15 minutes | Servings 9)

Ingredients

9 eggs

1/2 cup Swiss cheese, shredded

9 slices ham

1 teaspoon jalapeno pepper, deseeded and minced

Coarse salt and ground black pepper, to season

Directions

Preheat your oven to 380 degrees F. Spritz the sides and bottom of a muffin pan with cooking spray.

Coat each cup with a slice of ham; add jalapeno pepper, salt, black pepper, and Swiss cheese. Crack an egg into each cup.

Bake in for about 15 minutes or until the eggs are ser. Bon appétit!

Per serving: 137 Calories; 8.6g Fat; 1.8g Carbs; 12g Protein; 0.4g Fiber

412. Boston Lettuce Roll-Ups

(Ready in about 10 minutes | Servings 5)

Ingredients

10 thin ham slices

1 tomato, chopped

10 Boston lettuce leaves, washed and rinsed well

10 tablespoons cream cheese

1 red chili pepper, chopped

Directions

Drizzle fresh lemon juice over lettuce leaves. Spread cream cheese over each lettuce leaf. Add chopped tomatoes, chili pepper, and ham.

Place on a serving platter and serve immediately!

Per serving: 148 Calories; 10.2g Fat; 4.2g Carbs; 10.7g Protein; 0.8g Fiber

413. Cheese and Turkey Stuffed Pepper Bites

(Ready in about 15 minutes | Servings 5)

Ingredients

2 teaspoons olive oil

1 teaspoon mustard seeds

5 ounces ground turkey

10 mini bell peppers, cut in half lengthwise, stems and seeds removed

2 ounces garlic and herb seasoned chevre goat cheese, crumbled

Direction

In a frying pan, warm the oil over medium-high flame. Then, cook mustard seeds along with ground turkey for about 5 minutes, breaking apart with a fork. Season with salt and black pepper to taste.

Place the pepper halves on a parchment-lined baking pan. Spoon turkey mixture into each pepper half.

Top with cheese and bake in the preheated oven at 390 degrees F approximately 12 minutes. Enjoy!

Per serving: 198 Calories; 17.2g Fat; 3g Carbs; 7.8g Protein; 0.9g Fiber

414. Italian Caprese Skewers

(Ready in about 10 minutes | Servings 8)

Ingredients

16 grape tomatoes

8 ounces mozzarella, cubed

2 bell peppers, sliced

8 pieces Prosciutto

8 pieces Soppressata

Directions

Tread all ingredients onto bamboo skewers.

Season with salt to taste. Drizzle with 2 tablespoons of olive oil and wine vinegar if desired. Bon appétit!

Per serving: 141 Calories; 8.2g Fat; 3.3g Carbs; 12.9g Protein; 1g Fiber

415. Chicken Meatballs with Spinach and Cheese

(Ready in about 30 minutes | Servings 10)

Ingredients

1 egg, whisked
8 ounces spinach, chopped
1 ½ pounds ground chicken

8 ounces Parmigiano-Reggiano cheese, grated
1 teaspoon garlic, minced

Directions

Thoroughly combine all ingredients in a mixing bowl. Add in Italian spice mix.

Roll the meat mixture into 20 balls and place them on a lightly greased baking sheet.

Bake in the preheated oven at 385 degrees F for 20 to 25 minutes or until cooked through. Serve with toothpicks and enjoy!

Per serving: 207 Calories; 12.3g Fat; 4.6g Carbs; 19.5g Protein; 0.6g Fiber

416. Prosciutto Asparagus Bites

(Ready in about 25 minutes | Servings 6)

Ingredients

1 ½ pounds asparagus spears, trimmed
1/2 teaspoon granulated garlic

1/2 teaspoon paprika
1 tablespoon sesame oil
10 slices prosciutto

Directions

Begin by preheating your oven to 380 degrees F.

Toss the asparagus with granulated garlic, paprika, and sesame oil. Now, wrap asparagus spears in prosciutto slices, trying to cover the entire spear.

Bake in the preheated oven for about 20 minutes or until crisp-tender. Bon appétit!

Per serving: 119 Calories; 6.4g Fat; 6.3g Carbs; 10.2g Protein; 3.1g Fiber

417. Cheese and Cauliflower Balls

(Ready in about 35 minutes | Servings 2)

Ingredients

1 tablespoon butter, softened
1 ½ cups cauliflower florets
1 teaspoon Italian seasoning mix

1/2 cup Asiago cheese, grated
1 egg, beaten

Directions

Process the cauliflower in your blender until it has broken down into rice-sized pieces.

Cook the cauliflower in hot butter until it is golden and crisp-tender. Stir in Italian seasoning mix, Asiago cheese, and beaten egg.

Mix to combine well and shape the mixture into balls; flatten each ball with the palm of your hand. Place the balls on a parchment-lined baking pan.

Bake in the preheated oven at 400 degrees F for about 30 minutes. Bon appétit!

Per serving: 236 Calories; 19.2g Fat; 4.5g Carbs; 12.3g Protein; 1.6g Fiber

418. Creamy Anchovy Fat Bombs

(Ready in about 1 hour 10 minutes | Servings 10)

Ingredients

4 ounces canned anchovies, chopped
8 ounces cheddar cheese, shredded

1/2 yellow onion, minced
1 teaspoon fresh garlic, minced
6 ounces cream cheese, at room temperature

Directions

Mix all ingredients until everything is well combined; season with sea salt to taste. Let it chill in your refrigerator for 1 hour.

Roll the mixture into small balls and place on a serving platter.

Serve and enjoy!

Per serving: 122 Calories; 8.9g Fat; 3.2g Carbs; 7.3g Protein; 0g Fiber

419. Classic Vanilla Mini Muffins

(Ready in about 20 minutes | Servings 9)

Ingredients

1 teaspoon vanilla essence
3 ounces double cream
1 ½ cups almond meal

3 eggs
2 tablespoons coconut oil

Directions

Begin by preheating your oven to 370 degrees F.

Beat the eggs, coconut milk, and double cream until well combined.

In a separate mixing bowl, combine almond meal with vanilla and 1 teaspoon of baking powder. Add in zero-carb keto sweetener of choice.

Stir the egg mixture into dry almond mixture. Stir until everything is well incorporated.

Spoon the batter into a lightly-oiled muffin pan. Bake in the preheated oven for about 15 minutes. Enjoy!

Per serving: 85 Calories; 6.4g Fat; 3.1g Carbs; 4.1g Protein; 0g Fiber

420. Italian Keto Squares

(Ready in about 20 minutes | Servings 4)

Ingredients

2 cups mozzarella, shredded
1 ½ cups Romano cheese, grated

1 teaspoon Italian parsley
2 eggs, beaten
2 garlic cloves, crushed

Directions

Start by preheating your oven to 370 degrees F.

Thoroughly combine all ingredients until everything is well mixed.

Using a rolling pin, roll the dough out on a foil-lined baking sheet. Bake in the preheated oven for about 15 minutes until golden-brown around edges.

Cut into squares and serve. Bon appétit!

Per serving: 258 Calories; 12.2g Fat; 3.9g Carbs; 32.6g Protein; 1g Fiber

421. Wings with Marinara Sauce

(Ready in about 50 minutes | Servings 6)

Ingredients

3 pounds chicken wings
1/2 teaspoon paprika
1/2 teaspoon cayenne pepper
Sea salt and ground black pepper, to taste
2 cups marinara sauce

Directions

Begin by preheating your oven to 390 degrees F. Set a wire rack inside a rimmed baking pan.

Toss the chicken wings with paprika, cayenne pepper, salt, black pepper. Bake the wings in the preheated oven for 40 to 45 minutes or until done.

Serve hot wings with marinara sauce on the side. Bon appétit!

Per serving: 309 Calories; 8.2g Fat; 5.2g Carbs; 50g Protein; 1.2g Fiber

422. Bacon Dippers with Chinese Sauce

(Ready in about 45 minutes | Servings 5)

Ingredients

1/2 pound enoki mushrooms
5 slices bacon, cut into halves
2 tablespoons sesame oil
1 large clove of garlic, minced
1 teaspoon Chinese five-spice powder

Directions

Wrap enoki mushrooms with bacon and roll them up. Place the roll-ups on a foil-lined baking pan.

Bake in the preheated oven at 370 degrees F for 35 to 40 minutes, flipping once or twice.

Meanwhile, cook sesame oil, garlic and Chinese five-spice powder along with 1/2 cup of water. Cook until the sauce has reduced by half.

Serve immediately and enjoy!

Per serving: 323 Calories; 33.2g Fat; 4.4g Carbs; 1.5g Protein; 1.4g Fiber

423. Greek Cheese-Artichoke Dip

(Ready in about 25 minutes | Servings 10)

Ingredients

1/2 cup Greek-style yogurt
1/2 cup mayo
10 ounces canned artichoke hearts, drained and chopped
6 ounces cream cheese
20 ounces Monterey-Jack cheese, shredded

Directions

Begin by preheating your oven to 360 degrees F.

Thoroughly combine artichoke hearts, cream cheese, yogurt, and mayo in a lightly oiled baking dish. Pour in 1/2 cup of water.

Top with the shredded cheese and bake in the preheated oven for about 20 minutes or until hot and bubbly. Enjoy!

Per serving: 367 Calories; 31.7g Fat; 5.1g Carbs; 16.2g Protein; 2.4g Fiber

424. Double Cheese Balls with Pecans

(Ready in about 15 minutes + chilling time | Servings 10)

Ingredients

1/4 cup sour cream
1 teaspoon granulated garlic
3/4 cup pecans, finely chopped
10 ounces Swiss cheese, shredded
10 ounces cottage cheese

Directions

Mix the Swiss cheese, cottage cheese, sour cream, and garlic until everything is well incorporated. Add in Mediterranean herb mix, if desired.

Let it cool in your refrigerator at least 2 hours. Shape the mixture into small balls.

Roll the balls over the chopped pecans until they are well coated on all sides. Bon appétit!

Per serving: 199 Calories; 15.5g Fat; 4.7g Carbs; 11.3g Protein; 0.9g Fiber

425. Stuffed Celery Sticks

(Ready in about 15 minutes | Servings 6)

Ingredients

6 stalks celery, cut into halves
4 ounces Coby cheese, shredded
2 scallions, chopped
5 ounces shrimp
10 ounces cottage cheese, at room temperature

Directions

Spritz a frying pan with a nonstick cooking oil. Once hot, cook the shrimp for 2 to 3 minutes, flipping them over to ensure even cooking.

Chop the shrimp and place in a mixing bowl. Stir in in the cheese and scallions; season with salt and black pepper to taste. Stir until everything is well combined.

Divide the mixture between celery sticks and enjoy!

Per serving: 126 Calories; 6.2g Fat; 4.1g Carbs; 13.3g Protein; 0.4g Fiber

426. Bacon-Wrapped Poblano Bites

(Ready in about 35 minutes | Servings 16)

Ingredients

10 ounces cottage cheese, at room temperature

6 ounces Swiss cheese, shredded

1/3 teaspoon mustard seeds

16 poblano peppers, deveined and halved

16 thin slices bacon, sliced lengthwise

Directions

Start by preheating your oven to 395 degrees F.

Combine the cheese and mustard seeds in a mixing bowl.

Divide the mixture between poblano peppers. Wrap your peppers with bacon slices.

Bake in the preheated oven for about 30 minutes until the top is browned. Bon appétit!

Per serving: 183 Calories; 14g Fat; 5.9g Carbs; 9g Protein; 0.7g Fiber

427. Cream Cheese-Stuffed Mushrooms

(Ready in about 45 minutes | Servings 10)

Ingredients

1/4 cup mayonnaise

1/4 teaspoon mustard seeds

1/2 teaspoon celery seeds

20 button mushrooms, stalks removed

6 ounces cream cheese

Directions

Brush mushroom caps with a nonstick cooking spray; place them on a parchment-lined baking pan.

Bake mushroom caps in the preheated oven at 380 degrees F for 35 to 40 minutes until just tender and fragrant.

In a mixing bowl, combine cream cheese, mayo, mustard seeds, and celery seeds; season with the salt and black pepper to taste.

Spoon the mixture into the prepared mushroom caps and serve at room temperature. Enjoy!

Per serving: 103 Calories; 10g Fat; 1.9g Carbs; 2.5g Protein; 0.4g Fiber

VEGETARIAN

428. Easy Cauliflower Fritters

(Ready in about 15 minutes | Servings 5)

Ingredients

1 cup parmesan cheese, shredded

1 egg, beaten

1/2 cup almond meal

1 ½ pounds cauliflower florets

1 celery stalk, chopped

Directions

Process the cauliflower florets and celery in your food processor until they have broken down into rice-sized pieces.

Add in parmesan, egg, and almond meal. Mix until everything is well combined. Season with the salt and black pepper to taste.

Form the mixture into 5 equal patties.

In a nonstick skillet, heat 2 tablespoons of sesame oil. Once hot, fry the patties for 3 to 4 minutes per side. Serve warm and enjoy!

Per serving: 173 Calories; 10.7g Fat; 6.9g Carbs; 10.8g Protein; 2.9g Fiber

429. Avocado and Cucumber Salad

(Ready in about 5 minutes | Servings 4)

Ingredients

1 Lebanese cucumber, sliced

3 teaspoons fresh lemon juice

2 tablespoons extra-virgin olive oil

1 avocado, peeled, pitted and sliced

1/2 white onion, chopped

Directions

Combine avocado, onion, and cucumber in a salad bowl.

Drizzle lemon juice and extra-virgin olive oil over everything.

Taste, adjust seasonings, and serve well chilled. Bon appétit!

Per serving: 149 Calories; 14.3g Fat; 5.8g Carbs; 1.4g Protein; 3.6g Fiber

430. Greek Autumn Casserole

(Ready in about 1 hour 25 minutes | Servings 5)

Ingredients

1 cup Greek-style yogurt

5 eggs, beaten

1 ½ cups feta cheese, grated

1 pound aubergine cut into rounds

2 vine-ripe tomatoes, sliced

Directions

Toss the aubergine with 1 teaspoon of sea salt; let it sit for 25 minutes. Discard excess water and pat your aubergine dry with kitchen towel.

Now, place aubergine rounds in a lightly greased baking pan. Brush them with a nonstick oil and roast them at 380 degrees F for about 35 to 40 minutes or until tender.

Lay the roasted aubergine rounds on the bottom of a lightly greased casserole dish. Top with sliced tomatoes.

Then, whisk Greek yogurt with eggs. Pour the mixture over the roasted aubergine rounds. Top with feta cheese and continue to bake in the preheated oven at 365 degrees F for about 15 minutes. Enjoy!

Per serving: 226 Calories; 14.1g Fat; 6.8g Carbs; 16.3g Protein; 2.8g Fiber

431. Creamy Swiss Chard with Cheese

(Ready in about 15 minutes | Servings 6)

Ingredients

1 ½ pounds Swiss chard

1/2 cup vegetable broth

1 cup sour cream

1 yellow onion, chopped

2 garlic cloves, minced

Directions

Melt 2 tablespoons of butter in a sauté pan over medium-high heat. Sauté the onion for 3 to 4 minutes until tender and translucent.

Stir in the garlic and continue to cook until aromatic or about 30 seconds. Season with the salt and black pepper.

Stir in the Swiss chard and broth; continue to cook, partially covered, for 5 to 6 minutes over medium-low heat. Fold in the sour cream.

Ladle into individual bowls and serve warm.

Per serving: 149 Calories; 11.1g Fat; 6.6g Carbs; 5.4g Protein; 2.2g Fiber

432. Chanterelle Omelet with Peppers

(Ready in about 20 minutes | Servings 4)

Ingredients

6 eggs

1 cup Chanterelle mushrooms, chopped

1 white onion, chopped

2 bell peppers, chopped

2 tablespoons olive oil

Directions

In a frying pan, heat olive oil over moderate flame. Now, cook the mushrooms, onion, and peppers for 3 to 4 minutes until they are tender and fragrant.

Whisk the eggs until pale and frothy. Pour the eggs into the skillet and turn the heat to medium-low.

Let it cook for 4 to 5 minutes until the eggs are done and center of the omelet starts to look dry.

Serve warm and enjoy!

Per serving: 239 Calories; 17.5g Fat; 6.1g Carbs; 12.3g Protein; 1.8g Fiber

433. Japanese-Style Shirataki Noodle Ramen

(Ready in about 20 minutes | Servings 4)

Ingredients

1 ½ tablespoons ghee, melted
1 pound brown mushrooms, chopped

2 tablespoons green onions, chopped
4 cups roasted vegetable broth
8 ounces shirataki noodles

Directions

In a heavy-bottomed pot, melt the ghee over medium-high heat. Sauté the mushrooms for about 3 minutes or until they release liquid.

Add in green onions and continue sautéing an additional 2 minutes. Season with black pepper and salt to taste.

Add in the vegetable broth and bring to a boil. Turn the heat to simmer.

Continue to cook for about 10 minutes. Fold in the shirataki noodles and cook according to package directions. Bon appétit!

Per serving: 76 Calories; 5g Fat; 5.3g Carbs; 3.8g Protein; 0.9g Fiber

434. Vegetables in Creamy Sauce

(Ready in about 15 minutes | Servings 3)

Ingredients

1 white onion, chopped
1 bell pepper
1/2 pound cauliflower florets

1/2 pound savoy cabbage, shredded
1 cup double cream

Directions

Heat 2 tablespoons of olive oil in a saucepan over medium-high heat. Cook the onion until tender and fragrant about 4 minutes.

Stir in the bell pepper, cauliflower, and savoy cabbage; pour in 1 cup of water or mushroom soup.

Turn the heat to medium-low and let it cook for about 10 minutes until everything is heated through.

Fold in the double cream and let it simmer, partially covered, for about 3 minutes. Taste, adjust seasonings and serve warm.

Per serving: 256 Calories; 24g Fat; 6.5g Carbs; 3g Protein; 2.9g Fiber

435. Asparagus Frittata with Halloumi Cheese

(Ready in about 25 minutes | Servings 4)

Ingredients

5 whole eggs, beaten
10 ounces Halloumi cheese, crumbled
1/2 red onion, sliced

1 tomato, chopped
4 ounces asparagus, cut into small chunks

Directions

Heat 1 tablespoon of oil in a frying pan over medium-high heat; then, sauté the onion and asparagus for 3 to 4 minutes, stirring periodically to ensure even cooking.

Stir in tomato and cook for 2 to 3 minutes more. Place the sautéed vegetables in a lightly greased casserole dish.

Combine the eggs with cheese and pour the mixture over the vegetables. Bake in the preheated oven at 360 degrees F for 13 to 15 minutes.

Garnish with 2 tablespoons of Greek olives if desired. Enjoy!

Per serving: 376 Calories; 29.1g Fat; 4g Carbs; 24.5g Protein; 1g Fiber

436. Cheese and Kale Casserole

(Ready in about 35 minutes | Servings 4)

Ingredients

1 cup Cheddar cheese, grated
1 cup Romano cheese
4 eggs, whisked

2 tablespoons sour cream
6 ounces kale, torn into pieces

Directions

Begin by preheating your oven to 360 degrees F. Brush the sides and bottom of a casserole dish with a nonstick cooking spray.

Thoroughly combine the ingredients and pour the mixture into the casserole dish.

Bake in the preheated oven for about 35 minutes or until the top is golden brown. Salt to taste. Bon appétit!

Per serving: 384 Calories; 29.1g Fat; 5.9g Carbs; 25.1g Protein; 1.5g Fiber

437. Spicy Peppery Eggs

(Ready in about 15 minutes | Servings 2)

Ingredients

4 eggs, whisked
4 tablespoons full-fat yogurt
2 bell peppers, chopped

1 onion, sliced
3 ounces cheddar cheese, shredded

Directions

In a frying pan, heat 2 tablespoons of olive oil over medium-high heat. Sauté the peppers and onion for about 3 minutes until they have softened.

Whisk the eggs with yogurt. Pour the egg mixture into the frying pan. Season with pepper and salt to taste.

Cook the eggs for 5 to 6 minutes until they are set. Top with cheddar cheese and serve warm.

Per serving: 439 Calories; 36.7g Fat; 3.8g Carbs; 22.9g Protein; 0.1g Fiber

438. Old-Fashioned Green Chowder

(Ready in about 25 minutes | Servings 4)

Ingredients

1/2 cup scallions, chopped
2 zucchinis, sliced
1 celery stalk, chopped
4 ounces baby spinach
1 egg, beaten

Directions

In a heavy-bottomed pot, heat 1 tablespoon of oil over medium-high flame. Now, cook the scallions for about 3 minutes until tender and aromatic.

Add in 4 cups of water, zucchini, and celery; add in 1 tablespoons of vegetable bouillon powder, if desired.

Let it cook, partially covered, for about 15 minutes. Fold in spinach and continue to cook for 5 to 6 minutes more.

Afterwards, add in the egg and stir to combine well. Serve immediately, drizzled with melted butter, if desired.

Per serving: 85 Calories; 5.9g Fat; 3.8g Carbs; 3.7g Protein; 1.3g Fiber

439. Tofu Salad with Peppers

(Ready in about 15 minutes | Servings 4)

Ingredients

1 (14-ounce) tofu block, pressed and cubed
2 tablespoons fresh lemon juice
2 tablespoons extra-virgin olive oil
4 bell peppers, deveined and halved
2 scallions, chopped

Directions

Brush a frying pan with cooking spray. Cook the tofu cubes for about 3 minutes over medium-high heat; reserve.

Then, cook the peppers for 4 to 5 minutes, stirring periodically to ensure even cooking.

Toss the scallions and peppers with lemon juice and and olive oil. Top your salad with tofu cubes and enjoy!

Per serving: 155 Calories; 11.4g Fat; 6.4g Carbs; 8.6g Protein; 1.1g Fiber

440. Cheese and Zucchini Bake

(Ready in about 50 minutes | Servings 5)

Ingredients

2 zucchini, sliced
1/2 medium-sized leek, sliced
10 large eggs
3 tablespoons yogurt
2 cups Swiss cheese, shredded

Directions

Preheat your oven to 350 degrees F. Brush an oven-proof skillet with a nonstick cooking spray.

Place 1/2 of the zucchini in the skillet; place the leek slices on zucchini layer. Season with salt, and black pepper to your liking.

Add the remaining zucchini and leek.

Whisk the eggs and yogurt until well combined and frothy. Add the egg mixture and top with cheese.

Bake in the preheated oven for 35 to 40 minutes, until the top is hot and bubbly. Enjoy!

Per serving: 371 Calories; 32g Fat; 5.2g Carbs; 15.7g Protein; 0.3g Fiber

441. Dad's Keto Crêpes

(Ready in about 50 minutes | Servings 5)

Ingredients

2 tablespoons coconut oil
2 tablespoons toasted coconut
3 tablespoons peanut butter
4 eggs, well whisked
4 ounces cream cheese

Directions

In a mixing bowl, whisk the eggs and cream cheese until well combined.

Melt coconut oil in a frying pan over medium-high flame.

Cook each crêpe for 3 to 4 minutes per side. Serve with peanut butter and toasted coconut. Bon appétit!

Per serving: 248 Calories; 21.7g Fat; 5.7g Carbs; 9.1g Protein; 0.6g Fiber

442. Loaded Broccoli and Cheese Bake

(Ready in about 35 minutes | Servings 6)

Ingredients

3/4 pounds broccoli florets
6 eggs
6 ounces sour cream
1 cup vegetable broth
6 ounces Swiss cheese, shredded

Directions

Parboil broccoli in a pot of lightly-salted water for 2 to 3 minutes.

Brush the sides and bottom of a casserole dish with nonstick cooking spray. In a mixing bowl, combine the eggs, sour cream, and broth.

Place the broccoli florets on the bottom of the casserole dish. Pour the egg mixture over the broccoli. Top with Swiss cheese.

Bake in the preheated oven at 370 degrees for about 25 minutes. Bon appétit!

Per serving: 241 Calories; 16.3g Fat; 5.5g Carbs; 16.4g Protein; 1.5g Fiber

443. Authentic Zuppa alla Marinara with Broccoli

(Ready in about 30 minutes | Servings 3)

Ingredients

1 cup spinach leaves, torn into pieces
1 cup marinara sauce
4 ounces broccoli
2 tablespoons sesame oil
1 small-sized onion, chopped

Directions

Chopp the broccoli into small grain sized pieces; reserve.

Heat sesame oil in a frying pan over a moderate heat. Sauté the onion until tender and aromatic.

Stir in broccoli and cook for 2 to 3 minutes more. Add in marinara sauce along with 3 cups of water or vegetable broth. Season with Italian spice mix, if desired.

Bring to a boil; turn the heat to medium-low and continue to simmer for 20 to 25 minutes.

Fold in spinach leaves, cover, and let it sit in the residual heat for 10 minutes. Bon appétit!

Per serving: 130 Calories; 9.4g Fat; 8.8g Carbs; 2.9g Protein; 2.2g Fiber

444. Mexican Stuffed Peppers

(Ready in about 45 minutes | Servings 3)

Ingredients

1 ripe tomato, pureed
1 cup Mexican cheese blend
1 garlic clove, minced
3 bell peppers, halved, seeds removed
3 eggs, whisked

Directions

Preheat your oven to 380 degrees F. Brush the bottom and sides of a baking dish with a nonstick cooking spray.

Then, combine the eggs, cheese, and garlic; add in chili powder, if desired. Stuff the peppers and place them in the baking pan.

Pour the tomato puree into the baking dish. Bake, covered, for 35 to 40 minutes, until everything is thoroughly cooked. Bon appétit!

Per serving: 194 Calories; 13.9g Fat; 3.5g Carbs; 13.3g Protein; 0.7g Fiber

445. Pan-Fried Tofu with Vegetables

(Ready in about 15 minutes | Servings 2)

Ingredients

6 ounces firm tofu, pressed and cubed
1/2 avocado, pitted, peeled and sliced
2 cups enoki mushrooms
1 red bell pepper, sliced
4 tablespoons scallions, chopped

Directions

In a frying pan, heat 1 teaspoon of the olive oil over a moderate heat. Once hot, fry the tofu cubes for 3 to 4 minutes, stirring periodically; reserve.

In the same frying pan, heat the remaining teaspoon of olive oil. Now, sauté the scallions, peppers, and mushrooms for about 3 minutes or until they have softened.

Sprinkle the sautéed vegetables with salt and black pepper. Top with the reserved tofu. Garnish with avocado and serve.

Per serving: 217 Calories; 17g Fat; 7.5g Carbs; 11.5g Protein; 4.5g Fiber

446. Baked Avocado Egg Cups

(Ready in about 20 minutes | Servings 4)

Ingredients

1 cup Asiago cheese, grated
1/2 teaspoon dried rosemary
1 tablespoon fresh chives, chopped
2 avocados, pitted and halved
4 eggs

Directions

Start by preheating your oven to 410 degrees F.

Crack an egg into each avocado half. Season with salt and black pepper to taste.

Top with cheese and rosemary.

Bake in the preheated oven for 15 to 17 minutes. Garnish with fresh chives and enjoy!

Per serving: 300 Calories; 24.6g Fat; 5.4g Carbs; 14.9g Protein; 4.6g Fiber

447. Breakfast Keto Veggies

(Ready in about 25 minutes | Servings 4)

Ingredients

4 eggs
1 cup green cabbage, shredded
2 cups broccoli florets
1 shallot, sliced
2 bell peppers, deseeded and sliced

Directions

In a large skillet, heat 2 tablespoons of olive oil over medium-high heat. Cook the shallots and peppers until they've softened.

Fold in the cabbage and broccoli; pour in 1/2 cup of onion soup (preferably homemade). Turn the temperature to medium-low.

Continue to simmer for 10 to 13 minutes or until cooked through. Create four indentations in the vegetable mixture. Crack an egg into each indentation.

Cook for 8 to 11 minutes more until the eggs are cooked to desired doneness. Enjoy!

Per serving: 172 Calories; 11.1g Fat; 8g Carbs; 8.2g Protein; 2.8g Fiber

448. Green Cabbage with Tofu

(Ready in about 20 minutes | Servings 3)

Ingredients

1 (1.5-pounds) head green cabbage, cut into strips
1/2 cup vegetable broth
6 ounces tofu, diced
1/2 shallot, chopped
2 garlic cloves, finely chopped

Directions

Spritz a saucepan with a nonstick cooking oil. Fry the tofu in the preheated saucepan for about 5 minutes until crisp; reserve, keeping it warm.

Then, cook the shallot and garlic for 3 minutes longer until tender and aromatic. Stir in cabbage and beef bone broth.

Turn the temperature to simmer and let it cook, partially covered, for 10 to 12 minutes. Season with salt and pepper to taste.

Serve with reserved fried tofu and enjoy!

Per serving: 167 Calories; 11.8g Fat; 5.1g Carbs; 10.6g Protein; 2.4g Fiber

449. Roasted Asparagus Salad

(Ready in about 25 minutes | Servings 3)

Ingredients

3 tablespoons extra-virgin olive oil
1 cup cherry tomatoes, sliced
1 tablespoon Dijon mustard
1/2 lime, freshly squeezed
1 pound asparagus, trimmed

Directions

Place the asparagus spears on a lightly greased baking sheet and roast them at 390 degrees F for about 15 minutes.

In a small mixing dish, whisk the mustard, lime juice, and olive oil; add in minced garlic, if desired.

Cut the asparagus spears into small chunks and toss them with the prepared dressing. Top with cherry tomatoes and serve well-chilled.

Per serving: 159 Calories; 12.3g Fat; 6.1g Carbs; 5.8g Protein; 3.9g Fiber

450. Traditional Indian Saar

(Ready in about 30 minutes | Servings 4)

Ingredients

2 cups Indian masala sauce
1 cup full-fat yogurt
1 ½ tablespoons ghee
1 medium-sized leek, sliced
1 bell pepper, roughly chopped

Directions

Melt the ghee in a soup pot over a moderate heat. Now, cook the leek and peppers until they've softened.

Stir in Indian masala sauce and water, bringing to a boil; reduce the heat to medium-low. Let it simmer, covered, for 20 to 23 minutes.

Puree your soup in a blender and serve warm with yogurt on the side. Enjoy!

Per serving: 113 Calories; 5.5g Fat; 9.3g Carbs; 5.4g Protein; 2.5g Fiber

451. Roasted Cauliflower with Feta Cheese

(Ready in about 45 minutes | Servings 4)

Ingredients

1 pound cauliflower, halved
1 tablespoon Greek seasoning blend
1 cup feta cheese, crumbled
1 medium-sized leek, cut into 2-inch pieces
2 tablespoons olive oil

Directions

Pat cauliflower dry with paper towels.

Brush cauliflower and leeks with olive oil; sprinkle your veggies with Greek seasoning blend.

Place the cauliflower and leeks on a foil-lined baking sheet.

Roast in the predated oven at 380 degrees F for about 40 minutes, turning them over halfway through cooking. Serve with feta cheese and enjoy!

Per serving: 194 Calories; 15g Fat; 5.7g Carbs; 7.4g Protein; 2.5g Fiber

452. Broccoli Salad with Horseradish Mayo

(Ready in about 30 minutes | Servings 6)

Ingredients

1 tablespoon prepared horseradish
1 shallot, sliced
1/2 cup mayonnaise
6 cups broccoli florets
2 tablespoons balsamic vinegar

Directions

Roast the broccoli florets in the preheated oven at 420 degrees F for about 20 minutes until little charred.

Toss the roasted broccoli florets with the remaining ingredients; toss to combine well.

Serve at room temperature or well-chilled. Bon appétit!

Per serving: 170 Calories; 14.1g Fat; 7g Carbs; 3.1g Protein; 2.8g Fiber

453. Vegetable Noodles with Avocado Sauce

(Ready in about 10 minutes | Servings 3)

Ingredients

1 avocado, peeled and pitted
1/2 lemon, juiced and zested
1 zucchini
1 cucumber
2 garlic cloves, peeled

Directions

Spiralize the zucchini and cucumber.

In a frying pan, heat 2 tablespoons of olive oil over medium-high heat. Once hot, cook vegetable noodles for 5 to 6 minutes.

Meanwhile, puree the remaining ingredients until creamy and smooth. Pour the sauce over vegetable noodles and serve immediately.

Per serving: 181 Calories; 16.2g Fat; 6.9g Carbs; 2.1g Protein; 4.1g Fiber

454. Cream of Cauliflower and Ginger Soup

(Ready in about 20 minutes | Servings 4)

Ingredients

1 pound cauliflower florets
1/2 teaspoon ginger-garlic paste
3 cups vegetable broth
2 green onions, chopped
1 celery stalk, chopped

Directions

Preheat a heavy-bottomed pot over a medium-high heat. Sauté green onions until they are just tender and aromatic.

Stir in the celery, ginger-garlic paste, cauliflower, and vegetable broth, bringing to a boil. Immediately reduce heat to simmer.

Let it simmer for 15 to 16 minutes more or until everything is thoroughly cooked; remove from heat.

Puree the soup in your food processor and serve warm!

Per serving: 69 Calories; 1.5g Fat; 7g Carbs; 6.2g Protein; 3g Fiber

455. Cheesy Broccoli Casserole

(Ready in about 30 minutes | Servings 5)

Ingredients

1/2 cup heavy cream
1 pound broccoli florets
1 cup yellow onion, sliced
1 cup Colby cheese, shredded
2 cloves garlic, smashed

Directions

Start by preheating your oven to 380 degrees F. Brush the sides and bottom of a casserole dish with a nonstick cooking oil.

Parboil broccoli florets for about 3 minutes until just tender. Place the broccoli in the prepared casserole dish.

Stir in yellow onion and garlic. Now, whisk the heavy cream with the 1 cup of vegetable broth. Season with salt and black pepper to taste.

Pour the cream/broth mixture over the vegetables and bake at 390 degrees F for about 20 minutes.

Top with Colby cheese and continue to bake for 5 to 6 minutes more or until the top is hot and bubbly. Bon appétit!

Per serving: 194 Calories; 14.2g Fat; 7.2g Carbs; 9.3g Protein; 2.7g Fiber

456. Peppery Red Cabbage Soup

(Ready in about 30 minutes | Servings 6)

Ingredients

1 cup broccoli florets
1 pound red cabbage, shredded
1 cup tomato puree
2 tablespoons canola oil
2 bell peppers, chopped

Directions

Ina stockpot, heat the canola oil over medium-high heat. Sauté the bell peppers and broccoli for 4 to 5 minutes or until they are just tender and fragrant.

Stir in red cabbage and tomato puree along with 5 cups of water (or vegetable broth). Reduce heat to simmer.

Partially cover and let it simmer for 25 to 30 minutes. Enjoy!

Per serving: 82 Calories; 4.1g Fat; 6g Carbs; 2.1g Protein; 2.6g Fiber

457. Mediterranean-Style Zucchini Salad

(Ready in about 15 minutes | Servings 5)

Ingredients

1 ½ pounds zucchini, sliced
2 tomatoes, sliced
4 ounces goat cheese, crumbled
4 tablespoons extra-virgin olive oil, divided
1 red onion, sliced

Directions

Begin by preheating your oven to 420 degrees F.

Toss zucchini slices with 2 tablespoons of olive oil; season with Mediterranean spice mix. Place them on a baking sheet.

Roast in the preheated for about 11 minutes. Gently stir roasted zucchini with red onion and tomatoes.

Drizzle remaining 2 tablespoons of olive oil along with 2 tablespoons of vinegar. Top with goat cheese and serve immediately!

Per serving: 186 Calories; 13.5g Fat; 6.6g Carbs; 11.2g Protein; 2.2g Fiber

458. Mediterranean-Style Cauliflower Au Gratin

(Ready in about 1 hour | Servings 2)

Ingredients

5 ounces sour cream
2 eggs, whisked
3 ounces Provolone cheese, freshly grated
1/2 pound small cauliflower florets
2 scallions, chopped

Directions

Start by prehating your oven to 365 degrees F.

In a saucepan, barboil the cauliflower florets over medium-low heat until just tender. Place the cauliflower florets in a lightly oiled baking dish.

Thoroughly combine the scallions, eggs, sour cream, salt, and black pepper. Pour the cream/egg mixture over the cauliflower florets.

Top with grated Provolone cheese and cover with a piece of foil.

Bake for 40 to 45 minutes or until everything is thoroughly cooked. Bon appétit!

Per serving: 342 Calories; 23.3g Fat; 8g Carbs; 21.3g Protein; 2.7g Fiber

459. Cauliflower Tabbouleh Salad

(Ready in about 15 minutes | Servings 2)

Ingredients

1/2 cup cherry tomatoes, halved

1 Lebanese cucumber, diced

2 tablespoons extra-virgin olive oil

1 cup cauliflower florets

1/2 white onion, thinly sliced

Directions

Process the cauliflower in your food processor until it has broken into rice-sized chunks.

Cook cauli rice in a lightly-oiled frying pan over a moderate flame for about 9 minutes.

Toss cauliflower rice with onion, tomatoes, cucumber, and olive oil. Enjoy!

Per serving: 180 Calories; 16.1g Fat; 7g Carbs; 2.7g Protein; 2.7g Fiber

460. Classic Mushroom Stew

(Ready in about 20 minutes | Servings 4)

Ingredients

1 pound brown mushrooms, chopped

1/2 cup leeks, chopped

2 ripe tomatoes, pureed

1 teaspoon garlic, minced

1 medium-sized zucchini, diced

Directions

Heat a lightly-oiled soup pot over medium-high heat. Sauté the leeks and mushrooms until they are softened and mushrooms release liquid.

Now, stir in the garlic and zucchini, and continue to sauté for 2 to 3 minutes more or until they've softened.

Add in tomatoes along with 2 cups of water. Season with Sazón spice, if desired.

Cover part-way and continue to simmer for about 10 minutes. Enjoy!

Per serving: 108 Calories; 7.5g Fat; 7g Carbs; 3.14g Protein; 2.5g Fiber

461. Mediterranean Cauliflower Chowder

(Ready in about 30 minutes | Servings 4)

Ingredients

1 pound cauliflower florets

1 white onion, chopped

1 cup half and half

1 tablespoon butter, softened at room temperature

1/2 stalk celery, chopped

Directions

In a heavy-bottomed pot, melt the butter over medium-high flame. Sauté the celery and onion until they've softened.

Stir in the cauliflower; season with sea salt, black pepper, and Mediterranean spice mix, if desired; continue to sauté for a further 2 minutes.

Pour in 4 cups of water (or vegetable broth), bringing to a boil. Turn the heat to medium-low and continue to simmer for 20 to 25 minutes

Puree the chowder in your food processor and stir in the half and half. Continue to cook for 5 minutes more or until your chowder is thoroughly cooked. Enjoy!

Per serving: 172 Calories; 14.7g Fat; 7g Carbs; 3.1g Protein; 2.9g Fiber

462. Neufchatel Cheese Balls with Nuts

(Ready in about 10 minutes | Servings 6)

Ingredients

4 ounces Neufchatel cheese

4 ounces blue cheese

2 tablespoons fresh parsley, chopped

2 tablespoons fresh cilantro, chopped

8 tablespoons walnuts, finely chopped

Directions

In a mixing bowl, combine the cheese, parsley, and cilantro; season with the salt and black pepper to your liking.

Shape the mixture into 8 balls; roll them over the chopped walnuts until well coated. Serve well-chilled.

Per serving: 183 Calories; 15.9g Fat; 2.9g Carbs; 8.4g Protein; 0.9g Fiber

463. Mushroom Stroganoff with Sour Cream

(Ready in about 25 minutes | Servings 5)

Ingredients

2 tablespoons olive oil

1/2 cup onion, minced

1 ½ pounds button mushrooms, sliced

2 tablespoons marinara sauce

1 cup sour cream

Directions

Heat the olive oil in a large stockpot over the highest setting. Then, sauté the onion for 3 to 4 minutes until just tender and translucent.

Now, melt 1 tablespoon of butter in the same pot and cook the mushrooms for about 4 minutes until they release liquid. Add in marinara sauce and 4 cups of water (or vegetable stock).

Reduce the heat to simmer; cover part-way and continue to cook for a further 15 to 20 minutes.

Serve with sour cream and enjoy!

Per serving: 166 Calories; 13g Fat; 7g Carbs; 6g Protein; 1.6g Fiber

464. Keto Seed and Nut Granola

(Ready in about 30 minutes | Servings 10)

Ingredients

1/3 cup sunflower seeds
1/3 cup flaxseed meal
1 cup coconut, shredded, unsweetened
1 cup pecans, chopped
1/2 stick butter

Directions

Start by preheating your oven to 300 degrees F.

In a mixing bowl, combine all ingredients until everything is well incorporated. Pour in 1/4 cup water and stir again. Add in vanilla and cinnamon, if desired.

Spread the mixture in a thin layer on a parchment-lined cookie sheet. Bake in the preheated oven for 25 to 28 minutes.

Transfer to wire racks to cool completely. Devour!

Per serving: 162 Calories; 15.5g Fat; 4.6g Carbs; 3.2g Protein; 2.9g Fiber

465. Chinese Stir-Fry

(Ready in about 15 minutes | Servings 5)

Ingredients

1 ½ pounds Chinese cabbage, shredded
2 garlic cloves, minced
1 tablespoon Shaoxing wine
3 tablespoons sesame oil
1 shallot, sliced

Directions

In a wok, warm the sesame oil until sizzling. Once hot, cook the shallot and garlic for 2 to 3 minutes until they've softened. Add in Shaoxing wine to deglaze the pan.

Stir in Chinese cabbage and stir-fry for 5 to 6 minutes more. Season with salt and Sichuan peppercorns, if desired.

Serve in individual bowls and enjoy!

Per serving: 108 Calories; 8.5g Fat; 7.5g Carbs; 2.2g Protein; 2.3g Fiber

466. Breakfast Green Salad with Eggs

(Ready in about 15 minutes | Servings 3)

Ingredients

1 roasted pepper in oil, drained and chopped
1 tomato, diced
2 tablespoons extra-virgin olive oil
4 eggs
1/2 pound spinach

Directions

Place eggs in a saucepan and cover them with water by 1 inch. Let it boil for about 7 minutes over medium-high heat.

Toss the spinach, red pepper, tomato, and olive oil in a salad bowl. Drizzle 2 tablespoons of vinegar and olive oil over your vegetables.

Garnish with sliced eggs and enjoy!

Per serving: 156 Calories; 10g Fat; 7g Carbs; 10.4g Protein; 2.6g Fiber

467. Italian Insalata Caprese

(Ready in about 10 minutes | Servings 4)

Ingredients

1/2 cup mayonnaise
1/2 cup mozzarella cheese
8 ounces arugula
1 tomato, sliced
1/2 cup olives, pitted and halved

Directions

Toss the arugula, tomato, and olives in a salad bowl. Add in mayonnaise and toss again to combine well.

Top with mozzarella. Taste and adjust seasonings.

Serve garnished with fresh basil and enjoy!

Per serving: 245 Calories; 22.7g Fat; 3.9g Carbs; 6.3g Protein; 1.7g Fiber

468. Vegetable Stir Fry with Cheese

(Ready in about 20 minutes | Servings 3)

Ingredients

3 eggs
3 ounces Asiago cheese, shredded
2 cups white mushrooms, sliced
1 cup cauliflower rice
2 tomatoes, pureed

Directions

In a wok, heat 1 tablespoon of the sesame oil over medium-high flame. Sauté the mushrooms for 3 to 4 minutes until they release liquid; reserve.

Heat another 2 tablespoons of sesame oil. Now, cook the cauliflower rice for about 4 minutes or until tender. Return the reserved mushrooms to the wok.

Add in tomatoes and continue to cook for 2 to 3 minutes longer; season with Five-spice powder, if desired.

Heat 1 tablespoon of sesame oil; now, cook the eggs over a moderate flame for 4 to 5 minutes to desired doneness.

Top the vegetables with the fried eggs, garnish with cheese, and serve warm. Enjoy!

Per serving: 338 Calories; 28.4g Fat; 9.2g Carbs; 13g Protein; 2.2g Fiber

469. Greek-Style Zucchini Lasagna

(Ready in about 1 hour 20 minutes | Servings 2)

Ingredients

1/2 pound chestnut mushrooms, chopped
1/2 cup Greek-style yogurt
1/2 cup Provolone cheese, grated
1 large-sized zucchini, sliced lengthwise
1 cup tomato sauce with onion and garlic, no sugar added

Directions

Place the zucchini slices and 1 teaspoon of salt in a bowl with a colander; let it sit for 15 minutes and gently squeeze to discard the excess water.

Grill your zucchini for about 5 minutes and reserve.

Heat 1 tablespoon of olive oil in a frying pan over medium-high flame. Sauté the mushrooms until they are tender and fragrant. Add in the Greek spice mix if desired.

Stir in tomato sauce and continue to cook for 5 to 6 minutes longer.

Spread the mushroom sauce on the bottom of a lightly oiled casserole dish. Place the zucchini slices on top.

Mix Greek yogurt and Provolone cheese. Top your casserole with the cheese mixture.

Bake in the preheated oven at 380 degrees F for 42 to 45 minutes until the edges are hot and bubbly.

Per serving: 338 Calories; 23.3g Fat; 7.9g Carbs; 17.7g Protein; 3g Fiber

470. Braised Cabbage with Brown Mushrooms

(Ready in about 15 minutes | Servings 3)

Ingredients

2 tablespoons canola oil
2 cups brown mushrooms, sliced
3/4 pound green cabbage, shredded
1/2 cup cream of mushroom soup
1/2 cup onion, chopped

Directions

In a soup pot, heat canola oil over a moderate heat. Sauté the onion for about 4 minutes until translucent.

Fold in the mushrooms and continue sautéing for 3 to 4 minutes, stirring continuously to ensure even cooking.

Add in the cabbage and soup. Continue to simmer for about 9 minutes until cooked through. Bon appétit!

Per serving: 133 Calories; 9.4g Fat; 7.5g Carbs; 3.9g Protein; 4.3g Fiber

471. Festive Keto Coleslaw

(Ready in about 15 minutes | Servings 5)

Ingredients

4 tablespoons shallots, chopped
1 teaspoon garlic, minced
1 cup fresh cauliflower, chopped
1 cup green cabbage, shredded
1/3 cup mayonnaise

Directions

Place the shallots, garlic, cauliflower, and cabbage in a salad bowl.

Toss the vegetables with mayonnaise; you can add salt, pepper, and fresh lemon juice to taste.

Serve well chilled and enjoy!

Per serving: 121 Calories; 8.5g Fat; 6.8g Carbs; 3.3g Protein; 2.3g Fiber

472. Easy Family Ratatouille

(Ready in about 1 hour 10 minutes | Servings 6)

Ingredients

2 yellow onions, sliced
1 cup tomato sauce with onion and garlic, no sugar added
3 bell peppers, sliced
1 medium-sized Japanese eggplant, cut into rounds
2 medium-sized zucchinis, cut into rounds

Directions

Preheat your oven to 380 degrees F. Toss the vegetables with 3 tablespoons of extra-virgin olive oil.

Arrange the vegetables in the casserole dish. Add in tomato sauce along with Herbes de Provence, if used.

Cover with foil and bake for 30 to 35 minutes. Remove the foil and continue to bake an additional 25 minutes or until heated through.

Allow Ratatouille to rest for a couple of minutes before serving. Enjoy!

Per serving: 104 Calories; 7.2g Fat; 6.7g Carbs; 1.6g Protein; 2.7g Fiber

473. Middle Eastern Eggplant with Tahini

(Ready in about 30 minutes | Servings 7)

Ingredients

1 avocado, pitted, peeled and mashed
2 tablespoons tahini
1 teaspoon garlic paste
2 pounds eggplant, sliced
3 teaspoons avocado oil

Directions

Start by preheating your oven to 410 degrees F.

Brush the bottom of a baking sheet pan with nonstick cooking oil. Place the eggplant slices on the prepared pan; drizzle 2 teaspoons of avocado oil over eggplant slices.

Roast in the preheated oven approximately 20 minutes.

In the meantime, mix tahini with garlic paste; add in brown mustard, if desired.

Divide the tahini mixture between the eggplant slices and place under the preheated broiler for 4 to 5 minutes. Top with the mashed avocado and enjoy!

Per serving: 94 Calories; 6g Fat; 6.7g Carbs; 2.5g Protein; 4.1g Fiber

474. Skinny Avocado Smoothie Bowl

(Ready in about 5 minutes | Servings 2)

Ingredients

1/2 ripe avocado, peeled and pitted
2 teaspoons sunflower seeds
2 tablespoons sesame seeds
1 teaspoon ground cinnamon
1/2 cup canned coconut milk

Directions

Place all ingredients in a bowl of your food processor; add in 1/2 cup of water and process until creamy and smooth.

Divide your smoothie between two serving bowls and enjoy!

Per serving: 286 Calories; 28g Fat; 7.4g Carbs; 4.7g Protein; 2.4g Fiber

475. Swiss Cauliflower and Cheese Dip

(Ready in about 10 minutes | Servings 8)

Ingredients

5 ounces Swiss cheese, grated
1/2 teaspoon dried oregano
1/2 teaspoon dried basil
1 cup double cream
1/2 pound cauliflower

Directions

Parboil the cauliflower until crisp-tender; mash with a potato masher and season with the salt and black pepper to your liking.

Add in oregano and basil and stir to combine.

In a sauté pan, melt the cream and cheese over low heat. Stir in the mashed cauliflower and let it simmer for 5 minutes or until everything is heated through.

Bon appétit!

Per serving: 129 Calories; 10.4g Fat; 3.4g Carbs; 5.7g Protein; 0.7g Fiber

476. Classic Vegetable Chowder

(Ready in about 40 minutes | Servings 5)

Ingredients

1/4 cup dry white wine
1 cup heavy cream
1 cup celery, chopped
5 cups vegetable broth
1/2 cup shallots, chopped

Directions

Warm 1 tablespoon of olive oil in a soup pot until sizzling. Cook the shallots and celery until they've softened.

Stir in vegetable broth and wine and bring to a rolling boil. Turn the heat to simmer and continue to cook, partially covered, for 25 to 30 minutes.

Fold in the cream and continue to simmer for about 7 minutes. Enjoy!

Per serving: 131 Calories; 12.8g Fat; 2.5g Carbs; 2.2g Protein; 0.6g Fiber

477. Zucchini Noodles with Cheese (Zoodles)

(Ready in about 20 minutes | Servings 3)

Ingredients

2 green onions, chopped
2 vine-ripe tomatoes, pureed
3/4 pound zucchini, spiralized
1 cup Asiago cheese, shredded
2 green garlic stalks, chopped

Directions

Melt 1 tablespoon of butter in a saucepan over medium-high flame. Sauté green onions and garlic until they've softened.

Stir in pureed tomatoes, bringing the sauce to just below boiling point. Season with the salt and black pepper to your taste.

Continue to cook over low heat for about 15 minutes. Afterwards, fold in zucchini noodles and continue to cook for 3 to 4 minutes longer.

Garnish with Asiago cheese and serve warm.

Per serving: 241 Calories; 17.4g Fat; 6.2g Carbs; 13g Protein; 2.6g Fiber

478. Cream of Green Vegetable Soup

(Ready in about 25 minutes | Servings 4)

Ingredients

1 green bell pepper, chopped
1 medium zucchini, cut into chunks
4 cups vegetable broth
3 tablespoons olive oil
2 cups broccoli florets

Directions

Warm the olive oil in a stockpot over a moderate heat. Sauté the broccoli, pepper, and zucchini until tender and aromatic.

Pour in vegetable broth and cook until it comes to a boil. Turn the heat to medium-low.

Continue to simmer, partially covered, for 20 to 23 minutes. Puree your soup with an immersion blender and serve in individual bowls.

Per serving: 111 Calories; 10.4g Fat; 4.4g Carbs; 1.9g Protein; 1.5g Fiber

479. One-Skillet Keto Vegetables

(Ready in about 15 minutes | Servings 3)

Ingredients

2 bell pepper, deseeded and sliced
1 cup tomato sauce with herb and garlic, no sugar added
2 tablespoons sesame oil
1 yellow onion, sliced
1/2 cup cream of mushroom soup

Directions

Heat the sesame oil in a nonstick skillet over medium-high flame. Sweat yellow onion and peppers for about 4 minutes or until they are just tender.

Stir in tomato sauce and mushrooms soup; continue to simmer, partially covered, for 7 to 8 minutes.

Salt to taste and serve. Bon appétit!

Per serving: 118 Calories; 9.5g Fat; 6.1g Carbs; 1.9g Protein; 1.4g Fiber

480. Creamed Tahini and Broccoli Soup

(Ready in about 15 minutes | Servings 2)

Ingredients

2 tablespoons tahini butter
1/2 small-sized leek, chopped
1 cup spinach leaves
1/3 cup yogurt
1 2/3 cups broccoli florets

Directions

Melt 1 tablespoon of butter in a soup pot over a moderate heat. Sauté the leeks until tender and aromatic or about 4 minutes.

Add in the broccoli along with 2 cups of vegetable broth. When your mixture reaches boiling, reduce the temperature to a simmer.

Continue to cook, covered, for about 7 minutes.

Fold in the spinach; season with the salt and black pepper to taste; let it simmer for 2 to 3 minutes or until spinach leaves have wilted completely.

Puree your soup along with tahini butter. Serve with yogurt and enjoy!

Per serving: 220 Calories; 19g Fat; 8.4g Carbs; 4.4g Protein; 2.7g Fiber

481. Cheese Stuffed Peppers

(Ready in about 35 minutes | Servings 2)

Ingredients

3 bell peppers, deseeded and sliced in half
3 eggs
2 scallions, chopped
6 ounces cream cheese
4 Kalamata olives, pitted and sliced

Directions

Begin by preheating your oven to 380 degrees F. Brush a baking pan with a nonstick cooking oil.

Thoroughly combine the, scallions, cream cheese, and eggs; season with Greek spice mix, if desired.

Stuff the peppers with the cheese filling.

Bake in the preheated oven for 27 to 30 minutes until cooked through. Garnish with olives and serve warm.

Per serving: 387 Calories; 30.3g Fat; 5.3g Carbs; 22.7g Protein; 0.9g Fiber

482. Summer Vegetable Stew

(Ready in about 30 minutes | Servings 4)

Ingredients

4 tablespoons sour cream, well-chilled
1 summer zucchini, chopped
2 vine-ripe tomatoes
2 bell peppers, deseeded and chopped
1 small-sized shallot, chopped

Directions

Heat 2 teaspoons of sesame oil in a heavy-bottomed pot over medium-high flame. Sauté the bell peppers and shallot until they are just starting to lightly brown.

Stir in the zucchini, broth, tomatoes, and stir to combine. Bring to a rolling boil. Immediately reduce the heat to medium-low and let it simmer for 25 minutes until everything is thoroughly cooked.

Ladle into individual bowls and garnish with sour cream and fresh chives. Enjoy!

Per serving: 67 Calories; 3.8g Fat; 6g Carbs; 2.1g Protein; 1.7g Fiber

483. Cremini Mushroom Medley

(Ready in about 25 minutes | Servings 5)

Ingredients

1 pound cremini mushrooms, sliced
2 garlic cloves
2 cup tomato sauce with herbs, no sugar added
1 red onion, chopped
2 sweet Italian peppers, chopped

Directions

Heat 2 tablespoons of canola oil in a large stockpot over a moderate flame. Once hot, cook the onion and peppers until fragrant.

Add in the mushrooms and garlic and continue to sauté for 2 to 3 minutes or until just tender and fragrant.

Add in tomato sauce long with 2 cups of water (or cream of mushroom soup); reduce heat to medium-low and partially cover.

Continue to cook for 20 to 22 minutes or until thoroughly warmed. Ladle into soup bowls and serve. Bon appétit!

Per serving: 156 Calories; 11.9g Fat; 6.2g Carbs; 4.9g Protein; 2g Fiber

484. Italian Zoodles with Parmesan Cheese

(Ready in about 10 minutes | Servings 2)

Ingredients

1 medium-sized zucchini, sliced
1 ripe tomato, quartered
1/2 avocado, pitted and peeled
2 tablespoons sunflower seeds, hulled
2 tablespoons parmesan cheese, preferably freshly grated

Directions

Puree the avocado, sunflower seeds, and tomato until well combined. Add in 2 tablespoons of water if needed.

Season with salt and black pepper to taste. You can add Italian slice mix, if desired.

Spiralize your zucchini and divide zucchini noodles (zoodles) among two serving plates. Top your zoodles with avocado sauce.

Garnish with parmesan cheese and serve right away!

Per serving: 164 Calories; 13.3g Fat; 8.7g Carbs; 5.5g Protein; 4.9g Fiber

485. Creamed Broccoli Slaw

(Ready in about 10 minutes | Servings 2)

Ingredients

2 ounces mozzarella cheese
1/4 cup tahini dressing
1 cup broccoli florets
1 bell pepper, seeded and sliced
1 shallot, thinly sliced

Directions

Toss all ingredients, except for mozzarella cheese, in a salad bowl.

Top with the mozzarella cheese and serve well chilled. Enjoy!

Per serving: 323 Calories; 25.3g Fat; 6.8g Carbs; 15.7g Protein; 3.4g Fiber

486. Tom Kha Kai

(Ready in about 20 minutes | Servings 2)

Ingredients

1 cup vegetable broth
1 shallot, chopped
1/2 celery stalk, chopped
1/2 bell pepper, chopped
1 cup coconut milk, full-fat

Directions

Heat 1 teaspoon of coconut oil in a small pot; now, sauté the shallot, celery, and pepper until they've softened.

Pour in a splash of broth to scrape up the browned bits that stick to the bottom of the pot.

Pour in the remaining broth along with salt and pepper to taste and bring to a boil.

Turn the heat to simmer; continue to cook for 15 to 17 minutes or until thoroughly cooked. Pour in the coconut milk and stir for 2 minutes.

Garnish with fresh Thai basil, if desired. Enjoy!

Per serving: 273 Calories; 27.3g Fat; 5.7g Carbs; 5.2g Protein; 0.5g Fiber

487. Asparagus with Tangy Mayo Sauce

(Ready in about 15 minutes | Servings 5)

Ingredients

4 tablespoons sour cream
4 tablespoons shallots, minced
1/2 cup mayonnaise
1 ½ pounds asparagus, trimmed
4 tablespoons olive oil

Directions

Preheat your oven to 385 degrees F.

Drizzle the asparagus spears with olive oil. Season with sea salt and black pepper to taste. Roast in the preheated oven for about 10 minutes.

Whisk the shallots, mayonnaise, and sour cream until well combined. Serve the asparagus with the mayo sauce.

Per serving: 296 Calories; 28.4g Fat; 7g Carbs; 3.9g Protein; 3.3g Fiber

488. Cocoa Smoothie with Mint

(Ready in about 5 minutes | Servings 2)

Ingredients

1/4 teaspoon grated nutmeg
2 teaspoons granulated erythritol
1 cup milk
1/3 ripe avocado, peeled and pitted
3 teaspoons cacao powder, unsweetened

Directions

Place all ingredients in a bowl of your food processor; pour in 1/2 cup of water.

Blend until creamy and smooth.

Spoon into chilled glasses and serve right away!

Per serving: 140 Calories; 9g Fat; 6.6g Carbs; 3.7g Protein; 2.8g Fiber

DESSERTS

489. Birthday Walnut Cake

(Ready in about 25 minutes | Servings 10)

Ingredients

2 eggs
1 ½ cups walnut meal
1 stick butter, room temperature
1/3 cup full-fat milk
Buttercream Keto Frosting

Directions

Start by preheating your oven to 390 degrees F.

Beat the butter and milk with an electric mixer; gradually add in the eggs, one at a time, mixing continuously.

In a separate mixing bowl, combine walnut meal with 1 teaspoon of baking powder; add stevia and spices to taste.

Add this dry mixture to the wet mixture; mix to combine well.

Spoon the batter into a foil-lined baking pan. Bake for about 20 minutes. Frost the cake and serve well-chilled. Enjoy!

Per serving: 292 Calories; 29.1g Fat; 6g Carbs; 5.3g Protein; 2.4g Fiber

490. No Bake Hazelnut Cheesecake Parfaits

(Ready in about 10 minutes + chilling time | Servings 4)

Ingredients

4 ounces hazelnuts, ground
1 cup double cream
4 tablespoons cream cheese
1/2 teaspoon vanilla extract
1/2 teaspoon Swerve

Directions

Beat the cream until it starts to thicken. Slowly stir in the Swerve and continue mixing until stiff peaks form.

Fold in the cream cheese and vanilla extract. Afterwards, stir in the hazelnuts.

Serve well chilled!

Per serving: 341 Calories; 33.2g Fat; 7.6g Carbs; 6.6g Protein; 3.1g Fiber

491. Easy Almond Fudge Bars

(Ready in about 5 minutes | Servings 7)

Ingredients

3 tablespoons coconut oil
1/4 cup monk fruit powder
4 tablespoons coconut flakes
4 tablespoons cacao powder, no sugar added
1 cup almonds

Directions

Line a baking pan with a wax paper.

Blend all ingredients in your food processor until everything is well incorporated; scrape down the sides with a rubber spatula.

Press firmly into the prepared pan and freeze 10 minutes or until firm enough to slice.

Cut into squares. Store leftovers in the refrigerator or freezer. Enjoy!

Per serving: 78 Calories; 6.8g Fat; 4.7g Carbs; 0.5g Protein; 1g Fiber

492. Peanut Butter Balls

(Ready in about 35 minutes | Servings 10)

Ingredients

1/4 teaspoon ground cinnamon
1/2 cup erythritol
3/4 cup chunky peanut butter
3/4 cup peanuts, finely chopped
6 ounces chocolate, sugar-free, chopped

Directions

Mix all ingredients until smooth.

Place the batter in your refrigerator for 30 minutes or until firm enough to handle.

Shape the batter into bite-sized balls and place in your refrigerator until ready to serve. Bon appétit!

Per serving: 275 Calories; 23.2g Fat; 7.5g Carbs; 9.9g Protein; 5.3g Fiber

493. Smoothie Bowl with Raspberries

(Ready in about 5 minutes | Servings 1)

Ingredients

1/4 teaspoon vanilla extract
1 tablespoon cacao nibs, sugar-free
1/3 cup raspberries
3/4 cup almond milk
1/2 teaspoon Swerve sweetener

Directions

Blend the almond milk, Swerve, vanilla, and raspberries until creamy, smooth, and uniform.

Pour into the prepared bowl and top with cacao nibs. Enjoy!

Per serving: 90 Calories; 4.9g Fat; 6.5g Carbs; 4.2g Protein; 2g Fiber

494. Bavarian Vanilla Cream

(Ready in about 25 minutes + chilling time | Servings 4)

Ingredients

1 vanilla bean
4 tablespoons granulated Swerve
2 eggs
2 egg yolks
1 ½ cups heavy whipping cream

Directions

Separate the egg whites from the yolks. Beat the egg whites until they form clear bubbles. Stir in a pinch of coarse salt and beat the eggs until soft and rounded peaks are formed. Reserve.

In a saucepan, place the egg yolks, vanilla, Swerve, and whipping cream. Let it simmer over low heat until the mixture has thickened or 15 to 20 minutes.

Stir in the ground cloves and cinnamon to taste; mix to combine. Heat off.

Fold in the beaten egg whites; stir to combine again. Serve well chilled.

Per serving: 214 Calories; 21g Fat; 1.7g Carbs; 5g Protein; 0g Fiber

495. Pistachio Chocolate Candy

(Ready in about 10 minutes + chilling time | Servings 10)

Ingredients

1/4 cup pistachios, chopped
1/4 cup cocoa powder, unsweetened
2/3 cup double cream
9 ounces sugar-free chocolate, chopped
1/4 teaspoon pure vanilla extract

Directions

Place double cream in your microwave for 30 to 40 seconds. Stir in the chocolate, vanilla, and pistachios; whisk to combine.

Let the mixture sit in your refrigerator for 1 hour. Shape the mixture into small balls.

Roll these balls in cocoa powder and serve. Devour!

Per serving: 216 Calories; 18g Fat; 6.7g Carbs; 5.1g Protein; 4.5g Fiber

496. Vanilla Coconut Latte

(Ready in about 5 minutes | Servings 2)

Ingredients

1 cup coconut milk, unsweetened
1 vanilla bean, split lengthwise
8 drops vanilla liquid stevia
4 tablespoons coconut cream
1/2 cup brewed black coffee

Directions

Process all ingredients in your blender.

Pour your latte into two glasses filled with ice. Enjoy!

Per serving: 345 Calories; 35.3g Fat; 6.3g Carbs; 3.4g Protein; 3.3g Fiber

497. Velvety Coconut Cheesecake

(Ready in about 30 minutes | Servings 6)

Ingredients

1/2 cup coconut flour
7 ounces mascarpone cheese, at room temperature
1/2 cup heavy whipping cream
2 tablespoons cocoa powder
5 tablespoons coconut oil

Directions

Combine coconut flour, cocoa powder, and 3 tablespoons of coconut oil; add keto sweetener to taste. Press the crust into a lightly-oiled baking pan.

Then, mix mascarpone cheese and 2 tablespoons of coconut oil in your microwave.

Spread the filling over the crust. Top with heavy whipping cream. Place in your refrigerator until ready to serve.

Per serving: 236 Calories; 22.5g Fat; 4.9g Carbs; 6.1g Protein; 0.8g Fiber

498. Peanut Butter Cheesecakes Bowls

(Ready in about 10 minutes | Servings 2)

Ingredients

1/2 teaspoon vanilla extract
2 heaping tablespoons smooth peanut butter
2 ounces mascarpone cheese, at room temperature
1/2 cup double cream
1 teaspoon liquid Stevia

Directions

Beat mascarpone cheese with double cream and Stevia.

Add in the vanilla and continue mixing until everything is well incorporated.

Spoon the mixture into individual bowls; top each bowl with a teaspoon of peanut butter. Enjoy!

Per serving: 233 Calories; 19.2g Fat; 6g Carbs; 6.8g Protein; 0.9g Fiber

499. Ooey Gooey Chocolate Chunk Blondies

(Ready in about 30 minutes | Servings 2)

Ingredients

1/4 cup butter, melted
1 tablespoon milk
1/2 cup almond flour
1 egg, whisked
1/4 cup chocolate chips, unsweetened

Directions

Place the almond flour in a bowl; mix in cream of tartar and baking soda.

In the second bowl, whisk the egg, butter, and milk; add in keto sweetener of choice.

Stir the almond flour in to the egg/butter mixture; mix until everything is well incorporated. Fold in chocolate chips; add vanilla bean seeds, if desired.

Press the batter into a foil-lined baking pan. Bake in the preheated oven at 365 degrees F for about 20 minutes until the middle looks slightly underdone.

Place the baking pan on a wire rack and let your blondies cool down. Store your blondies in an airtight container up to 3 days at room temperature.

Per serving: 347 Calories; 34g Fat; 5.2g Carbs; 5.7g Protein; 2.8g Fiber

500. Valentine's Day Blueberry Cheesecake

(Ready in about 1 hour 10 minutes | Servings 2)

Ingredients

A handful of fresh blueberries
4 tablespoons butter, room temperature
1/2 cup almond flour
6 ounces ricotta cheese, at room temperature
2 eggs, whisked

Directions

In a bowl, thoroughly combine butter and almond flour. Press the crust into a parchment-lined baking pan and freeze for 30 minutes.

Using an electric mixer, whip ricotta cheese with granulated keto sweetener of choice (e.g. erythritol or xylitol).

Fold in the eggs, one at a time, and continue to mix until everything is well incorporated. Spread the filling over the prepared crust.

Bake at 430 degrees F for 10 minutes; decrease the oven temperature to 350 degrees F and bake for about 25 minutes.

Garnish with fresh blueberries and serve.

Per serving: 598 Calories; 58.9g Fat; 7.4g Carbs; 13.3g Protein; 2g Fiber

501. Pecan Pie Candy

(Ready in about 10 minutes | Servings 2)

Ingredients

3 tablespoons cocoa powder
2 tablespoons coconut oil
1/4 cup coconut butter
1 teaspoon liquid Stevia
1/4 cup pecans, ground

Directions

Thoroughly combine all ingredients until well mixed.

Spoon the batter into candy molds and freeze until ready to serve. Devour!

Per serving: 436 Calories; 47.6g Fat; 6.9g Carbs; 3.4g Protein; 4.5g Fiber

502. Easiest Mug Cake Ever

(Ready in about 10 minutes | Servings 2)

Ingredients

4 tablespoons full-fat milk
4 tablespoons Monk fruit powder
4 tablespoons psyllium husk flour
2 tablespoons ground flax seed
5 tablespoons almond flour

Directions

In a lightly-oiled mugs, mix all ingredients until well combined.

Place in your microwave for 1 minute. Enjoy!

Per serving: 143 Calories; 10.7g Fat; 5.7g Carbs; 5.7g Protein; 2.6g Fiber

503. Coconut Bark with Cranberries

(Ready in about 1 hour 10 minutes | Servings 12)

Ingredients

1/2 cup butter, melted
1/2 teaspoon liquid Stevia
1/3 cup cranberries
1 ½ cups coconut flakes, unsweetened

Directions

In your food processor, blend all ingredients until smooth and creamy.

Press the batter into a foil-lined baking pan.

Place in your refrigerator until firm enough to slice or about 1 hour. Cut into squares and enjoy!

Per serving: 107 Calories; 11.1g Fat; 2.5g Carbs; 0.4g Protein; 0.9g Fiber

504. Favorite Chia Pudding

(Ready in about 10 minutes+ chilling time | Servings 2)

Ingredients

3/4 cup coconut milk
2 tablespoons Swerve
1/2 teaspoon vanilla paste
4 tablespoon chia seeds
2 tablespoons shredded coconut, unsweetened

Directions

Thoroughly combine chia seeds, vanilla, coconut milk, and Swerve.

Spoon the pudding in storage containers and let it refrigerate overnight.

Divide the pudding between 2 bowls. Garnish with the shredded coconut and devour!

Per serving: 225 Calories; 20.3g Fat; 7.7g Carbs; 3.8g Protein; 4.7g Fiber

505. Chocolate Candy with Peanuts

(Ready in about 1 hour 5 minutes | Servings 6)

Ingredients

1/2 cup coconut oil
1/4 cup Xylitol
4 tablespoons roasted peanuts, ground
1/2 cup peanut butter, no sugar added
1/4 cup cocoa powder, unsweetened

Directions

Melt the coconut oil and combine it with peanut butter.

Add in the cocoa powder and Xylitol; mix to combine well. Freeze for about 1 hour.

Roll the mixture into small balls; roll these balls over the ground peanuts and serve well-chilled.

Per serving: 328 Calories; 32.6g Fat; 7.7g Carbs; 6.9g Protein; 2.7g Fiber

506. Nana's Coconut Cookies

(Ready in about 25 minutes | Servings 8)

Ingredients

2 tablespoons coconut oil
2 cups coconut flour
1/4 cup monk fruit powder
1 tablespoon coconut milk
1 egg, whisked

Directions

Whip the coconut oil, coconut milk, and egg until smooth and uniform. In another bowl, combine coconut flour with monk fruit; stir in baking powder.

Add the dry flour mixture to the wet mixture and mix until everything is well combined. Roll the mixture into bite-sized balls; place the balls on a foil-lined cookie pan and flatten them with a fork.

Bake at 350 degrees F for about 15 minutes. Bon appétit!

Per serving: 142 Calories; 13g Fat; 5.2g Carbs; 3.5g Protein; 2.4g Fiber

507. Easy Molten Cake

(Ready in about 20 minutes | Servings 4)

Ingredients

3 ounces bakers' chocolate, sugar-free
4 eggs
1 tablespoon unsweetened cocoa powder
4 ounces butter
2 tablespoons almond meal

Directions

Start by preheating your oven to 380 degrees F. Pour 2 cups of water into a baking dish.

Beat the eggs and butter until well mixed. Melt the chocolate and add the melted chocolate to the mixing bowl.

Fold in the almond meal and cocoa powder; add in Swerve to taste. Spoon the mixture into four buttered ramekins.

Place the ramekins into the baking dish. Bake in the preheated for 10 to 12 minutes. Invert each cake onto a serving plate. Bon appétit!

Per serving: 478 Calories; 45g Fat; 7.6g Carbs; 10.6g Protein; 4.9g Fiber

508. Fluffy and Nutty Cookies

(Ready in about 20 minutes | Servings 6)

Ingredients

6 tablespoons pecans, chopped
1 tablespoon butter
3 tablespoons coconut milk
2 tablespoons peanut butter
1 cup coconut flour

Directions

In a mixing bowl, combine coconut flour and pecans; add in 2-3 tablespoons of xylitol. In a separate bowl, combine coconut milk, peanut butter, and melted butter.

Mix the flour mixture and dry ingredients on medium-high speed until well combined. Shape the dough into bite-sized balls and flatten them with your hands.

Bake in the preheated oven at 330 degrees F approximately 10 minutes until golden brown on the bottom. Bon appétit!

Per serving: 184 Calories; 16.5g Fat; 6.4g Carbs; 5g Protein; 3.8g Fiber

509. Flax Seed and Pecan Porridge

(Ready in about 10 minutes + chilling time | Servings 2)

Ingredients

1/2 cup canned coconut milk
2 tablespoons golden flaxseeds, ground
A few drops of liquid Stevia
2 tablespoons pecans, ground
2 tablespoons coconut flour

Directions

In a saucepan, bring 2/3 cup of water and coconut milk to a boil.

Add in pecans, coconut flour, golden flaxseeds, and liquid Stevia. Then, reduce the heat to medium-low.

Continue to simmer for 2 to 3 minutes or until slightly thickened. Serve well-chilled.

Per serving: 327 Calories; 32g Fat; 6.7g Carbs; 4.8g Protein; 4.9g Fiber

510. Chocolate Pound Cake

(Ready in about 30 minutes | Servings 12)

Ingredients

1/3 cup cocoa powder, unsweetened
2 cups almond meal
1 cup coconut butter
2/3 cup full-fat milk, unsweetened
1 cup Swerve

Directions

Begin by preheating your oven to 365 degrees F.

Mix the almond meal, Swerve, and cocoa powder; add in 1 teaspoon of baking powder and stir again.

Add in the coconut butter and milk; add in butterscotch extract, if desired, and mix again until well combined.

Spoon the batter into a lightly buttered baking pan. Bake in the preheated oven for about 20 minutes.

Place on a wire rack to cool and serve.

Per serving: 296 Calories; 27g Fat; 5.6g Carbs; 10.8g Protein; 2.7g Fiber

511. Basic Keto Brownies

(Ready in about 1 hour | Servings 10)

Ingredients

1/2 cup coconut oil
3 ounces baking chocolate, unsweetened
5 tablespoons coconut flour
1/2 cup cocoa powder, unsweetened
4 eggs

Directions

Start by preheating your oven to 330 degrees F.

Thoroughly combine the coconut flour and cocoa powder; add in 1/2 teaspoon of baking powder.

Whisk the eggs with a keto sweetener, of choice; add in the melted coconut oil and chocolate.

Gradually stir the dry ingredients into the egg mixture, whisking constantly. Scrape the batter into a buttered baking pan.

Bake in the preheated oven for 45 to 50 minutes or until a tester inserted into the middle of your brownie comes out dry. Enjoy!

Per serving: 205 Calories; 19.5g Fat; 5.4g Carbs; 4.7g Protein; 3.2g Fiber

512. Avocado Chocolate Pudding

(Ready in about 5 minutes + chilling time | Servings 2)

Ingredients

1/2 ripe avocado, pitted and peeled
2 ounces cream cheese

4 tablespoons unsweetened cocoa powder
4 tablespoons almond milk
1/4 cup swerve sweetener

Directions

Blend all of the above ingredients until well combined.

Serve in dessert bowls and enjoy!

Per serving: 163 Calories; 14.6g Fat; 9.8g Carbs; 4.7g Protein; 5.9g Fiber

513. Peanut Butter Squares

(Ready in about 10 minutes + chilling time | Servings 10)

Ingredients

1 stick butter, room temperature
1/3 cup Swerve
1/2 cup unsweetened coconut flakes

1/3 cup unsweetened cocoa powder
1/3 cup peanut butter

Directions

Place the butter and peanut butter in your microwave for 30 seconds or until they have melted.

Stir in the other ingredients and mix again.

Pour the mixture into a foil-lined baking sheet. Freeze for 1 hour or until firm enough to slice. Devour!

Per serving: 122 Calories; 11.7g Fat; 4.9g Carbs; 1.5g Protein; 1.4g Fiber

514. Coconut and Chocolate Fudge

(Ready in about 25 minutes | Servings 2)

Ingredients

1/4 cup coconut flour
1/3 cup coconut oil
2 ounces sugar-free dark chocolate, melted

2 tablespoons ground flax
1/3 cup xylitol

Directions

Thoroughly combine the ground flax, coconut flour, and xylitol in a bowl; add in 1/2 teaspoon of baking powder.

In a separate bowl, whisk the coconut oil and melted chocolate.

Stir the wet mixture into the dry mixture and mix until everything is well combined. Scrape the batter in a foil-lined baking pan.

Bake in the preheated oven at 370 degrees F for about 20 minutes or until a toothpick comes out dry. Devour!

Per serving: 405 Calories; 40g Fat; 8.8g Carbs; 6.3g Protein; 5.3g Fiber

515. Almond Cheesecake Bars

(Ready in about 40 minutes | Servings 2)

Ingredients

8 tablespoons monk fruit powder
1 egg, beaten
3 ounces cream cheese

2 tablespoons coconut oil, at room temperature
1/2 cup almond flour

Directions

Mix the eggs, coconut oil, almond flour, and 4 tablespoons of monk fruit powder in a bowl. Spread this mixture onto the bottom of a wax paper-lined baking pan.

Beat the cream cheese with the remaining 4 tablespoons of monk fruit. Spoon this mixture over the crust.

Bake in the preheated oven at 365 degrees F for about 20 minutes. Store in your refrigerator until ready to serve. Garnish with slivered almonds and enjoy!

Per serving: 509 Calories; 48g Fat; 8.4g Carbs; 13.2g Protein; 3.9g Fiber

516. Autumn Keto Crepes

(Ready in about 15 minutes | Servings 6)

Ingredients

4 tablespoons pumpkin puree, sugar-free
4 eggs

6 ounces ricotta cheese, at room temperature
1 cup almond meal
1/2 cup pecans, fine ground

Directions

Combine almond meal and pecans along with 1/2 teaspoon of baking powder.

Add in the eggs, one at a time, whisking after each addition. Add in ricotta cheese and pumpkin puree. Mix again to combine well.

In a lightly greased pan, cook your pancakes for about 3 minutes on each side. Serve with favorite keto toppings. Bon appétit!

Per serving: 260 Calories; 21.7g Fat; 6.9g Carbs; 11.6g Protein; 3.8g Fiber

517. Homemade Crunch Bars

(Ready in about 30 minutes | Servings 10)

Ingredients

1 1/3 cup peanut butter
1 egg
1/2 cup hemp hearts

1 cup walnuts, ground
1/2 cup granulated Swerve

Directions

Strat by preheating your oven to 370 degrees F.

Mix all ingredients until everything is well combined. Scrape the batter into a parchment-lined baking pan.

Bake in the preheated oven for about 12 minutes. Bon appétit!

Per serving: 190 Calories; 17.1g Fat; 5.9g Carbs; 5.9g Protein; 2.7g Fiber

518. Old-Fashioned Cinnamon Cookies

(Ready in about 20 minutes | Servings 2)

Ingredients

2 tablespoons coconut flour
1/3 cup monk fruit powder
1/4 teaspoon cinnamon
1 egg, whisked
1/3 cup almond butter, at room temperature

Directions

Begin by preheating an oven to 350 degrees F.

Thoroughly combine all ingredients until well mixed.

Roll the mixture into balls and place them on a cookie sheet. Then, flatten each ball with the palm of your hand.

Bake for about 15 minutes until golden on the bottom. Bon appétit!

Per serving: 316 Calories; 27g Fat; 9.1g Carbs; 11.1g Protein; 5.3g Fiber

519. Almond Orange Cheesecake

(Ready in about 15 minutes + chilling time | Servings 12)

Ingredients

3 tablespoons Swerve
17 ounces mascarpone cream
2 tablespoon orange juice
1 ½ cups almond flour
1 stick butter, room temperature

Directions

Mix 2 tablespoons of Swerve, almond flour, and butter. Press the crust into a foil-lined baking pan.

Mix the remaining tablespoons of Swerve with mascarpone cheese and orange juice; mix until everything is well combined.

Spread the filling onto the crust and serve well-chilled.

Per serving: 150 Calories; 15.4g Fat; 2.1g Carbs; 1.2g Protein; 0.1g Fiber

520. Peanut Butter Cheesecake Balls

(Ready in about 35 minutes | Servings 6)

Ingredients

6 ounces cream cheese
2 tablespoons butter
4 tablespoons confectioners' Swerve
1/3 cup cocoa powder, unsweetened
1 cup peanut butter

Directions

Mix all of the above ingredients until creamy and smooth.

Freeze for 30 to 40 minutes before serving. Enjoy!

Per serving: 406 Calories; 40.5g Fat; 6.7g Carbs; 7.5g Protein; 2.5g Fiber

521. Restaurant-Style Cupcakes

(Ready in about 20 minutes | Servings 9)

Ingredients

6 eggs, beaten
2 tablespoons flaxseed meal
1/3 cup coconut flour
1/2 cup coconut oil, melted
3 tablespoons granulated Swerve

Directions

Begin by preheating your oven to 365 degrees F. Line a muffin tin with cupcake liners.

In a mixing bowl, whisk the eggs with the coconut oil and Swerve until pale and frothy. In the second bowl, combine flaxseed meal and coconut flour along with 1 teaspoon of baking powder.

Add the dry mixture to the wet mixture and mix to combine. Scrape the batter into the muffin tin.

Bake in the preheated oven for about 15 minutes. Bon appétit!

Per serving: 163 Calories; 17g Fat; 1.5g Carbs; 2.3g Protein; 0.9g Fiber

522. Decadent Chocolate Soufflé

(Ready in about 15 minutes | Servings 4)

Ingredients

3 eggs
1 ½ ounces butter, melted
1 ½ ounces heavy cream
4 tablespoons cocoa powder, unsweetened
2 tablespoons coconut flour

Directions

In a mixing bowl, combine coconut flour and cocoa powder along with 1/2 teaspoon of baking powder.

In a separate bowl, beat the eggs, butter, and heavy cream; add the wet mixture to the dry mixture, add in a keto sweetener of choice and mix again.

Divide the batter into four buttered ramekins.

Bake in the preheated oven at 360 degrees F for 8 to 11 minutes or until the middle is still soft. Bon appétit!

Per serving: 168 Calories; 15.8g Fat; 6g Carbs; 4.5g Protein; 2.5g Fiber

523. Chocolate Cheesecake Mousse

(Ready in about 1 hour 10 minutes | Servings 3)

Ingredients

1 teaspoon caramel extract
4 tablespoons cocoa powder, unsweetened
1/2 cup Swerve
2 ounces cream cheese, at room temperature
1/2 cup double cream

Directions

Beat the cream cheese and double cream until firm peaks form.

Add in the caramel extract, cocoa powder, and Swerve. Mix to combine well.

Refrigerate at least 1 hour and enjoy!

Per serving: 154 Calories; 14.8g Fat; 6g Carbs; 2.8g Protein; 2.4g Fiber

524. Chocolate Yogurt Popsicles

(Ready in about 10 minutes + chilling time | Servings 8)

Ingredients

5 tablespoons cocoa powder

1 3/4 cups plain yogurt

1/2 teaspoon pure vanilla essence

3/4 cup Swerve

4 tablespoons full-fat milk

Directions

Blend all of the above ingredients in your food processor.

Pour into popsicle molds and freeze for at least 6 hours. Devour!

Per serving: 58 Calories; 2.6g Fat; 5.5g Carbs; 3.1g Protein; 1.2g Fiber

525. Mom's Vanilla Cheesecake

(Ready in about 40 minutes | Servings 8)

Ingredients

10 ounces cream cheese, at room temperature

2 egg

9 tablespoons xylitol

3 tablespoons coconut oil

1 cup almond flour

Directions

Begin by preheating your oven to 330 degrees F. Pour hot water into a large pan, until it's 3/4- inch deep.

Mix the coconut oil, almond flour, and 3 tablespoons of xylitol to make the crust. Press the crust into the bottom of a lightly buttered springform pan.

Bake in the preheated oven for 7 to 8 minutes.

Then, mix the cheese and the remaining 6 tablespoons of xylitol. Fold in the eggs, one at a time, mixing after each addition at low-medium speed.

Spoon the filling over the prepared crust and spread evenly. Lower the springform pan into the pan with water.

Bake for about 30 minutes or until the center is still jiggle while the edges are set. Allow your cheesecake to cool at room temperature. Bon appétit!

Per serving: 256 Calories; 24.3g Fat; 5g Carbs; 6.1g Protein; 1.6g Fiber

526. Summer Penuche Fudge

(Ready in about 45 minutes | Servings 10)

Ingredients

2 ounces baker's chocolate, sugar-free

1/2 cup almond butter

1 teaspoon Stevia

1/2 stick butter

2 tablespoons tahini (sesame paste)

Directions

Melt the butter and mix it with tahini, almond butter, Stevia, and chocolate. Add in cinnamon to taste.

Spread the mixture on the bottom of a parchment-lined baking pan.

Freeze for 40 to 50 minutes before slicing and serving. Devour!

Per serving: 176 Calories; 18.3g Fat; 3.2g Carbs; 1.8g Protein; 1.2g Fiber

527. Greek Cheesecake with Pecans

(Ready in about 2 hours 20 minutes | Servings 10)

Ingredients

1 cup pecan flour

36 ounces cream cheese, room temperature

4 eggs

1 ½ cups xylitol

4 tablespoons butter, melted

Directions

Combine pecan flour, 1 cup of xylitol, and butter until well combined. Press the crust into a lightly buttered springform pan. Freeze for 30 minutes.

Meanwhile, beat the cream cheese with eggs and 1/2 cup of xylitol. Remove crust from freezer and pour in the prepared filling.

Bake in the preheated oven for 55 to 60 minutes until top of cheesecake turns golden.

Allow your cheesecake to cool at room temperature. Enjoy!

Per serving: 483 Calories; 47.2g Fat; 5.8g Carbs; 10.3g Protein; 1.7g Fiber

528. Café-Style Fudge

(Ready in about 10 minutes + chilling time | Servings 6)

Ingredients

1 tablespoon instant coffee granules

4 tablespoons confectioners' Swerve

4 tablespoons cocoa powder

1 stick butter

1/2 teaspoon vanilla extract

Directions

Beat the butter and Swerve at low speed.

Add in the cocoa powder, instant coffee granules, and vanilla and continue to mix until well combined.

Spoon the batter into a foil-lined baking sheet. Refrigerate for 2 to 3 hours. Enjoy!

Per serving: 144 Calories; 15.5g Fat; 2.1g Carbs; 0.8g Protein; 1.1g Fiber

529. Coconut and Seed Porridge

(Ready in about 15 minutes | Servings 2)

Ingredients

6 tablespoons coconut flour

1/2 cup canned coconut milk

4 tablespoons double cream

2 tablespoons flaxseed meal

1 tablespoon pumpkin seeds, ground

Directions

In a saucepan, simmer all of the above the ingredients over medium-low heat. Add in a keto sweetener of choice.

Divide the porridge between serving bowls and enjoy!

Per serving: 300 Calories; 25.1g Fat; 8g Carbs; 4.9g Protein; 6g Fiber

530. Pecan and Lime Cheesecake

(Ready in about 30 minutes + chilling time | Servings 10)

Ingredients

1 cup coconut flakes
20 ounces mascarpone cheese, room temperature

1 ½ cups pecan meal
1/2 cup xylitol
3 tablespoons key lime juice

Directions

Combine the pecan meal, 1/4 cup of xylitol, and coconut flakes in a mixing bowl. Press the crust into a parchment-lined springform pan. Freeze for 30 minutes.

Now, beat the mascarpone cheese with 1/4 cup of xylitol with an electric mixer.

Beat in the key lime juice; you can add vanilla extract, if desired.

Spoon the filling onto the prepared crust. Allow it to cool in your refrigerator for about 3 hours. Bon appétit!

Per serving: 296 Calories; 20g Fat; 6g Carbs; 21g Protein; 3.7g Fiber

531. Rum Butter Cookies

(Ready in about 10 minutes + chilling time | Servings 12)

Ingredients

1/2 cup coconut butter
1 teaspoon rum extract
4 cups almond meal

1 stick butter
1/2 cup confectioners' Swerve

Directions

Melt the coconut butter and butter. Stir in the Swerve and rum extract.

Afterwards, add in the almond meal and mix to combine.

Roll the balls and place them on a parchment-lined cookie sheet. Place in your refrigerator until ready to serve.

Per serving: 400 Calories; 40g Fat; 4.9g Carbs; 5.4g Protein; 2.9g Fiber

532. Fluffy Chocolate Chip Cookies

(Ready in about 10 minutes + chilling time | Servings 10)

Ingredients

1/2 cup almond meal
4 tablespoons double cream
1/2 cup sugar-free chocolate chips

2 cups coconut, unsweetened and shredded
1/2 cup monk fruit syrup

Directions

In a mixing bowl, combine all of the above ingredients until well combined. Shape the batter into bite-sized balls.

Flatten the balls using a fork or your hand.

Place in your refrigerator until ready to serve.

Per serving: 104 Calories; 9.5g Fat; 4.1g Carbs; 2.1g Protein; 2.6g Fiber

533. Chewy Almond Blondies

(Ready in about 55 minutes | Servings 10)

Ingredients

1/2 cup sugar-free bakers' chocolate, chopped into small chunks
1/4 cup erythritol

2 tablespoons coconut oil
1 cup almond meal
1 cup almond butter

Directions

In a mixing bowl, combine almond meal, almond butter, and erythritol until creamy and uniform.

Press the mixture into a foil-lined baking sheet. Freeze for 30 to 35 minutes.

Melt the coconut oil and bakers' chocolate to make the glaze. Spread the glaze over your cake; freeze until the chocolate is set.

Slice into bars and devour!

Per serving: 234 Calories; 25.1g Fat; 3.6g Carbs; 1.7g Protein; 1.4g Fiber

534. Light Greek Cheesecake

(Ready in about 1 hour 35 minutes | Servings 6)

Ingredients

10 ounces whipped Greek yogurt cream cheese
6 tablespoons butter, melted

2 cups confectioner's Swerve
2 eggs
2 cups almond meal

Directions

Start by preheating your oven to 325 degrees F.

Combine the almond meal and butter and press the crust into a lightly buttered springform pan.

Beat the Greek-style yogurt with confectioner's Swerve until everything is well mixed. Fold in the eggs, one at the time, and mix well to make sure that everything is being combined together.

Pour the filling over the crust. Bake in the preheated oven for about 35 minutes until the middle is still jiggly. Your cheesecake will continue to set as it cools. Bon appétit!

Per serving: 471 Calories; 45g Fat; 6.9g Carbs; 11.5g Protein; 4g Fiber

535. Fluffy Chocolate Crepes

(Ready in about 40 minutes | Servings 2)

Ingredients

1/4 cup coconut milk, unsweetened
2 egg, beaten
1/2 cup coconut flour

1 tablespoon unsweetened cocoa powder
2 tablespoons coconut oil, melted

Directions

In a mixing bowl, thoroughly combine the coconut flour and cocoa powder along with 1/2 teaspoon of baking soda.

In another bowl, whisk the eggs and coconut milk. Add the flour mixture to the egg mixture; mix to combine well.

In a frying pan, preheat 1 tablespoon of the coconut oil until sizzling. Ladle 1/2 of the batter into the frying pan and cook for 2 to 3 minutes on each side.

Melt the remaining tablespoon of coconut oil and fry another crepe for about 5 minutes. Serve with your favorite keto filling. Bon appétit!

Per serving: 330 Calories; 31.9g Fat; 7.1g Carbs; 7.3g Protein; 3.5g Fiber

536. Crispy Peanut Fudge Squares

(Ready in about 1 hour | Servings 10)

Ingredients

1/2 cup peanuts, toasted and coarsely chopped
1 vanilla paste

2 tablespoons Monk fruit powder
1 stick butter
1/3 cup coconut oil

Directions

Melt the butter, coconut oil, and vanilla. Add in Monk fruit powder and mix to combine well.

Place the chopped peanuts in an ice cube tray. Pour the batter over the peanuts.

Place in your freezer for about 1 hour. Bon appétit!

Per serving: 218 Calories; 21.2g Fat; 5.1g Carbs; 3.8g Protein; 0.7g Fiber

537. Almond Butter Cookies

(Ready in about 15 minutes + chilling time | Servings 8)

Ingredients

1 ½ cups almond butter
1/2 cup sugar-free chocolate, cut into chunks

1/2 cup double cream
1/2 cup Monk fruit powder
3 cups pork rinds, crushed

Directions

Melt almond butter and Monk fruit powder; add in crushed pork rinds along with vanilla, if desired.

Spread the mixture onto a cookie sheet and place in your refrigerator.

Microwave the chocolate with double cream; spread the chocolate layer over the first layer. Place in your refrigerator until ready to serve. Enjoy!

Per serving: 322 Calories; 28.9g Fat; 3.4g Carbs; 13.9g Protein; 0.6g Fiber

538. Basic Almond Cupcakes

(Ready in about 35 minutes | Servings 9)

Ingredients

1 cup almond milk, unsweetened
2 tablespoons coconut oil

1/2 cup almond meal
1/4 cup Swerve
3 eggs

Directions

Mix all of the above ingredients until well combined. Line a muffin pan with cupcake liners.

Spoon the batter into the muffin pan.

Bake in the preheated oven at 350 degrees F for 18 to 20 minutes or until a toothpick comes out dry and clean. Enjoy!

Per serving: 134 Calories; 11.6g Fat; 2.9g Carbs; 5.4g Protein; 1.3g Fiber

539. Blueberry Cheesecake Bowl

(Ready in about 10 minutes + chilling time | Servings 8)

Ingredients

2 cups cream cheese
1/2 cup blueberries
1/2 teaspoon coconut extract

6 tablespoons pecans, chopped
1/4 cup coconut cream

Directions

Beat the cream cheese and coconut cream until well mixed.

Fold in the coconut extract, pecans, and 1/4 cup of blueberries and mix again. Refrigerate for 2 to 3 hours.

Serve garnished with the remaining 1/4 cup of blueberries. Enjoy!

Per serving: 244 Calories; 24.2g Fat; 4.7g Carbs; 3.7g Protein; 1g Fiber

540. Energy Chocolate Chip Candy

(Ready in about 10 minutes + chilling time | Servings 10)

Ingredients

2 tablespoons milk
1/2 cup peanut butter, melted
1 cup coconut flour

1/4 cup erythritol
1/4 cup chocolate chips, sugar-free

Directions

Mix all of the above ingredients until everything is well combined.

Spoon the mixture into an ice-cube tray.

Place in your refrigerator for about 2 hours. Bon appétit!

Per serving: 102 Calories; 7.8g Fat; 5.8g Carbs; 2.6g Protein; 1.8g Fiber

541. Fudgy Mug Brownie

(Ready in about 10 minutes | Servings 2)

Ingredients

2 eggs
1/2 teaspoon Monk fruit powder

2 dollops heavy whipping cream
1/2 cup coconut milk
2 tablespoons coconut flour

Directions

Whip the eggs and coconut milk until well combined.

In another bowl, mix the coconut flour and Monk fruit powder; add vanilla and cinnamon to taste.

Add the egg mixture to the dry mixture and stir to combine well. Scrape the batter into microwave-safe mugs.

Microwave for about 1 minute 30 seconds. Garnish with a dollop of whipping cream and serve!

Per serving: 336 Calories; 31.5g Fat; 6g Carbs; 9.1g Protein; 3.1g Fiber

542. Basic Keto Brownies

(Ready in about 1 hour 25 minutes | Servings 10)

Ingredients

1/2 cup butter, melted
1 ¼ cups coconut flour
1 teaspoon baking powder

1/3 cup cocoa powder, unsweetened
1 cup Xylitol

Directions

Start by preheating your oven to 355 degrees F.

Mix all ingredients until everything is well combined. Spread the batter onto the bottom of a parchment-lined baking pan.

Bake in the preheated oven for 15 to 20 minutes or until a toothpick comes out dry and clean. Transfer to wire racks until firm enough to slice. Bon appétit!

Per serving: 123 Calories; 12.9g Fat; 3.1g Carbs; 0.9g Protein; 1.7g Fiber

543. Dad's Rum Brownies

(Ready in about 30 minutes | Servings 8)

Ingredients

6 ounces butter, melted
3 ounces baking chocolate, unsweetened and melted

1 cup almond flour
2 eggs
2 tablespoons rum

Directions

Start by preheating your oven to 365 degrees F.

Thoroughly combine almond flour and baking powder. In another bowl, combine the eggs, butter, chocolate and rum. Add the flour mixture to the wet mixture.

Spoon the batter into the bottom of a foil-lined baking pan.

Bake in the preheated oven approximately 20 minutes. Enjoy!

Per serving: 245 Calories; 23.2g Fat; 3.1g Carbs; 3.1g Protein; 1.8g Fiber

544. Chia Smoothie Bowl

(Ready in about 5 minutes | Servings 2)

Ingredients

1/2 cup coconut milk
2 tablespoons chia seeds
4 tablespoons powdered erythritol

A pinch of freshly grated nutmeg
4 tablespoons peanut butter

Directions

Blend all ingredients in your food processor.

Serve in individual bowls and devour!

Per serving: 280 Calories; 16g Fat; 7g Carbs; 25g Protein; 4g Fiber

545. Chocolate Cheesecake Fudge

(Ready in about 35 minutes + chilling time | Servings 6)

Ingredients

16 ounces cream cheese, at room temperature
2 tablespoons unsweetened cocoa powder

3/4 cup coconut flour
1/3 cup butter, at room temperature
6 ounces sour cream

Directions

Combine the coconut flour and butter; press the crust into the bottom of a lightly buttered baking pan; freeze for 30 minutes.

Make the filling by mixing the cream cheese, sour cream, and cocoa powder, add in Erythritol to taste. Spoon the filling over the crust.

Bake in the preheated oven at 420 degrees F for 8 to 10 minutes; decrease temperature to 365 degrees F and continue to bake for 15 to 20 minutes more.

Enjoy!

Per serving: 411 Calories; 38g Fat; 7.5g Carbs; 5.8g Protein; 1.1g Fiber

546. Favorite Keto Frisuelos

(Ready in about 20 minutes | Servings 6)

Ingredients

1 tablespoon butter, melted
3 eggs
2 ounces double cream

4 ounces mascarpone cheese
6 tablespoons confectioners' Swerve

Directions

Whisk the eggs until pale and frothy. Fold in double cream and mascarpone cheese. Mix until everything is well combined. Add maple extract and salt to taste.

Melt the batter in a frying pan over medium-high heat.

Spoon 1/6 of the batter into the hot frying pan. Cook for 2 to 3 minutes per side. Repeat until you run out of the ingredients. Serve with confectioners' Swerve. Enjoy!

Per serving: 137 Calories; 12.3g Fat; 3.2g Carbs; 4.1g Protein; 0g Fiber

547. Candy Bar Cheesecake Balls

(Ready in about 10 minutes + chilling time | Servings 10)

Ingredients

9 ounces sugar-free chocolate chips

2 ounces butter, at room temperature

9 ounces mascarpone cheese, at room temperature

1 teaspoon butterscotch extract

2 cups powdered erythritol

Directions

In a mixing bowl, combine the butter, mascarpone cheese, erythritol, chocolate chips, and butterscotch extract.

Refrigerate for 2 hours and then, shape the mixture into bite-sized balls. Bon appétit!

Per serving: 293 Calories; 26g Fat; 5.6g Carbs; 5.3g Protein; 1g Fiber

548. Old-Fashion Coffee Mousse

(Ready in about 15 minutes + chilling time | Servings 4)

Ingredients

1/2 teaspoon instant coffee

1 teaspoon pure coconut extract

2 cups double cream

4 egg yolks

6 tablespoons Xylitol

Directions

Warm double cream in a saucepan over low heat. Let it cool at room temperature.

Then, combine the egg yolks, instant coffee, coconut extract, and Xylitol; whisk to combine well.

Spoon the egg mixture into the lukewarm cream. Cook the mixture over the lowest setting until the liquid has thickened slightly.

Serve well-chilled and enjoy!

Per serving: 289 Calories; 27.6g Fat; 5g Carbs; 5.9g Protein; 0g Fiber

549. Blueberry Pot de Crème

(Ready in about 10 minutes | Servings 1)

Ingredients

2 tablespoons Greek-style yogurt

1 tablespoon peanut butter

1 tablespoon chia seeds

1/2 avocado, pitted and peeled

2 tablespoons blueberries

Directions

Blend the avocado, blueberries, and Greek-style yogurt in your food processor. Add in Swerve to taste.

Garnish with peanut butter and chia seeds. Bon appétit!

Per serving: 235 Calories; 17.7g Fat; 8.9g Carbs; 8.1g Protein; 7g Fiber

550. Chocolate Blechkuchen

(Ready in about 30 minutes + chilling time | Servings 8)

Ingredients

1 cup almond meal

3 eggs

1/3 cup coconut oil

1/4 cup powdered erythritol

1/4 cup cocoa powder, unsweetened

Directions

Start by preheating your oven to 330 degrees F.

Combine the almond meal and cocoa powder; add in 1/2 teaspoon of baking powder and mix until well combined.

Fold in the eggs, one at a time, whisking after each addition. Add in coconut oil and powdered erythritol.

Press the batter into a buttered springform pan. Bake in the preheated oven for about 20 minutes. Frost the cake with whipped cream, if desired.

Per serving: 182 Calories; 17.1g Fat; 5.8g Carbs; 5.5g Protein; 3.1g Fiber

FAVORITE KETO RECIPES

551. Walnut Crunch Bars

(Ready in about 30 minutes | Servings 10)

Ingredients

1/2 stick butter, softened
1/2 cup chia seeds
1 cup walnuts, ground

1/2 cup granulated Swerve
2/3 cup peanut butter, chunk-style

Directions

Start by preheating your oven to 350 degrees F.

Mix the walnuts and Swerve. Then, combine the peanut butter and regular butter.

Add the butter mixture to the dry walnut mixture; stir in chia seeds and mix again to combine.

Pour into a foil-lined baking sheet. Bake in the preheated oven approximately 12 minutes. Cut into squares and enjoy!

Per serving: 207 Calories; 17.9g Fat; 5.9g Carbs; 7.1g Protein; 3.3g Fiber

552. Chuck Roast with Tomato Sauce

(Ready in about 3 hours | Servings 5)

Ingredients

2 ½ pounds chuck roast
1/2 cup celery, chopped
2 vine-ripe tomatoes, pureed

1 ½ tablespoons lard, room temperature
1/2 cup leeks, sliced

Directions

In a soup pot, melt the lard over medium-high flame. Cook the leeks and celery until they've softened or about 5 minutes.

Spread the sautéed mixture on the bottom of a lightly greased casserole dish.

Add in the tomatoes and chuck roast; season with salt and black pepper to taste. Roast in the preheated oven at 320 degrees F for 2 hours 40 minutes.

Bon appétit!

Per serving: 359 Calories; 16.4g Fat; 5.1g Carbs; 47.5g Protein; 1.2g Fiber

553. Spicy Turkey Curry

(Ready in about 1 hour | Servings 4)

Ingredients

3 teaspoons sesame oil
1/2 cup curry paste
1/2 cup turkey consommé

1 pound turkey wings, boneless and chopped
1 cup unsweetened coconut milk, preferably homemade

Directions

Heat sesame oil in a wok over medium-high flame. Brown the turkey wings on all sides for about 6 minutes.

Add in the remaining ingredients and stir to combine. Season with salt and black pepper.

Let it simmer for 40 to 45 minutes or until thoroughly cooked. Enjoy!

Per serving: 295 Calories; 19.5g Fat; 2.9g Carbs; 25.5g Protein; 0g Fiber

554. Winter Pork Soup

(Ready in about 30 minutes | Servings 5)

Ingredients

1 celery stalk, chopped
5 cups beef bone broth
2 teaspoons olive oil

1 pound ground pork
2 shallots, chopped

Directions

In a heavy-bottomed pot, heat 1 teaspoon of the olive oil over a medium-high flame. Brown the ground pork, beaking apart with a wide spatula; reserve.

Heat the remaining teaspoon of olive oil and sauté the shallot and celery until they are tender.

Pour in the beef bone broth and bring to a boil. Stir in the reserved pork. Reduce the heat and continue to simmer, partially covered, for 20 to 25 minutes.

Salt to taste and serve warm. Bon appétit!

Per serving: 292 Calories; 20.6g Fat; 1.6g Carbs; 23.6g Protein; 0.3g Fiber

555. Easiest Pulled Pork Ever

(Ready in about 3 hours | Servings 4)

Ingredients

1 ½ pounds Boston butt
3 tablespoons apple cider vinegar
1 cup tomato sauce

1/2 teaspoon chipotle powder
1 teaspoon black peppercorns, whole

Directions

Start by preheating your oven to 320 degrees F. Place all ingredients in a lightly oiled casserole dish.

Bake in the preheated oven for 2 hours 50 minutes, checking it every 25 to 30 minutes.

Shred the pork with two forks and serve with cooking juices on the side. Enjoy!

Per serving: 338 Calories; 21.2g Fat; 4.4g Carbs; 30.8g Protein; 1.2g Fiber

556. Bœuf à la Bourguignonne

(Ready in about 1 hour 20 minutes | Servings 5)

Ingredients

1 ½ pounds shoulder steak, cut into cubes
1 cup red Burgundy wine
1 onion, chopped

1 celery stalk, chopped
1 tablespoon Herbs de Provence

Directions

Preheat a lightly oiled stockpot over a medium-high flame. Now, cook the shoulder steak for about 7 minutes.

Pour in a splash of wine to deglaze the pan.

Stir in the Herbs de Provence, onion, celery, and the remaining wine; pour in 3 cups of water. Bring to a boil and immediately reduce the heat to medium-low.

Partially cover, and allow it to simmer for about 1 hour. Enjoy!

Per serving: 217 Calories; 5.5g Fat; 3.9g Carbs; 30g Protein; 0.4g Fiber

557. Holiday-Style Chicken Salad

(Ready in about 20 minutes + chilling time | Servings 2)

Ingredients

1/2 head Romaine lettuce, torn into pieces
1 small-sized celery stalk, chopped
2 chicken thighs, skinless
1/4 cup mayonnaise
1/2 cucumber, sliced

Directions

In a frying pan, cook the chicken thighs over medium-high heat until thoroughly cooked.

Shred the meat, discarding the bones. Transfer the meat to a salad bowl.

Fold in the remaining ingredients; gently stir to combine. Place in your refrigerator until ready to serve. Bon appétit!

Per serving: 456 Calories; 29g Fat; 6.7g Carbs; 40.1g Protein; 3.7g Fiber

558. Country-Style Pork Burgers

(Ready in about 20 minutes | Servings 6)

Ingredients

1 ½ cups Romano cheese, grated
2 garlic cloves, finely minced
1/2 cup onion, finely minced
2 pounds ground pork
1 serrano pepper, deseeded and minced

Directions

Combine all ingredients in a mixing bowl. Roll the mixture into 6 equal patties.

Grill your patties for about 7 to 8 per side. Serve on keto buns garnished with your favorite keto toppings. Enjoy!

Per serving: 515 Calories; 35.4g Fat; 2.6g Carbs; 44.3g Protein; 0.2g Fiber

559. Melt-in-Your-Mouth Chicken Breasts

(Ready in about 20 minutes | Servings 4)

Ingredients

2 chicken breasts
2 tablespoons butter, melted
8 ounces Ricotta cheese, room temperature
4 slices bacon, chopped
1/4 cup scallions, chopped

Directions

Start by preheating your oven to 370 degrees F.

Spread the melted butter all over the chicken breasts. Season them with salt and pepper to taste.

Fry the chicken for about 8 minutes over medium-high heat. Place the chicken in a lightly oiled casserole dish.

Top with cheese and bacon and bake for 12 to 15 minutes or until heated through. Garnish with fresh scallions and serve warm!

Per serving: 295 Calories; 19.5g Fat; 2.9g Carbs; 25.5g Protein; 0g Fiber

560. Korean-Style Chicken Casserole

(Ready in about 30 minutes | Servings 2)

Ingredients

3/4 pound chicken breast fillets, chopped into bite-sized chunks
1/2 teaspoon Korean seasoning mix
1 bell pepper, deveined and chopped
2 ripe tomatoes, chopped
1/2 cup sour cream

Directions

Start by preheating your oven to 380 degrees F.

Brush the sides and bottom of a casserole dish with 1 tablespoon of olive oil. Add the chicken and Korean seasoning mix to the casserole dish.

Season with the salt to taste. Add in the pepper and tomatoes. Top with sour cream.

Bake in the preheated oven for 20 to 25 minutes and enjoy!

Per serving: 410 Calories; 20.7g Fat; 6.2g Carbs; 50g Protein; 1.5g Fiber

561. Tender St. Louis-Style Ribs

(Ready in about 2 hours 10 minutes | Servings 5)

Ingredients

2 tablespoons Swerve sweetener
1 cup tomato sauce, no sugar added
2 pounds St. Louis-style pork ribs
4 tablespoons sesame oil
2 garlic cloves, pressed

Directions

Sprinkle the pork ribs with salt and black pepper to taste. Place them on a foil-lined casserole dish.

Cover with the foil and bake in the preheated oven at 365 degrees F approximately 1 hour 20 minutes.

Meanwhile, combine sesame oil, Swerve sweetener, tomato sauce, and garlic in a mixing bowl. Spread the glaze over the pork ribs.

Turn the temperature to 400 degrees F and continue to bake an additional 30 minutes. Bon appétit!

Per serving: 370 Calories; 21.2g Fat; 4.3g Carbs; 38.8g Protein; 1.1g Fiber

562. Z'paghetti Bolognese

(Ready in about 30 minutes | Servings 3)

Ingredients

2 zucchinis, spiralized
2 medium-sized tomatoes, pureed
3/4 pound ground pork
3 teaspoons olive oil
2 cloves garlic, pressed

Directions

In a frying pan, heat the oil over a moderate heat. Now, cook ground pork for about 5 minutes or until browned.

Then, sauté the garlic for 30 seconds more or until aromatic.

Stir in the pureed tomatoes and bring to a boil; turn the heat to medium-low and let it simmer for a further 20 to 25 minutes.

Add in the zoodles and continue to simmer for 2 minutes more. Bon appétit!

Per serving: 357 Calories; 28.7g Fat; 4g Carbs; 20.2g Protein; 1.1g Fiber

563. Italian-Style Turkey Fillets

(Ready in about 1 hour | Servings 6)

Ingredients

1 ½ pounds turkey breasts
6 ounces Asiago cheese, sliced
2 tablespoons extra-virgin
olive oil

2 bell peppers, thinly sliced
2 garlic cloves, sliced

Directions

Lightly grease the sides and bottom of a casserole dish with olive oil.

Sprinkle the turkey with Italian seasoning mix.

Using a small knife, create slits in turkey breasts; stuff with garlic, cheese, and bell peppers.

Bake in the preheated oven at 365 degrees F for 50 to 55 minutes or until heated through. Bon appétit!

Per serving: 347 Calories; 22.2g Fat; 3g Carbs; 32g Protein; 0.5g Fiber

564. Pistachio Praline Truffles

(Ready in about 10 minutes + chilling time | Servings 10)

Ingredients

1/4 cup pistachios, chopped
1/4 teaspoon pure vanilla
extract
2/3 cup double cream

9 ounces sugar-free chocolate,
chopped
1/4 cup cocoa powder,
unsweetened

Directions

Melt double cream; stir the chocolate, vanilla, and pistachios into the warm cream.

Mix to combine and place the mixture in the refrigerator.

Shape the mixture into bite-sized balls and roll them over cocoa powder. Bon appétit!

Per serving: 216 Calories; 18g Fat; 6.7g Carbs; 5.1g Protein; 4.5g Fiber

565. Fluffy Chocolate Chip Cookies

(Ready in about 10 minutes + chilling time | Servings 10)

Ingredients

1/2 cup almond meal
4 tablespoons double cream
1/2 cup sugar-free chocolate
chips

2 cups coconut, unsweetened
and shredded
2 tablespoons golden flaxseed
meal

Directions

Thoroughly combine all of the above ingredients; add in a keto sweetener of choice. Shape the mixture into balls.

Arrange the balls on a foil-lined baking pan. Flatten the balls using a fork or your hand.

Let it cool in your refrigerator for about 2 hours. Bon appétit!

Per serving: 104 Calories; 9.5g Fat; 4.1g Carbs; 2.1g Protein; 2.6g Fiber

567. Easy Sopressata Sandwiches

(Ready in about 10 minutes | Servings 2)

Ingredients

4 slices Sopressata
2 eggs
4 thin zucchini slices, cut
lengthwise

2 slices provolone cheese
1 red bell pepper, sliced thinly

Directions

Melt 1 tablespoon of butter in a skillet over a moderate flame. Cook the eggs for about 5 minutes.

Place one zucchini slice on each serving plate. Place the cheese, Sopressata, and bell peppers on the zucchini sliceS.

Top with the fried eggs; sprinkle with salt and black pepper; top with the remaining zucchini slices and serve immediately!

Per serving: 352 Calories; 26.5g Fat; 6.6g Carbs; 22.1g Protein; 0.6g Fiber

568. Chuck Roast with Vegetables

(Ready in about 20 minutes | Servings 5)

Ingredients

1 ½ pounds chuck, cut into
bite-sized cubes
2 tablespoons olive oil

2 bell peppers, deveined and
sliced
2 cups cauliflower florets
1 red onion, sliced

Directions

Heat the olive oil in a saucepan over medium-high heat. Sear the beef for about 10 minutes until browned; reserve.

Sauté the onion in the same saucepan until tender and fragrant. Then, add the peppers and cauliflower along with the reserved beef and 1/4 cup of water to the saucepan; bring to a boil.

Turn the heat to simmer; let it simmer approximately 10 minutes or until everything is thoroughly cooked. Bon appétit!

Per serving: 261 Calories; 14.3g Fat; 4g Carbs; 30.1g Protein; 1.2g Fiber

569. Mediterranean-Style Chicken Drumettes

(Ready in about 25 minutes | Servings 5)

Ingredients

1 ½ pounds chicken drumettes
2 bell peppers, sliced
2 tablespoons Greek cooking
wine

1 red onion, cut into wedges
2 tablespoons olive oil

Directions

Begin by preheating an oven to 410 degrees F. Brush the sides and bottom a casserole dish with 1 tablespoon of olive oil.

Heat the remaining tablespoon of olive oil in a nonstick skillet over medium-high heat. Sear the chicken drumettes for about 5 minutes on each side or until browned.

Deglaze the pan with Greek cooking wine. Place the chicken drumettes in the prepared casserole dish. Add in 1/2 cup of water or chicken broth.

Place red onion and peppers on the chicken drumettes.

Season with Mediterranean spice mix, if desired. Roast for about 20 minutes and serve warm.

Per serving: 218 Calories; 9.1g Fat; 4.2g Carbs; 28.6g Protein; 0.7g Fiber

570. French-Style Filet Mignon

(Ready in about 15 minutes | Servings 6)

Ingredients

2 pounds pork filet mignon, cut into bite-sized chunks
1 tablespoon Dijon mustard
1 cup double cream
2 teaspoons lard, at room temperature
Flaky salt and ground black pepper, to season

Directions

In a large saucepan, melt the lard over medium-high heat; once hot, sear the filet mignon for about 3 minutes on each side. Season with salt and pepper.

Add in the mustard and double cream. Let it simmer, partially covered, for 5 to 6 minutes or until the sauce has thickened and reduced.

Bon appétit!

Per serving: 301 Calories; 16.6g Fat; 2.3g Carbs; 34.2g Protein; 0.2g Fiber

571. Summer BBQ Pork

(Ready in about 1 hour 15 minutes | Servings 5)

Ingredients

2 pounds pork loin roast, trimmed
1 ½ tablespoons olive oil
1 tablespoon fresh lemon juice
1 tablespoon pork rub seasoning blend
1 tablespoon stone-ground mustard

Directions

Brush the pork with the olive oil, lemon juice, pork rub seasoning blend, and mustard.

Grill the pork loin roast over indirect heat for about 50 minutes.

Serve with mashed cauliflower, if desired. Bon appétit!

Per serving: 386 Calories; 20.1g Fat; 0.1g Carbs; 48g Protein; 0.1g Fiber

572. Italian Pepper and Goat Cheese Omelet

(Ready in about 15 minutes | Servings 3)

Ingredients

6 eggs, whisked
1 teaspoon Italian seasoning blend
1/2 cup goat cheese, shredded
3 ounces bacon, diced
1 Italian pepper, chopped

Directions

Fry the bacon in the preheated nonstick skillet for about 5 minutes; set aside.

Then, sauté Italian pepper for 2 minutes or until fragrant and tender. Pour the eggs into the skillet.

Add in Italian seasoning blend. Cook until the eggs are set about 5 minutes. Top with the reserved bacon and goat cheese.

Fold your omelet in half and serve warm!

Per serving: 481 Calories; 43.3g Fat; 4.8g Carbs; 17.2g Protein; 0.6g Fiber

573. Buttery Chicken Drumettes (Murgh Makhani)

(Ready in about 40 minutes | Servings 4)

Ingredients

1 pound chicken drumettes
Fresh juice of 1/2 lemon
3 tablespoons butter, melted
1 garlic clove, sliced
2 tablespoons white wine

Directions

Arrange the chicken drumettes in a parchment-lined roasting pan. Brush chicken drumettes with melted butter.

Add in the garlic, lemon, and wine; season with the salt and pepper to your liking.

Bake in the preheated oven at 430 degrees F for 35 to 40 minutes. Garnish with fresh scallions. Bon appétit!

Per serving: 209 Calories; 12.2g Fat; 0.4g Carbs; 23.2g Protein; 0.1g Fiber

574. Kid-Friendly Cheeseburgers

(Ready in about 15 minutes | Servings 3)

Ingredients

1 pound ground beef
1 tablespoon olive oil
3 slices Colby cheese
1 white onion, sliced
1 teaspoon burger seasoning mix

Directions

In a mixing bowl, combine the ground meat with the burger seasoning mix.

Shape the mixture into three equal patties.

In a frying pan, warm the olive oil until sizzling. Once hot, fry your burgers for 4 to 5 minutes. Turn them over, top with cheese and cook for a further 4 to 5 minutes.

Garnish with onions and serve right away!

Per serving: 533 Calories; 35.1g Fat; 4.8g Carbs; 46g Protein; 0.8g Fiber

575. Japanese-Style Porterhouse Steak

(Ready in about 20 minutes + marinating time | Servings 6)

Ingredients

2 pounds porterhouse steak, cut into 6 thin slices
4 tablespoons sake

4 tablespoons olive oil
2 cloves garlic, pressed
8 tablespoons rice vinegar

Directions

Place all of the above ingredients in a large ceramic dish. Cover and let it marinate for about six hours.

Grill the porterhouse steak over medium heat, basting with the reserved marinade. Cook for 6 to 7 minutes per side.

Season with salt and pepper to taste. Bon appétit!

Per serving: 299 Calories; 17.7g Fat; 1.1g Carbs; 31.5g Protein; 0.1g Fiber

576. Bell Pepper Keto Nachos

(Ready in about 35 minutes | Servings 3)

Ingredients

3 bell peppers, cut into halves
1/2 cup onion, finely chopped
1 pound chorizo sausage

6 ounces 1/4 cup pico de gallo
3/4 cup full-fat Mexican blend cheese, shredded

Directions

Start by preheating your oven to 390 degrees F. Spritz the bottom and sides of a casserole dish with cooking spray.

Arrange the peppers in the casserole dish.

Heat 2 tablespoons of olive oil in a saucepan over a moderate heat. Cook the onions and chorizo until the onion is tender and chorizo in no longer pink or about 6 minutes.

Stir in cup pico de gallo along with the salt and pepper to taste. Divide the filling between pepper halves.

Bake in the preheated oven for about 22 minutes. After that, top with cheese and place the dish under the preheated broiler for 5 minutes more or until cheese is hot and bubbly on the top. Enjoy!

Per serving: 507 Calories; 40.7g Fat; 8.8g Carbs; 24.5g Protein; 1.6g Fiber

577. Ham and Mushroom Mini Frittatas

(Ready in about 25 minutes | Servings 6)

Ingredients

6 slices ham, chopped
1 cup mushrooms sliced
2 bell peppers, chopped

8 eggs, beaten
1 cup goat cheese, shredded

Directions

Start by preheating your oven to 350 degrees F. Cook the ham in a preheated skillet over the highest setting; reserve.

In the pan drippings, cook the mushrooms and peppers for 3 to 4 minutes or until tender and fragrant.

Remove from the heat. Spoon the mixture into the prepared muffin cups; pour in the eggs and top with goat cheese.

Bake for about 15 minutes or until they are just set in the center. Lastly, loosen the frittatas from the muffin cups using a rubber spatula and slide them onto a serving platter. Bon appétit!

Per serving: 157 Calories; 8.7g Fat; 3.1g Carbs; 14.5g Protein; 0.3g Fiber

578. Caesar Salad Skewers

(Ready in about 20 minutes | Servings 3)

Ingredients

1 chicken breasts
4 ounces ham
2 ounces mozzarella cheese, cubed

1 cup cherry tomatoes
2/3 cup mayonnaise

Directions

Preheat a lightly greased grill pan over medium-high heat. Fry the chicken until golden brown on the top.

Alternate pieces of chicken breasts, ham, mozzarella cheese, and cherry tomatoes onto bamboo skewers. Serve with mayonnaise for dipping. Bon appétit!

Per serving: 157 Calories; 8.7g Fat; 3.1g Carbs; 14.5g Protein; 0.3g Fiber

579. Shrimp and Broccoli Kabobs

(Ready in about 20 minutes | Servings 3)

Ingredients

2 tablespoons sesame oil
1 ½ pounds shrimp, deveined
2 cups broccoli florets

1 red bell pepper, sliced
1 onion, cut into wedges

Directions

Heat 1 tablespoon of sesame oil in a frying pan over medium-high heat. Then, cook the shrimp, stirring continuously to ensure even cooking. Season with salt and pepper to your liking.

In the same pan, heat the remaining tablespoon of sesame oil and sauté the broccoli, peppers and onion until just tender or about 6 minutes. Season with Cajun spice mix, if desired.

Tread the cooked shrimp onto skewers, alternating with sautéed vegetables. Serve on a nice serving platter and enjoy!

Per serving: 314 Calories; 10.5g Fat; 8.7g Carbs; 47.5g Protein; 2.4g Fiber

580. Salmon Stuffed Celery

(Ready in about 20 minutes | Servings 4)

Ingredients

1 cup dry white wine

3 cloves garlic, smashed

2 salmon fillets

8 oz cream cheese, softened

4 medium celery stalks

Directions

Bring wine and garlic to a boil in a saucepan. Immediately reduce temperature to simmer and add in salmon fillets. Partially cover.

Allow salmon fillets to simmer for 9 to 11 minutes. Flake the salmon and stir in the cream cheese.

Fill the celery sticks with the salmon mixture and serve immediately. Enjoy!

Per serving: 379 Calories; 23.2g Fat; 3.8g Carbs; 37.1g Protein; 0.3g Fiber

581. Marble Fat Bombs

(Ready in about 20 minutes | Servings 12)

Ingredients

1 cup walnut

1 cup peanuts

2 tablespoons Monk fruit powder

1/2 cup coconut oil

4 tablespoons unsweetened cocoa powder

Directions

Process walnuts, peanuts, Monk fruit powder, and coconut oil in your blender until creamy and smooth. Separate the batter into two halves.

Stir the cocoa powder into the first half.

Spoon the first half of the batter into muffin silicone cups. Spoon the cocoa mixture over the first layer.

Freeze for 30 to 40 minutes and enjoy!

Per serving: 251 Calories; 21.8g Fat; 9.5g Carbs; 7.6g Protein; 2.2g Fiber

582. Easy Keto Tortilla

(Ready in about 20 minutes | Servings 10)

Ingredients

4 eggs

1 cup almond milk

1/2 cup almond meal

1/2 cup walnut, ground

1/2 teaspoon coarse salt

Directions

Whisk the eggs until pale and frothy; pour in the almond milk and whisk to combine well.

Add in almond meal, ground walnut, and salt; stir again to combine well.

Cook your tortilla in the preheated skillet until you run out of ingredients. Serve with your favorite keto toppings and enjoy!

Per serving: 120 Calories; 9.8g Fat; 3.1g Carbs; 5.9g Protein; 0.9g Fiber

583. Keto Dinner Rolls

(Ready in about 30 minutes | Servings 6)

Ingredients

3 egg whites

2 eggs

1/3 cup almond meal

1/3 cup coconut flour

1 teaspoon baking powder

Directions

Start by preheating your oven to 360 degrees F.

Whisk the eggs until pale and frothy. Add in the remaining ingredients along with 1/4 cup of boiling water.

Beat with an electric mixer until everything is well combined. Divide the dough into six balls. Flatten the balls and arrange them on a foil-lined cookie sheet.

Then, bake for 20 to 25 minutes or until done. Bon appétit!

Per serving: 98 Calories; 7.8g Fat; 2.2g Carbs; 5.9g Protein; 1g Fiber

584. Gingerbread Keto Granola

(Ready in about 30 minutes | Servings 10)

Ingredients

2 cups unsweetened and shredded coconut

1 ¼ cups cup pecan halves

1/2 cup pepitas

1 teaspoon ginger

1/2 cup Erythritol

Directions

Start by preheating an oven to 290 degrees F; coat a large roasting pan with parchment paper.

Combine all ingredients in a mixing bowl. Add in vanilla essence, if desired.

Spread the mixture in an even layer onto the parchment-lined pan. Bake for about 25 minutes, rotating the pan halfway through.

Serve with keto toppings of your choice. Bon appétit!

Per serving: 176 Calories; 17.1g Fat; 5g Carbs; 3.4g Protein; 2.9g Fiber

585. Rich and Easy Keto Pizza

(Ready in about 25 minutes | Servings 4)

Ingredients

6 eggs

10 ounces cheddar cheese, shredded

6 tablespoons marinara sauce

3 ounces pepperoni, sliced

3 ounces Soppressata, sliced

Directions

Start by preheating your oven to 390 degrees F.

Combine the eggs and cheddar cheese until well mixed.

Spread the batter in an even layer onto the parchment-lined baking sheet. Bake in the preheated oven for about 13 minutes until the top is golden brown.

Turn the oven temperature to 440 degrees F.

Spoon marinara sauce over the crust. Top with pepperoni and Soppressata. Continue to bake approximately 10 minutes or until thoroughly cooked. Bon appétit!

Per serving: 600 Calories; 48.7g Fat; 3.2g Carbs; 35.4g Protein; 0.5g Fiber

586. Summer Bulletproof Coffee

(Ready in about 5 minutes | Servings 1)

Ingredients

1 tablespoon coconut oil, melted
1 teaspoon vanilla extract
1 cup coffee

1 teaspoon granular Swerve
1 tablespoon heavy whipping cream

Directions

In your blender, mix the coconut oil, vanilla, coffee, and Swerve until well combined.

Place ice cubes in a tall glass. Pour your coffee into the glass.

Top with heavy whipping cream and enjoy!

Per serving: 183 Calories; 19.3g Fat; 0.9g Carbs; 0.6g Protein; 0g Fiber

587. Protein Blackberry Smoothie

(Ready in about 5 minutes | Servings 2)

Ingredients

2 cups coconut milk
1/3 cup blackberries
1 tablespoon coconut oil, melted

3 tablespoons collagen protein
A pinch of grated nutmeg

Directions

Blend all ingredients until creamy, uniform, and smooth.

Spoon into two tall glasses and enjoy!

Per serving: 228 Calories; 14.3g Fat; 9.3g Carbs; 8g Protein; 0g Fiber

588. Coconut Hasty Pudding

(Ready in about 10 minutes | Servings 2)

Ingredients

1 cup unsweetened coconut, shredded
1 tablespoon flax seeds

1 tablespoon pumpkin seeds
1 tablespoon sunflower seeds
1/2 cup full-fat coconut milk

Directions

In a saucepan, stir all ingredients along with 1/2 cup of water.

When the mixture comes to a boil, immediately reduce temperature to simmer. Continue to simmer for about 3 minutes until thoroughly cooked.

Serve in individual bowls and enjoy!

Per serving: 352 Calories; 40.1g Fat; 9.4g Carbs; 8.5g Protein; 6g Fiber

589. Basic Keto Griddlecake

(Ready in about 35 minutes | Servings 6)

Ingredients

6 eggs
6 tablespoons almond flour
1 teaspoon baking powder

4 tablespoons heavy cream
1 stick butter, melted

Directions

Beat the egg until pale and frothy.

Stir in almond flour and baking powder; add a pinch of salt. Stir in the cream and melted butter.

Bake in a preheated waffle maker until your run out of ingredients. Serve with your favorite keto toppings. Enjoy!

Per serving: 397 Calories; 37.3g Fat; 6.7g Carbs; 11.5g Protein; 3.5g Fiber

590. Breakfast Egg Muffins with Ham

(Ready in about 25 minutes | Servings 4)

Ingredients

10 eggs
4 ounces cream cheese
4 ounces Pepper-Jack cheese, shredded

4 ounces ham, chopped
1 red bell pepper, chopped

Directions

Start by preheating your oven to 360 degrees F. Spritz a muffin pan with a nonstick cooking oil.

Mix all of the above ingredients in the order listed above. Spoon the mixture into the prepared muffin pan.

Bake in the preheated oven for about 18 minutes or until cooked through. Bon appétit!

Per serving: 383 Calories; 28.4g Fat; 3.5g Carbs; 27.5g Protein; 0.2g Fiber

591. Double Cheese and Bacon Fat Bombs

(Ready in about 15 minutes | Servings 6)

Ingredients

4 ounces Romano cheese
4 ounces cream cheese, at room temperature

1/2 teaspoon garlic powder
6 tablespoons bacon bits

Directions

Mix the cheese and garlic powder until well combined. Freeze for 10 minutes.

Shape the mixture with an ice cream spoon into balls. Roll the balls over bacon bits.

Place in your refrigerator until ready to serve. Bon appétit!

Per serving: 196 Calories; 17.4g Fat; 1.7g Carbs; 8.9g Protein; 0g Fiber

592. Chicken Liver Pate with Cognac

(Ready in about 15 minutes | Servings 10)

Ingredients

6 ounces butter
1 red onion, chopped
1 clove garlic, finely chopped
1 ½ pounds chicken livers
1 tablespoon Cognac

Directions

Melt the butter in a saucepan over medium-high heat. Now, cook the onion until tender and aromatic or about 3 minutes.

Add in the garlic and continue to cook for 1 minute more or until aromatic. Add in chicken livers and continue to cook for 5 minutes longer.

Transfer the ingredients to the bowl of your food processor. Add in cognac and puree the ingredients until creamy and smooth.

Keep in your refrigerator until ready to serve. Bon appétit!

Per serving: 211 Calories; 17.4g Fat; 1.6g Carbs; 11.8g Protein; 0.2g Fiber

593. Old-School Custard

(Ready in about 20 minutes | Servings 2)

Ingredients

1/2 cup double cream
1/4 cup coconut milk
2 egg yolks
1/4 cup Xylitol
1/2 teaspoon pure vanilla essence

Directions

In a saucepan, warm the cream and coconut milk over medium-low heat. Heat off.

Whisk in the egg yolks, Xylitol, and vanilla essence.

Cook over the lowest setting for about 17 minutes, whisking continuously. Bon appétit!

Per serving: 179 Calories; 16.6g Fat; 2.9g Carbs; 4.2g Protein; 0g Fiber

594. Beef Salad Cups

(Ready in about 15 minutes | Servings 5)

Ingredients

1 tablespoon olive oil
1 ½ pounds ground beef
1 onion, chopped
1 bell pepper, chopped
18 leaves Bibb lettuce

Directions

Heat olive oil in a frying pan over medium-high heat. Now, cook ground beef for about 4 minutes or until no longer pink.

Add in onion and continue to cook for 3 minutes more or until fragrant.

Add in bell pepper and remove from the heat. Season with salt and pepper to taste.

Double-up the lettuce leaves and fill them with the beef mixture. Serve and enjoy!

Per serving: 315 Calories; 20.3g Fat; 6.2g Carbs; 21g Protein; 2.6g Fiber

595. Vanilla Ice Cream

(Ready in about 15 minutes | Servings 2)

Ingredients

1 cup full-fat coconut milk
1/4 cup granulated Swerve
A pinch of salt
A pinch of grated nutmeg
1 teaspoon pure vanilla extract

Directions

Thoroughly combine all ingredients.

Freeze the mixture until firm. Enjoy!

Per serving: 276 Calories; 28.3g Fat; 7.2g Carbs; 2.7g Protein; 2.6g Fiber

596. Easy Blueberry Crumble

(Ready in about 35 minutes | Servings 6)

Ingredients

1 cup blueberries
1/4 cup granulated Swerve
1/2 cup almond meal
1/2 cup unsweetened coconut flakes
4 tablespoons coconut oil

Directions

Start by preheating your oven to 355 degrees F. Place blueberries on the bottom of a lightly oiled baking dish.

Mix the remaining ingredients in a bowl. Sprinkle evenly over the blueberries.

Bake in the center of the oven for about 33 minutes until the fruit is bubbling. Serve in dessert bowls garnished with whipped cream, if desired. Devour!

Per serving: 116 Calories; 11.3g Fat; 4.6g Carbs; 0.4g Protein; 1.2g Fiber

597. Cheese Eggplant Crisps

(Ready in about 45 minutes | Servings 3)

Ingredients

1/2 pound eggplant, peeled and thinly sliced
1 teaspoon Cajun seasoning mix
1/2 cup almond meal
3 ounces parmesan cheese, grated
2 tablespoons sesame oil

Directions

Sprinkle the eggplant slices with 1 teaspoon of salt; let them stand for about 30 minutes. Squeeze the eggplant slices and discard the excess water.

Toss the eggplant slices with the other ingredients. Roast in the preheated oven at 390 degrees F for about 13 minutes.

Serve with your favorite keto sauce on the side. Bon appétit!

Per serving: 264 Calories; 21.1g Fat; 9.1g Carbs; 10.4g Protein; 3.3g Fiber

598. Bacon and Avocado Bites

(Ready in about 5 minutes | Servings 5)

Ingredients

4 ounces Feta cheese
1 avocado, mashed
1 garlic clove, minced
2 tablespoons Kalamata olives, chopped
4 ounces bacon, cooked and chopped

Directions

Mix feta cheese, avocado, garlic, and olives in a bowl; season with salt and pepper to taste.

Shape the mixture into balls with a cookie scoop. Roll them over bacon bits.

Keep in your refrigerator until ready to use. Enjoy!

Per serving: 224 Calories; 19.9g Fat; 4.9g Carbs; 6.9g Protein; 2.8g Fiber

599. Cheese Cauliflower Breadsticks

(Ready in about 15 minutes | Servings 5)

Ingredients

1 egg
1 pound cauliflower rice
1 cup Cheddar cheese, shredded
1 cup Romano cheese, shredded
1/2 teaspoon dried Italian seasoning

Directions

Start by preheating your oven to 450 degrees F. Line a rimmed baking sheet with parchment paper.

Beat the eggs until pale and frothy. Stir in the remaining ingredients and stir until everything is well incorporated.

Spread the batter about a 1/4-inch-thick on the prepared baking sheet.

Bake approximately 10 minutes until the cheese is turning brown in spots. Bon appétit!

Per serving: 244 Calories; 18g Fat; 5.1g Carbs; 15.6g Protein; 1.8g Fiber

600. Greek-Style Citrus Marinated Olives

(Ready in about 10 minutes | Servings 10)

Ingredients

1/4 cup extra virgin olive oil
3 cloves garlic, pressed
2 cups Kalamata olives
2 tablespoons fresh lemon juice
1 tablespoon Greek herb mix

Directions

In a saucepan, heat the olive oil over a moderate heat. Now, cook the garlic for about 1 minute until it is pale golden.

Add in the olives along and continue to cook for 2 to 3 minutes. Remove from the heat.

Stir in the lemon juice and Greek herb mix. Serve warm at room temperature. Enjoy!

Per serving: 81 Calories; 8.3g Fat; 2.1g Carbs; 0.2g Protein; 0.9g Fiber